William Franklin Willoughby

A Workingman's Insurance

William Franklin Willoughby

A Workingman's Insurance

ISBN/EAN: 9783743313903

Manufactured in Europe, USA, Canada, Australia, Japa

Cover: Foto ©ninafisch / pixelio.de

Manufactured and distributed by brebook publishing software (www.brebook.com)

William Franklin Willoughby

A Workingman's Insurance

WORKINGMEN'S INSURANCE

BY

WILLIAM FRANKLIN WILLOUGHBY
UNITED STATES DEPARTMENT OF LABOR

NEW YORK: 46 East 14th Street
THOMAS Y. CROWELL & COMPANY
BOSTON: 100 Purchase Street

COPYRIGHT, 1898,
BY T. Y. CROWELL & CO.

Norwood Press
J. S. Cushing & Co. — Berwick & Smith
Norwood Mass. U.S.A.

PREFACE.

The publication of a work upon a subject in which the American public has as yet manifested but comparatively little interest, and concerning which the American literature consists of a single government report and one or two articles in periodicals, demands that something be said in explanation of its production.

Though the question of workingmen's insurance is one that is but barely entering upon the stage of discussion in this country, in Europe it has assumed a position of great practical importance. To-day there is not a country on the Continent in which this question does not occupy the foremost place among measures actively considered for improving the condition of the laboring classes. In the modern movement for economic reform there is probably no one subject that offers so many features of paramount importance. As a social measure, it presents the most radical step to improve the condition of the laboring classes that has been undertaken since the rise of the modern industrial system. As a subject of political philosophy, it involves important questions concerning the proper sphere of the state, and the manner in which state powers shall be exercised.

The novelty of the vast scheme of compulsory insurance, put into operation within the last ten years by the German and Austrian governments, has directed attention strongly to these two countries; and it has erroneously been thought that the question of workingmen's insurance is something both of recent birth and restricted to these two countries. Such is not the case. The general compulsory insurance of workingmen is an innovation; but their optional insurance, either by private institutions, or institutions operated under the auspices of the state, has occupied a prominent place among workingmen's institutions for over fifty years.

In the only available source of information concerning this question in the English language, that of the report of Mr. Brooks for the United States Department of Labor, the author has limited himself strictly to a consideration of compulsory insurance. Though much less striking in character, the great results achieved through purely voluntary insurance, by means of such institutions as the Friendly Societies of Great Britain, the *Sociétés de Secours Mutuels* of France, Belgium, and other countries, and the long-established pension and aid funds organized by the great railway, mining, and other companies in the various countries of Europe and in America, are of far greater interest to American students.

In the present work, therefore, it is our intention, not only to describe the experiment of compulsory insurance, but to consider all of the various methods by which workingmen make provision through common action for the time when they shall be incapacitated for work. The history of the insurance institutions and the present condition of the problem will be given for each country separately. In this account the leading type of each insurance system will be singled out for specially careful consideration. Thus, Germany and Austria will enable us to study compulsory insurance; France, Belgium, and Italy state, but voluntary, insurance; England and France the two leading types of mutual aid societies; and France and the United States insurance funds organized by employers for the benefit of their employés.

This description of conditions, however, will be but a part of our work. If our inquiry is to be other than a series of disconnected chapters, there should be some consideration of the problem itself; that is, of the general principles upon which its solution must rest. Our study, therefore, will consist of two fairly distinct parts: first, that of the problems of workingmen's insurance, involving a consideration of the grounds upon which the demand for the insurance of workingmen rests, the reasons which have given rise to the present pronounced movement in its favor, and the nature of the actuarial and other problems involved; and, secondly, a description of the systems of workingmen's insurance that have been organized in each country, and the present position of the problem in each at the present time.

Some apology possibly ought to be made for the large number of tables that have been given in carrying out this second part of our work. Insurance problems, however, are essentially statistical in character; and the operations of insurance institutions can adequately be shown in no other way. Had the institutions dealt with been at all familiar to American students, the number of tables might have been curtailed. Such not being the case, and the only sources of information, the official reports, being accessible to but few, it was thought that the presentation of the more important details would be of real value. The tables, moreover, are not mere exhibits. They are in all cases integral parts of the text, and serve to present concisely the history or operations of the institutions under consideration. In the conversion of foreign into United States money, the tables in use in the United States Treasury Department have been followed.

But few references to authorities have been made. In the preparation of this work reliance has been placed almost exclusively upon official reports and documents, the titles of which are given in an appendix. Unfortunately, in a number of instances, the publication of these reports is somewhat delayed, but in all cases the latest possible figures have been given.

CONTENTS.

	PAGE
PREFACE	iii

CHAPTER I.

THE PROBLEM OF WORKINGMEN'S INSURANCE.

1. Introductory	1
2. The Nature of Workingmen's Insurance . .	5
3. The Organization of Workingmen's Insurance .	15
4. Systems of Insurance	22

CHAPTER II.

WORKINGMEN'S INSURANCE IN GERMANY.

1. Introduction	29
2. Insurance against Sickness	36
3. Insurance against Accidents	59
4. Insurance against Old Age and Invalidity . .	75

CHAPTER III.

WORKINGMEN'S INSURANCE IN AUSTRIA.

1. Introduction	88
2. Insurance against Sickness	90
3. Insurance against Accidents	100

CHAPTER IV.

Workingmen's Insurance in France.

1. Introduction	112
2. State Insurance Institutions	116
3. Mutual-Aid Societies	131
4. Employers' Insurance Funds	149
5. The Present Problem of Workingmen's Insurance	172
6. The Insurance of Mine Employés	185

CHAPTER V.

Workingmen's Insurance in Belgium.

1. Introduction	191
2. The National Savings and Old-Age Insurance Bank	192
3. Miners' Insurance Funds	195
4. Mutual-Aid Societies	202
5. National Bank for the Assistance of Workingmen Injured by Accidents	203
6. Employers' Insurance Funds	204
7. The Present Problem of Workingmen's Insurance	204

CHAPTER VI.

Workingmen's Insurance in Italy.

1. Introduction	206
2. Insurance against Accidents	208
3. Insurance against Old Age and Invalidity	218
4. Insurance against Sickness	219

CHAPTER VII.

WORKINGMEN'S INSURANCE IN OTHER COUNTRIES OF CONTINENTAL EUROPE.

1. Introduction 220
2. Switzerland 220
3. Scandinavian Countries 226
4. Other Countries 231

CHAPTER VIII.

WORKINGMEN'S INSURANCE IN ENGLAND.

1. Introduction 233
2. Friendly Societies 235
3. Government Insurance 262
4. Employers' Liability 264
5. Proposed Schemes for Old Age Insurance . . 276

CHAPTER IX.

WORKINGMEN'S INSURANCE IN THE UNITED STATES.

1. Introduction 282
2. Railroad Employés' Relief Departments . . 284
3. Insurance Work of Labor Organizations . . 318
4. Employers' Liability 327

CHAPTER X.

CONCLUSION 330

APPENDIX I.

                                              PAGE
INSURANCE AGAINST UNEMPLOYMENT 361

APPENDIX II.

BIBLIOGRAPHICAL NOTE 379

WORKINGMEN'S INSURANCE.

CHAPTER I.

The Problem of Workingmen's Insurance.

Introductory.—The problem of workingmen's insurance is but one phase of the general labor movement. It is but a part of that great effort now being made by modern society so to modify conditions that the situation of the actual wielders of the tools of production shall be improved. In its complete development it comprehends the care and indemnification of all wage-earning men and women in case they are incapacitated for work, either temporarily or permanently, as the result of an accident or sickness, and the grant to them of a pension after they are no longer able to work on account of physical disability or old age. Under it no one need look forward with apprehension to the privations consequent upon sickness or accident. The ever-constant dread of dependent old age is wiped out at a stroke. It constitutes therefore the latest and most radical measure to grant thorough-going relief in the chief cases of suffering to which the wage-earning classes are now exposed.

The field of events to which the principles of insurance can be applied is an extended one. Under the head of workingmen's insurance, however, it is usual to consider but the four branches: that against accidents; that against sickness; that against old age and invalidity; and that against lack of employment. Of these, we are here primarily concerned with but the first three. The effort to provide for the fourth through insurance methods has only lately been seriously attempted. The considerations involved in out-of-work insurance, moreover, are of so special a character, that it has not been deemed desirable to consider them in connection with the other kinds of insurance. An account of the principal efforts in this direction, however, will be given in a supplemental chapter. Our study proper, therefore, will relate entirely to the three branches of insurance against accidents, sickness, and old age and invalidity.

Before entering upon this study, however, it is desirable first to clear the ground by the consideration of a number of points common to the general question of insurance. It is of importance that these considerations be perfectly understood, for they go to the root of the whole matter, and determine whether insurance of any kind is an institution that it is desirable to develop.

First of all, it should be noted that not a little misapprehension exists in regard to the true nature of insurance. Insurance is not an end in itself. It is but a means to an end. It is a mere device, a machine employed for the purpose of accomplishing certain objects, the adoption of which should depend upon the manner in which it performs its functions, and the economy with which it can be operated. It is primarily a savings institution by which men are assisted to make provision for future contingencies; and, secondly, a scheme by which men agree to share the risk of certain contingencies to which all are liable.

Secondly, the objection has been raised against workingmen's insurance that its introduction tends to lessen individual responsibility. Personal economy, it is said, is replaced by aid from an outside source. As regards the justice of this criticism, however, everything depends upon the method of insurance that is adopted. There is evidently a wide difference, in this respect, between compulsory and voluntary, and between state and privately organized insurance. In the idea of insurance itself there is certainly no room for such a criticism. Among the well-to-do, insurance has reached the point where by many it is considered as almost a moral obligation on the part of the head of a family. How much more desirable is it then for the workingman to whom the slightest sickness or accident means immediate and acute distress! When the former takes out an accident or life insurance policy, he does not feel that he has in the slightest degree sacrificed his independence; nor is there any reason why the latter should feel so under similar circumstances. The great extension of insurance within recent years has been due to the perfecting of insurance institutions, whereby policy holders are made to feel, not only that they have absolute security, but that they are getting the worth of their money. The movement for workingmen's insurance is but a similar effort to develop or create institutions adapted to the peculiar conditions of the wage-earning classes, whereby the same advantage of security against times of need can be enjoyed. In insurance itself, therefore, there is no sacrifice of the principle of self-help. It is, on the contrary, a device to provoke it.

Thirdly, it is important to notice the fundamental difference between the modern movement for insurance, and all previous efforts to provide for workingmen when incapacitated for labor. The modern movement for insurance represents the effort to substitute for the old relief funds, which too often were founded upon a charitable basis, institutions founded upon scientific principles, whereby each workingman himself provides by regular payments for the relief he will probably need. The significance of this difference can be seen in the use of the word "insurance" instead of "relief." The history of the insurance movement is, in many respects, analogous to that of the triumph of organized charity over indiscriminate alms-giving. It, however, goes a step further. Its object is to replace relief by a system under which each makes use of a fund that he himself has assisted to create. This gradual evolution from relief to insurance constitutes the key by which the history of workingmen's aid funds must be interpreted.

Finally, there should be noted the great change introduced in the question through the entrance of the state upon the field as the dominant agent. It is this feature that gives the greatest significance to the problem at the present time. From a purely private, the question has suddenly become a political one. The question is no longer that of state control of private institutions, but that of the compulsory use of insurance facilities provided by the state. It will be seen that the extent to which this intervention of the state has been carried constitutes the chief difference between the various insurance systems that are now in operation.

The Nature of Workingmen's Insurance. — The three kinds of insurance to which our study relates, though similar in general purpose, and together constituting a harmonious scheme, yet present distinct problems. Not only do the demands for each rest upon different grounds, with the result that the acceptance of one form by no means implies that the others should be adopted as well; but, were the organization of all three determined upon, the technical difficulties of their administration would demand that each should be kept independent. Such, at least, has been the experience of those countries in which workingmen's insurance has been highly developed. It is the purpose of the sections that immediately follow to indicate the necessity for this separation, the peculiar problems involved in each kind of insurance, the grounds upon which the introduction of each can be urged, the elements that must be taken into consideration in the practical work of organizing and administering any scheme, and, finally, the various methods and systems that have actually been followed for the provision of workingmen's insurance. This information once gained, the reader will be in a position to study in a more critical spirit the detailed description of the experience of each country as given in the subsequent chapters.

Of the necessity for each kind of insurance, that providing assistance in case of accidents, rests upon much the strongest grounds. No one not familiar with the conditions under which large industries are prosecuted, or with statistics of their operation, can realize the frequency of accidents to employés in such industries as railway transportation, mining, building, construction, and other work. Thus the statistician of the Interstate Commerce Commission reports that on an average each year one out of every 31 employés is injured, and one out of every 318 killed. If the accidents resulting to trainmen alone be considered, the figures show that one out of every 10.6 employés in this class of occupations is injured, and one out of every 111 killed.[1] While equally exact statistics cannot be obtained for other industries, information, as far as it has been compiled, shows that the industries of coal mining, stone quarrying, bridge building, and construction work of all kinds, and the great industries of iron and steel manufacture, are scarcely less dangerous. It is evident, then, that the occurrence of industrial accidents is productive of enormous suffering. It is only when a question such as this is looked at from the general standpoint of all labor, that the magnitude of the problem is

[1] Average for the five years 1889 to 1893.

realized. The direct result of accidents, moreover, represents but a comparatively small portion of the suffering caused by them. Socially speaking, the greatest hardships are those which result to workingmen's families in consequence of the financial distress caused by the stoppage of the laborer's earning capacity. But a small proportion of the working classes make any adequate provision for contingencies. In Europe, in nine cases out of ten, and in this country in a great many cases, a serious accident to a workingman means an immediate demand for charitable assistance in some form or other. It is to remedy this state of affairs, and to lessen at least the financial distress, that the aid of insurance has been invoked.

The especial development in recent years of the demand for the insurance of workingmen against accidents finds its explanation in a number of causes. First in importance is that of the increase in the system of production upon a large scale. While the general feeling is that the introduction of high power and complicated machinery has resulted in the increase in the number and severity of accidents, it is impossible to state this as a fact based upon statistical records. It is certain, however, that under modern conditions there has been a very great increase in the number of accidents beyond the control of the workingmen themselves. Interpretation of the common law has for the most part absolved employers from obligation on their account. Recourse has therefore more and more been had to insurance, as the best means of indemnification.

A second cause is found in the gradual change of sentiment in regard to the question upon whom should fall the burden of the loss resulting from accidents to labor. Strange as it may at first seem, the demand for the insurance of workingmen has been the logical, one might almost say, the inevitable, result of efforts to reform the law relating to the liability of employers for accidents to their employés. The process by which this result has been reached presents an exceedingly interesting example of the evolution of a social problem, and is well worth following.

Prior to the modern movement that we are now considering, the prevailing law in Europe, as well as in this country, was substantially that known as the common-law liability of employers. This principle, briefly stated, was that the employer is responsible only for those accidents resulting directly from his fault or the fault of his agents, whose orders the injured person was in duty bound to follow. The application of this law meant that the employer bore the consequences of those accidents only that were due to his fault and then only when such fault was clearly established by proof; while the workingman bore the results, not only of accidents due to his own fault, but of all fortuitous accidents, of accidents caused by his fellow-employés, and those whose occurrence, which, though due to the fault of the employer, could not be so legally proven.

It is scarcely necessary to call attention to the injustice of this rule under existing conditions. At the time that popular approval sanctioned the custom and gave it the force of law, the employé was in intimate relations with his employer. Should an accident occur, it was an easy matter to determine the responsibility. The growth of production on a large scale has, however, made this principle very largely inapplicable. Under modern conditions, the employé is often one of a thousand workingmen, working in a system of so great complexity that it is frequently impossible to trace responsibility. Under the above rule, therefore, it was, with few exceptions, upon the employé that fell the suffering caused by accidents. The hardships that this régime entailed upon the workingmen became more and more marked as the development of the great industries went on. The first step in the movement to lessen them was therefore the rise of the purely legal question of employers' liability. As yet there was little or no suggestion of insurance.

The most grievous injustice of the old law was that provision which threw the burden of proof upon the employé, in any attempt to recover damages. The first modification demanded was, therefore, for what was called the "inversion of proof"; that is, that the law be so changed that the employer should be liable for damages unless he could prove that he was in no way at fault.

It was soon apparent, however, that this measure represented but a very limited measure of reform; that, even if it were gained, the workingmen would be indemnified for but a small proportion of their injuries. The discussion that was had upon the subject brought out the fact that a large proportion of accidents were due, either to chance, or to occurrences practically beyond human control, or at least to causes, the responsibility for which could not be located. To the two classes of accidents due to the fault of the employer and of the employé, there was added a third, that due to the industry itself. This third class constitutes what in Europe is called the "*risque professional,*" or trade risk, being the dangers for the most part inherent in the prosecution of the industry itself. Statistics which began to be collected showed that less than 12 per cent of accidents could be attributed to the direct fault of employers. Considerably over 50 per cent were found to be due to the third cause.

As soon as this fact became recognized, the query naturally arose why the burden of these latter accidents should be made to rest exclusively upon the employés. It was argued that it was the industry that caused them, and that it was upon the industry that in some way the support of their consequences should be made to fall. In other words, there seemed to be no reason why this liability should not constitute as legitimate an item of the cost of production, to be taken into consideration and borne by the employer, as that of the breaking of machinery, fire, or loss in any other way. Moreover, as far as these accidents were preventible by the exercise of forethought, such forethought must, for the most part, be exercised by the employer, who determines the conditions under which the industry is carried on, the tools that must be made use of, etc. This reasoning once understood, the movement for reform took the wider form of a demand that the industry, that is the employer, should be made responsible for all accidents not clearly the fault of the injured person himself.

Further than this it would seem that the principle of employers' liability could not go. Unfortunately, however, practical results showed that with this secured scarcely more than a beginning had been made. Though, theoretically, the legal position of the laborer was infinitely improved, practically he still had to endure the hardships resulting from a great many accidents. The legal question had been solved, but the social problem remained. As matters then stood, the workingman could only recover damages as the result of an action at law, with the consequent delays, expense, and uncertainties, which he was in no position to bear. More and more the feeling developed, that if the employer was to be made really responsible for accidents to his employés, some better method must be devised by which this aid to the workingmen could be made more certain, and immediately available.

It was at this point that the agency of insurance was invoked. By it, it was merely sought to establish in advance the amount of the indemnity that would be paid, in proportion to the severity of the injury, and to ensure its immediate payment, by requiring employers either to insure their employés for these sums in a private or state institution, or themselves to maintain insurance funds. The employer would thus insure himself against accidents, exactly as he had done against fire. In demanding this, the advocates of insurance were encouraged by the fact that on the Continent a great many employers had long recognized the justice of this position, and had voluntarily practised this system, with the most happy results. From a legal question, therefore, the question of accidents to labor has, by a natural process of evolution, become the social one of insurance. In Europe proper, this evolution is complete, and it may almost be said that there is not a country in which the attempt to reach a solution of the question through a change of the laws relating to employers' liability has not been abandoned in favor of some measure providing for the extension of workingmen's insurance against accidents.

Turning now to insurance against sickness, we find that not only has the problem arisen in quite another way, but that its advisability rests upon quite other grounds. In the first place, the insurance of workingmen against sickness is founded upon no such claim of natural justice as is that of indemnification for accidents. In the latter instance, the industry is only made to bear the expense of the damages which inevitably result from its conduct, and the expense can fairly be called a legitimate item of the cost of production. Except in the comparatively few cases of trade maladies resulting from the use of injurious substances, sickness is not the direct result of conditions of labor. Insurance against it, therefore, cannot be urged as a right. The demand for it must rest upon other ground.

The desirability of such insurance, however, is none the less great. Sickness being a contingency that practically every one must experience, it is of great importance that all should make provision for its occurrence. If workingmen would make such provision by personal savings, nothing further could be desired. The habit of economy, however, is a characteristic that is naturally present in but few men. It is, however, one that is susceptible of development in almost all, if opportunities for saving are afforded. This insurance does. It offers to the working classes the best method by which they can provide for the times when illness will prevent them from working. It does not promise to do anything directly for them, but merely offers a device by which they can aid themselves.

The modern movement for insurance against sickness, moreover, unlike that against accidents, has a long and rich history in the various mutual-aid societies organized by men for their mutual assistance when sick, and in the numerous voluntary relief funds organized under various auspices for the benefit of workingmen. The study of sick insurance, therefore, involves the consideration of such interesting classes of institutions as the Friendly Societies of Great Britain, the *Sociétés de Secours Mutuels* of the Continent, and the aid funds organized by the large employers of labor, or by labor organizations. The existence of all of these institutions has to be taken into account. In fact, the present problem of sick insurance is almost wholly that of the reform or reorganization of existing institutions, in order that they may become more effective, and reach a larger proportion of the working population.

If sickness is a contingency to be anticipated by all, old age and ultimate invalidity is scarcely less so. The two most pitiful facts of modern industrial conditions, says Mr. Morley, in defining in a recent speech the position of the liberal party in Great Britain, are the sight of men capable of and willing to work, without an opportunity to do so, and the old laborer, after a life of toil, reduced to want. Nothing shows the real economic helplessness of the working classes as the fact that, though old age is a condition that must be looked forward to by all, but few workingmen are able by their unaided efforts to make a suitable provision for it. Insurance frankly recognizes this, and seeks to provide a way by which this condition of affairs can be remedied.

In many respects the considerations here involved are similar to those discussed in the case of insurance against sickness. The difference lies in the fact that the working classes have utterly failed to develop any institutions similar to their sick funds for the creation of pensions in their old age. Attempts have been made, but the task has been beyond their power. As a result, the history of old-age insurance is almost entirely contained in such state insurance institutions as the national old-age insurance banks of France and Belgium.

The essential features of old-age insurance, that differentiate it from both accident and sick insurance, lie chiefly in the principles upon which any system for its provision must rest. These differences will be treated in the consideration of the practical problems involved in the organization and administration of each kind of insurance to which we now pass.

The Organization of Workingmen's Insurance. — Insurance is a true science. The organization of any scheme, if it be established upon a basis financially sound, and with the relative rights of different classes of members equitably adjusted, involves the observance of a great many conditions. First, the character of the occurrences insured against must be accurately defined and determined; secondly, a tariff of dues must be fixed, so that each member will pay an amount proportional to the risk he runs of ultimately becoming a charge upon the fund; and, thirdly, a machinery for the collection of dues and the payment of benefits must be created. These elements are obviously different for each kind of insurance. The old relief measures knew no such distinctions. They were aid funds in which the fortunate aided the unfortunate. Scientific insurance seeks to replace this by the organization of a scheme by which each one makes provision for sickness, accident, or old age, according to the likelihood that he will need relief. To establish such a system requires as the first step that each risk should be considered separately.

The necessity for this is especially important as regards sick and accident insurance on the one hand, and old-age and invalidity insurance on the other. The former are fundamentally different from the latter, in that members thus insured are constantly enjoying the benefits for which they are making payments, while in the latter they are making deposits for a deferred benefit. In the first case, therefore, the account between the fund and the insured is always balanced. No matter when members leave the fund, they make no sacrifice or carry with them any rights. If they have paid ten dollars dues during the year, they have received the equivalent in knowing that they would have been provided for if they had been sick or injured during that period. In the second case, however, *i.e.* in old-age insurance, the members receive no immediate equivalent. Their contributions are taken from them in return for an ultimate claim that they may have for a pension when invalidated for work. The longer they remain members, therefore, the greater becomes their claim upon the fund.

This difference necessitates an entirely different scheme of insurance. In the case of insurance against accidents and sickness, it is but necessary to make the simple calculation of the probable number and severity of cases of accidents or sickness, and fix dues accordingly. In old-age and invalidity insurance, on the other hand, this determination of probable expenditures is an exceeding difficult matter. Indeed, it furnishes the most intricate problem with which insurance has to deal. Here the accounts of each year cannot be considered by themselves. To secure a proper adjustment of receipts and expenditures, it is necessary to calculate probable receipts and expenditures for a period of thirty, forty, or even fifty years in advance. It is evident that when any given body of men are first brought under a system for providing old-age pensions, the number who will reach the age entitling them to a pension during the first few years will be exceedingly small, and the consequent demands upon the fund correspondingly slight. As the system becomes older, however, the number of pensioners will constantly increase, the maximum not being reached for many years. The demands upon the fund will, moreover, increase at an even greater ratio, since pensioners once entered upon the fund remain a constant charge until their death. A condition of equilibrium, therefore, will not be reached until the number of deaths equals the number of new pensioners.

At the beginning, therefore, a condition of affairs is encountered where receipts are stationary, while expenditures are increasing in an almost geometrical ratio. Under these circumstances, it is manifestly unjust to make the contributions of each year meet the expenditures of that year, as is done in the case of insurance against accidents and sickness. Clear as this point is, it has been grossly disregarded in many instances. One of the most frequent and most dangerous errors made in the past in the organization of pension funds has been the neglect of this point, and the throwing upon the future, charges that were really incurred in former years.

This determination of probable charges in the future, and the fixing of dues so that each year will bear its just burdens, is, moreover, but one of the elements complicating the problem. Another equally important consideration is that of fixing dues so that justice will be done as between members of different ages. In the case of insurance against accidents and sickness, the risk does not vary greatly with the ages of members. In old-age insurance, the question of age constitutes the essential element. Instead of a single schedule of dues, therefore, it is necessary to have one graduated according to the ages of members upon joining the scheme. In other words, the total amount of dues paid by each member during his connection with the fund should, on an average, represent an amount sufficient to constitute, according to his chances of life, a fund for the payment to him of the pension he has contracted for.

To make these necessary calculations, there is required statistical data covering a long period of years and relating to a number of different classes of facts. The primary basis must of course be tables of mortality. Here, however, the ordinary mortality tables in use by life-insurance companies can only serve as a guide. In order to make sufficiently accurate calculations, it is necessary to have tables specially applicable to the different classes of workingmen, or at least to workingmen as distinct from the general population. Again, life-insurance tables are based on what are called "good risks," only those determined by medical examinations to be physically sound being accepted as policy holders. Workingmen's insurance, on the other hand, if it is to accomplish its highest aim, must include practically all workingmen, whatever their chances of life.

Up to this point we have been considering the question as one purely of old-age pensions. The problem is rendered much more complex by the fact that it is desirable to combine with this a partial system of life insurance. As insurance of workingmen has for its object the protection of the families of workingmen, as much as the workingmen themselves, provision is generally made for the pensioning of the widows and orphans of workingmen dying either before or after they have entered upon the enjoyment of their pensions. Still another complication is that whereby pensions are provided for members who become invalidated for work before reaching the minimum age at which pensions begin to run. All of these risks should be calculated separately, their total representing the insurance risk of each member.

The differences between old-age, and accident and sick insurance have been treated at some length, since there enters into them many of the most important questions involved in workingmen's insurance. Sufficient has certainly been said to show that old-age and invalidity insurance cannot well be combined with that of insurance against accidents or sickness. The grounds for the separation of the last two, though not so imperative, are yet of great strength. They can, however, be briefly stated.

The first relates to the basis upon which dues should be established. Not only should employers, in one case, and employés in the other, be the persons who should make the payments, but the determination of the amount of the dues should be made in quite different ways in the case of the two insurances. In the case of sickness, the problem is a comparatively simple one. It is but necessary to determine the average frequency and duration of cases of sickness, and fix dues accordingly. In general, no account need be taken of the occupation of members. There is a considerable body of data in existence from which such morbidity tables can be prepared, such as the results of the operations of the German and Austrian insurance systems, of the Friendly Societies of England, and of the mutual-aid societies of France and Belgium.

In the case of insurance against accidents, the problem is a much more complicated one. The risk of accident varies greatly in different industries. As it would be unjust to make the employers in one industry pay for accidents occurring in another, it becomes necessary to organize a special schedule of charges for each industry, or even for each occupation. To do this, it is necessary to have statistics of accidents for each industry and occupation, covering a considerable number of years, and showing in detail, not only the absolute number of accidents, but their proportion to the total number of employés, the results of the accidents, the number of days those receiving injuries are incapacitated for work, etc. In other words, it is desirable to have tables of the probabilities of accidents and the loss of time they cause, or, as it is called, the "coefficient of risk" for each industry and each occupation.

Great difficulty was experienced in the beginning of the movement for the insurance of workingmen in Europe, on account of the lack of information on these points. Germany, prior to the introduction of her system of insurance, was forced to make elaborate statistical investigations, in order to obtain data upon which to base its organization. Switzerland, as a part of a series of elaborate investigations concerning workingmen's insurance that she has been making with a view to the introduction of a system of compulsory insurance, has collected statistics of all accidents during a period of three years. Fortunately, some data concerning accidents to employés in the important industries of railway transportation and mining exist in almost every country, though it is far from satisfactory on such points as the severity of the accidents, the number of days lost from work by the sufferers, etc. The data on all of these points are, however, becoming daily more complete. However perfect these statistics may be, it is nevertheless necessary that each insurance organization should keep detailed and exact records of its own experiences. The differences in the conditions of production are such that the general tables should always be checked by the results of each institution.

The second reason for keeping independent the two systems, lies in the difficulties of their practical administration. In the case of accident, as in that of old-age insurance, the best results can be obtained by having the work more or less centralized. This is in order to give stability, and prevent the demands on the funds from fluctuating greatly from year to year. In the case of sick insurance, however, every consideration demands that the work should be localized as far as possible. This is not due simply to the fact that the amount of sickness in a community is fairly constant, but that simulation and imposition may be guarded against. The great evil inherent in sick insurance is the encouragement of members to simulate illness in order to obtain the benefit. The only method by which this can be at all controlled, is to organize the insurance on the plan of the small mutual-aid society, where every member knows his fellow-associates. Under these conditions, each member is directly interested in the financial condition of his society, and feels at the same time that any benefit wrongfully received must be paid by his companions. Simulation and malingering have been the greatest difficulties with which the German and Austrian systems have had to contend, and it is yet an open question whether they can successfully cope with the evil.

Systems of Insurance. — In the foregoing pages we have dealt only with the nature of insurance operations, the reasons for keeping separate the various kinds, and some of the more important points involved in the organization of any insurance scheme. We now pass to the various kinds of institutions, or systems, that have been devised for putting into practice the principles that we have been considering.

In Europe, the position has now been reached where there is a practical consensus of opinion that only in the development of insurance can there be found an adequate and rational method of providing for the relief of workingmen in cases of accidents, sickness, or old age. But if there is a consensus of opinion in regard to the need for insurance, it is far otherwise as regards the best system by which it can be accomplished. The great point of difference is as to the part that the government should play in the movement. There is probably no other question about which the contest of the principles of state action and private initiative is being more fiercely fought. The extent to which the state has intervened in providing insurance for the working classes constitutes the essential difference between the various systems that have been created. Using this principle, therefore, as a basis for classification, it will be found that all schemes of workingmen's insurance can be referred to four distinct classes.

I. Starting with that system in which the influence of the state is most prominent, we have, first, the system of compulsory state insurance. Here the state intervenes to the fullest extent. It practically takes over the insurance business, as far as the working classes are concerned, and makes of it a branch of the regular operations of the government. Furthermore, it makes obligatory upon the specified classes of the population that it hopes to benefit, the utilization of the system that it provides. It is important here to notice the essential difference between compulsory insurance and state insurance, as the two terms are frequently confused. The state may make insurance compulsory, and itself do little or nothing toward the provision of insurance institutions. On the other hand, the state may create insurance institutions, and leave it entirely to the free choice of workingmen whether they will take advantage of its benefits or not. Or, finally, it may make insurance obligatory, and itself provide the institution.

The best types of compulsory insurance are, of

course, those of Germany and Austria, where insurance against accidents, sickness, and old age is obligatory in the first, and against accidents and sickness in the second, for practically the entire laboring population. In the provision of institutions for their insurance, however, every possible use has been made of voluntary and locally organized funds, the creative power of the state being only invoked when such institutions did not exist. The interference of the state, therefore, is as far as possible limited to seeing that the amount of the insurance given is equivalent to the required standard, that the amount of dues is neither excessive nor too small in amount, and to determining the persons upon whom the payment of these dues shall fall.

Compulsory insurance has also gained a foothold in France. By the enactment of the law of June 29, 1894, the insurance of all mine employés against the three contingencies of sickness, accidents, and old age is made obligatory upon all coal operators of the country. Roumania also created a similar system in 1895; and Belgium has had for over fifty years a general system of miners' insurance which, if not actually, is for all intents and purposes compulsory upon mine owners.

II. The system in which the action of the state is next most prominent is that of voluntary state insurance. Here the state, instead of compelling workingmen to insure themselves, endeavors, by the creation of suitable institutions, and the offering of special inducements, to lead workingmen voluntarily to insure themselves. In doing this it but pursues a policy identical with that which has dictated the creation of national systems of savings banks. It is manifest that a state institution possesses important advantages over those privately organized. It offers a guarantee of security that no private concern can afford; it obtains notoriety and appeals to the imagination of the people as a government undertaking; it is in great part relieved from the expenses of advertising, the payment of commissions to agents, etc.; and, finally, it does not have to realize any profits. When we come to consider the various systems that have been created, it will be seen that state insurance has its disadvantages as well. It is sufficient in this place, however, simply to mention some of the advantages, in order to show the reasons that have dictated its development.

The best examples of state voluntary insurance are found in France, Belgium, and Italy. The first country has had in existence for a great many years three independent insurance departments, providing respectively insurance against accidents, old age and invalidity, and death. Belgium has also had in operation a similar institution for old-age insurance; and Italy has more recently entered this field, by creating in 1883, a national bank for the insurance of workingmen against accidents.

III. The third system is that of institutions privately organized, but controlled and aided by the state. This system occupies a sort of intermediary position between state and purely voluntary institutions. Unlike the other systems, it does not represent the deliberate creation of a state scheme, but arises in this wise. The laboring classes have organized purely voluntary institutions for their mutual assistance in cases of accidents or sickness. In time these societies reached such a position of importance, that the state was forced to enact special legislation in regard to them. This legislation was originally intended but to secure their honest and efficient management. But as the great good accomplished by them became more and more evident, the state, in addition to assuming a certain control over their operations, sought to aid their development in various ways, either by conferring upon them certain privileges, or even by granting them regular cash subsidies. The result of this twofold interference, to control and to aid, has been to create of these societies, in a number of instances, something like national systems of insurance. This movement is at the present time in full force. The tendency is for the state to carry its regulation further and further; to make these societies more uniform, both as regards their organization and operations; and thus to make of them general systems. The most important examples of this class are the Friendly Societies of Great Britain and the *Sociétés de Secours Mutuels* of France, Belgium, Italy, Switzerland, and other countries of the Continent. Under this class, also, come, to a greater or less extent, the aid funds organized in connection with labor or other organizations, though in these the interference of the state is reduced to a minimum.

IV. The fourth class of institutions is that wherein the state does not interfere at all, and consists of those funds voluntarily created by employers of labor for the purpose of aiding their employés in cases of sickness or accidents, or of providing them with a moderate pension when they are too old to work. This form of insurance is especially applicable to industries that must be carried on on a large scale, such as those of railway transportation, mining, the iron and steel industries, etc. In this country there are but few such funds, the relief departments of several of our railway systems forming the only important examples. In Europe, however, these funds are very numerous. In France and Belgium there is scarcely a railway, mining corporation, or other large industrial company, that does not maintain some sort of a fund of this description; and, in England, to cite no others, most, if not all, railway companies have such institutions.

These funds, though generally alike, differ widely in specific features. The work of many is of a very valuable character, while others have features which make them very objectionable institutions. One of the most important points of difference is that of the extent to which the workingmen are made to contribute to the support of the funds and are allowed to participate in their management.

In the foregoing we have been able to do little more than indicate some of the general considerations with which workingmen's insurance has to deal, and to make a classification of the kinds of insurance institutions that have been created in the different countries. It is difficult to discuss details, except in connection with the study of the organization and operations of actual institutions. The presentation and examination of the actual difficulties with which workingmen's insurance has to contend, and the various considerations that must be taken into account in any attempt to provide institutions for that purpose, have therefore been left to the chapters that follow.

CHAPTER II.

Workingmen's Insurance in Germany.

Introduction. — It is to Germany, more than to any other country, that one must turn to study workingmen's insurance in its most complete development. More than ten years have elapsed since the first law was enacted looking towards the introduction of a general system of compulsory insurance of workingmen. Since then, law after law extending the system has been placed upon the statute books, until to-day there is in practical operation a complete and harmonious system for the triple insurance of practically all workingmen of the empire against accidents, sickness, and old age and invalidity. There is thus afforded an opportunity of studying the question of workingmen's insurance in all of its branches, as applied to the same body of workingmen.

In order to appreciate the true spirit of the German workingmen's insurance legislation, to comprehend the part that it now plays in the industrial life of the people, and the attitude from which it is now regarded, it will be necessary to examine, at least briefly, the original causes which gave birth to it, and the political circumstances which hastened its development.

The present system of compulsory state insurance, often termed the boldest experiment in social legislation ever attempted, had its impelling causes in three distinct circumstances: that of the development of a political philosophy which accorded to the state the widest attributes for the purpose of improving social conditions; that of the rapid rise of a social democracy, which, impatient at the feeble improvement accomplished under the existing organization of society, avowedly sought a complete destruction of the existing social fabric in order to introduce a new régime; and that of the beneficial results already accomplished through partly voluntary and partly compulsory insurance societies.

The philosophical principles underlying German social legislation in its modern development may, in a measure, be said to take its rise from the works of Fichte. To him, at least, should be ascribed the greatest influence in shaping thought upon this subject in the early years of the movement. The works which he wrote in 1796 and 1800 rest upon an interpretation of equality and property, the logical consequence of which is socialism. Lassalle acknowledges his great indebtedness to him as the source from which he derived the inspiration for many of his teachings. Fichte's interpretation of the sphere of the state was that of one which should not only include the police power, but permit the fullest utilization of the powers of the state to improve the conditions of the people. Sismondi is another writer who may be mentioned as contributing powerfully toward moulding opinion in favor of the wide use of the state's power for the accomplishment of social reform.

These philosophical writers, represented by Fichte

and Sismondi, were the logical forerunners, and laid the basis for the system of the modern school of economists, whose advocacy of a wide extension to the powers of the state has earned for them the designation of socialists of the chair. The advocacy of the introduction of compulsory insurance by this school long antedated the introduction of a definite proposal looking toward that end. This fact should not be lost sight of. Compulsory insurance is far from an original conception of Bismarck. The matter of compulsory insurance did not become one of practical politics until it had received a thorough discussion and academic consideration on the part of the most distinguished economists of the country.

The first definite proposal for the adoption of compulsory insurance seems to have originated with Dr. Schaeffle, the leader of the state socialists, as well as their most voluminous writer. His efforts in this field have caused him to be called the father of compulsory state insurance. Certainly to no one else is the country more indebted for a careful study of all of the elements involved in such a scheme. His conception of the idea dates from at least as early as 1867. In that year he published a work, *Kapitalismus und Socialismus*, in which is elaborated a complete scheme of state insurance. After 1870, the discussion became general. In 1874, the *Verein für Social-Politik* made workingmen's insurance the subject of a special investigation, the result of which, however, was a declaration against insurance by the state in favor of insurance regulated by the state. The most distinguished economists, however, followed the lead of Schaeffle, and pronounced themselves in favor of compulsion. Chief among these may be mentioned Wagner, whose writings were of great influence in bringing about the ultimate triumph of this principle. Schaeffle, who, as we have seen, had indicated a plan as early as 1867, after laboring without ceasing fifteen years longer upon its elaboration, presented in his new book, appearing in 1881, *Der Korporative Hülfskassenzwang*, a scheme of insurance in which all the elements were worked out in the minutest details. In this plan can be found all the essentials of the legislation now in force.

It is evident from the foregoing, that compulsory insurance was not a scheme unexpectedly sprung upon the nation by the government, but was rather the putting into practice of a scheme resting upon a philosophical basis carefully worked out after years of discussion. The framers of the insurance laws had but to avail themselves of the principles established by this investigation.

This long preparation, the preliminary studies of economists of the first rank, explains the rapidity with which the laws were elaborated and enacted by the German government. The reason for the complete conversion of the government to the idea of compulsory insurance, and the occasion for its introduction, however, were due to political conditions. Compulsory insurance was avowedly taken up by Bismarck, for the purpose of checking the rapid growth of the social democratic party. His purpose was to outbid socialism in its own field. There is, however, an important distinction between the socialism of Bismarck and that of the social democratic party. The state socialism of Bismarck aims to remedy social ills through the instrumentality of the present political organization, while the socialism of the social democratic party — Marxist socialism — was avowedly revolutionary, and sought for a change in industrial conditions through the complete annihilation of the existing political fabric, and the building anew upon its ruins. There is no doubt that energetic measures were required, if this form of socialism was to be checked. Politically, the socialists were not strong before the Franco-German War of 1870–71. In 1872 they polled but 125,000 votes. In 1874 the vote had risen to 350,000; in 1877, to nearly half a million. Oppressive legislation was resorted to, but socialism could not be thus suppressed. With remarkable boldness, then, Bismarck changed his tactics, and attempted to guide where he could not arrest.

But compulsory insurance was not merely a system of social reform elaborated by economists, and taken up by the government as a measure of political necessity. The system inaugurated in 1883 was but the last step, though a long one, in the elaboration of means already in existence in Germany for the insurance of workingmen. For more than a generation insurance constituted one of the definite attributes of the trade guilds, and as such was recognized and regulated by law. In Prussia, the industrial ordinances of January 15, 1845, and the legislation of February 9, 1849, and April 3, 1854, contained provisions regarding relief and insurance funds, the purpose and result of which was to give to such institutions the greatest possible development. The law of 1854 was of especial importance, for by it the principle of compulsion was recognized, through the power given to the communes and other governmental authorities, not only to compel the formation of insurance societies, but to compel certain classes of employers to defray one-half the cost of their maintenance. The number of these societies at the end of the year 1876, that is to say, just before the new law of April 8, 1876, which regulated them anew, went into force, was 5239, with 869,204 members. In 1880 official statistics showed 839,602 members of registered friendly societies, 200,000 members of societies not registered, and 220,000 members of the special miners' societies, or a total of 1,259,602 members. In the mining industry, workingmen's insurance was practically universal. Theoretically and practically, therefore, the way was prepared for a general system of obligatory insurance.

The conditions leading up to and making possible a general system of workingmen's insurance have now been described. The actual formation of a plan, however, its introduction, and the rapidity with which its enactment and organization was secured, were due to the indomitable energy, the persistent efforts, and the unslacking courage with which obstacles were met and overcome of one man. Workingmen's insurance as it exists in Germany to-day is the creation of Chancellor Bismarck.

Though the system in its entirety, that of the triple insurance of workingmen against accidents, sickness, and invalidity or old age, required nearly a decade for its elaboration, the whole scheme was fully thought out and determined upon before a step was taken. That it was organized piecemeal was due to practical difficulties. In considering, then, the different kinds of insurance, it is important to remember that each is but a part of one general harmonious system, in which each of the three supplements and complements the others.

The plan of operations comprehended the organization of insurance against accidents as the initial step. In January, 1881, the first move was made by the introduction into the Reichstag of a bill providing for the creation of this form of insurance. This proposition was rejected; and, such was the opposition developed, that the early adoption of any plan seemed desperate. At this moment the Emperor intervened with his famous message to the Reichstag of November 17, 1881. In this communication, which is often called the "monument of the new social order," the complete scheme of workingmen's insurance is elaborated and unequivocally recommended. This message was productive of immediate effect. Heretofore there had been some doubt whether the Emperor was in thorough accord with his minister in his programme for social reform. All uncertainty was now removed. The enactment of the insurance laws was seen to be the most earnest wish of the sovereign. On the 8th of May, 1882, the government again took the initiative, and introduced two separate measures, relating, the one to insurance against accidents, and the other to insurance against sickness. Their introduction was simultaneous, because an intimate relationship existed between the two. Under these propositions, disability for work for thirteen weeks or less, though the result of an accident, was assimilated with cases of sickness, and the indemnification therefor made a charge upon the sick fund.

The second of the propositions, that providing for insurance against sickness, was the first to be passed, June 15, 1883. The bill providing for insurance against accidents was enacted into law the following year, July 6, 1884. It was not until five years later, June 22, 1889, that a law relating to the third branch of workingmen's insurance, that against old age and invalidity, was passed, and the complete scheme, as planned by Bismarck and outlined by the Emperor in his message of 1881, definitely organized.

Insurance against Sickness. — The preparation of a law concerning insurance against sickness presented unusual difficulties on account of the prior existence of institutions for this purpose. Though these private institutions had failed to secure for all workingmen the benefits of insurance, they had yet accomplished a great deal of good, and their operations had entered so thoroughly into the life of the working classes, that their preservation was desirable. The problem was, therefore, to devise a system by which insurance could be made general and compulsory, and at the same time existing institutions be modified as little as possible.

The preliminary steps leading to the introduction of the measure providing for compulsory insurance against sickness, and its final enactment, June 15,

1883, have been described in the Fourth Special Report of the United States Department of Labor, and need not be repeated here. According to this law, insurance against sickness, through one or the other means provided by the law, was made obligatory upon all workingmen and officials employed in mines, quarries, factories, or other industrial establishments, whose yearly wages did not exceed 2000 marks ($476). Permission, moreover, was given to the communes to make insurance obligatory upon small masters and mechanics, and to certain other classes voluntarily to become members of the system. April 10, 1892, a new law was enacted, going into effect January 1, 1893, by which the obligation of insurance was still further extended, so as to include persons employed in commercial firms, offices, etc. It will thus be seen that the fundamental principles followed in determining the classes to be subjected to compulsion were that they should be employés; that is, men not working on their own account, and should receive wages not exceeding 2000 marks a year.

The desirability of decentralizing, as far as possible, the administration of sick insurance was fully appreciated by the German government. Sick insurance was therefore entrusted to a large number of separate societies, each of which was made absolutely independent of the others as regards its receipts and expenditures. Together they were to constitute a single system only through the obligation to make annual reports, and to conform to the requirements of the law as regards the granting of a minimum amount of relief, the methods of raising and investing funds, etc. In many respects the ideal form of a sick-relief organization is that of a mutual-aid society among workingmen of the same locality and industry, and, if possible, of the same establishment. As the organization of such societies was practicable only in a limited number of cases, the law had to make provision for other kinds of organizations. The scheme thus provided for insurance societies of eight different kinds, through the affiliation with any one of which the requirements of the act could be fulfilled. These eight classes were, and are, as follows: —

(1) The Communal Sick Association (*Gemeindekrankenversicherung*). This is the loosest and least homogeneous of the eight. Into it are gathered all workingmen who cannot conveniently be included in the other kinds of associations. They constitute, to use the apt term of M. Bodenheimer, the "proletariat" of insurance.

(2) The Local Sick Association (*Ortskrankenkasse*). This is the most important of all of the associations. Through it are insured all industrial workers proper, who, because they are engaged in small establishments, cannot well be organized into factory or trade-guilds societies.

(3) The Factory Sick Association (*Betriebs[Fabrik]-krankenkasse*). Employers, if they have fifty laborers, may form for themselves independent associations, and, if the conditions are such as to make it desirable, they may be compelled to do so. Each industrial establishment is thus made to bear its own burdens. Practically, the only difference between the Factory and the Local Association is, that in the former

there is only one, while in the latter there are several employers. It will be remembered that a great many factory associations had already been formed by large manufacturing and mining establishments before the passage of the compulsory law.

(4) The Building-Trades Sick Association (*Baukrankenkasse*). On account of the intermittent character of construction work, it was found necessary to provide a special organization for the insurance of workingmen thus employed.

(5) The Trade-Guild Sick Association (*Innungskrankenkasse*). The various trade guilds in a good many cases had created funds for the benefit of their members prior to the enactment of the present law. The government, wishing to interfere with their operations as little as possible, made them one of the kinds of institutions for sick insurance, thus giving to members the privilege of insuring themselves in this way instead of through the other organizations.

(6) The Free Association, or Friendly Society (*Hülfskasse*). These were the old voluntary relief societies existing prior to the passage of the law, which in general were based upon no community of industry or trade-union membership. The government, in framing its measure, only allowed these societies to remain because they were compelled to do so. In them the burden of insurance is borne entirely by the persons insured, and the employers assist in no way. At the same time, the amount of relief granted is less than that given by the government-organized institutions. Nevertheless, a most deter-

mined effort was made by their members for their preservation. It was concerning their fate that the greatest fight in the Reichstag was waged. The result was a compromise, permitting the insurance conditions to be fulfilled through them, but leaving the entire expense upon their members as formerly. It is now well recognized, however, that this was a compromise in name only. The superior advantages offered by the other institutions are such that sooner or later this form of association will be crushed out.

(7) Independent State Association (*Landesrichtliche Hülfskasse*). These are sick associations organized under the auspices of the particular states of the empire, which the government was unwillingly forced to allow to remain in operation. Their disappearance, however, is but a matter of time.

(8) The Miners' Associations (*Knappsschaftskasse*). Insurance in the mining industry had been compulsory long before the enactments of the law of 1883. A general system of compulsory insurance by means of *Knappsschaftskasse*, as they were called, was therefore already in existence. As its operation was in every sense satisfactory, miners were expressly exempted from the operation of the law of 1883, and allowed to insure themselves through their own system. Practically, the only change made regarding them was to require them to modify their constitutions, when necessary, so that the minimum amount of relief, as established by the law of 1883, would in all cases be granted. The main difference between these societies and those organized by the law, is that they are not sick insurance associations solely, but

provide for old-age and invalidity pensions as well. As they are not made a part of the general system, reports of their operations are not included in the general reports concerning sick insurance. In the consideration of the practical results of sick insurance given further on, the results of their operations, therefore, cannot be included. Constituting an independent system, they will have to be studied apart.

Whatever the kind of association, the law provides that the following minimum of aid must be granted to members when sick:—

1. Free medical attendance and medicine from the beginning of their illness, if such illness lasts three days or more.

2. In case of incapacity for work, an indemnity for each working day, from the third day of illness, equal to one-half the daily wages of the insured, or else, in special cases, free hospital treatment, together with half the sick benefit.

3. In case of death, a cash benefit to the deceased's family for burial expenses amounting to twenty times the average daily wage; and

4. Sick relief to women during four weeks after confinement.

The total money value of this minimum relief is estimated to be equal to three-fourths of the average wages upon which the calculation is based. A great deal of latitude, however, is given the individual societies in determining each for itself the extent to which it will grant relief in excess of this minimum. Thus the law permits them to make the value of the relief granted equal to the full amount of the wages of the recipient, to extend the period during which sick relief is given so as to embrace an entire year, instead of thirteen weeks, and to women during their confinement from four to six weeks. The daily cash indemnity may also be raised from 50 to 75 per cent, and the burial money from 20 to 40 times the average daily wages. Benefits may also be paid for the first three days of the illness, as well as for Sundays and holidays; and, finally, the relief may even be extended to other members of the family and to convalescents.

The expense of the insurance is borne jointly by the workingmen and their employers, in the proportion of two-thirds and one-third respectively. The amount of the contributions that can be demanded is limited by law to from one to one and a half per cent of the usual local daily wages of ordinary laborers, in the case of certain associations, and cannot exceed from two to three per cent of the average daily wages of the class of workingmen insured, in the case of others. As a usual thing, it is the employer who makes the entire contribution, recouping himself by retaining the laborer's share from the latter's wages. Apart from the matter of contributions, the whole burden of administration falls upon the employer. It is upon him that rests the obligation to see that all of his employés are insured, to keep the record of the date of employment and of leaving of each employé, to see that all the rules concerning insurance are complied with, etc. All of this work must be done at his own expense, and therefore does not figure in any way in the expenses of administration.

Briefly to recapitulate then: insurance against sickness has not been accomplished through the creation of a central institution, or even of a central administration, as in the case of insurance against accidents and old age, but by a multitude of separate relief societies, each having a separate existence, and only joined together in one system by the general provision that a minimum amount of relief must be granted, and that annual reports must be made to a central authority. Each association has its own constitution, indicating the branches of industry for which it is founded, the classes of persons subjected to insurance, the nature and importance of the aid granted, the amount of dues, the method of government of the association, the revision of the constitution, etc. Each association is governed by officers elected by its members. In general, with the single exception of compulsion upon the part of workingmen to become members, the organization and work of these associations differ but little from that of ordinary mutual-aid societies existing in France, England, and other countries.

This system has now been in operation something over ten years. The German government annually publishes detailed statistics of its operations, and, as these figures constitute the most important data relating to the insurance of workingmen against sickness that exists, it will be desirable to consider the results in some detail.

As a social study, the statistical material furnished by any scheme of workingmen's insurance is of value, for two purposes: first, as showing the financial operations of the insurance system; and, secondly, as giving information concerning the frequency, character, and causes of accidents, sickness, or invalidity among the working classes. The second class of information is of interest apart from any connection it may have with the method of insurance employed. It will be conducive to clearness, therefore, to consider the question of the number of persons insured and the amount of sickness experienced, quite apart from the financial operations. This information is indispensable in order to understand the operations of the insurance scheme itself. There is first given a table, on the following page, showing the number and membership of each kind of insurance association for each year since the organization of the system.

These figures show at a glance the magnitude of the operations of sick insurance in Germany. The number of persons insured at the end of 1885 was 4,294,173. In 1893 the average number was 7,106,804, while the number at the end of the year was 6,754,735. Adding to this latter figure the number of miners insured in their special funds, 478,119, we find at the end of 1893 a grand total of 7,232,854 persons in the German Empire compulsorily insured against sickness. It is interesting to know what percentage this number is of the total population of the empire. This calculation has not been made in all of the annual reports. In 1889, however, the percentage was stated to be 13.4; in 1890, 13.8; in 1891, 14.1; in 1892, 13.9; and, in 1893, 14.2. It will thus be seen that an almost con-

WORKINGMEN'S INSURANCE IN GERMANY. 45

stantly increasing percentage of the population has been brought under the sick-insurance system. The present number includes practically the entire body

AVERAGE NUMBER AND MEMBERSHIP OF SICK INSURANCE ASSOCIATION, 1885-1893.

Year.	Communal.		Local.		Factory.		Building Trades.	
	Number.	Members.	Number.	Members.	Number.	Members.	Number.	Members.
1885	7,024	586,584	3,693	1,534,888	5,473	1,261,200	83	12,115
1886	7,170	629,069	3,739	1,701,305	5,615	1,314,216	105	12,897
1887	7,343	628,985	3,754	1,909,046	5,724	1,374,683	98	17,311
1888	6,874	770,959	3,783	2,220,731	5,807	1,434,667	115	28,627
1889	7,334	1,025,896	3,984	2,542,997	5,892	1,543,717	124	37,208
1890	7,606	1,101,364	4,064	2,746,025	6,044	1,673,531	109	29,058
1891	7,732	1,166,893	4,181	2,900,004	6,162	1,730,308	110	27,293
1892	7,802	1,179,845	4,220	2,998,378	6,257	1,742,838	108	29,743
1893	7,847	1,236,736	4,306	3,240,371	6,361	1,782,614	93	31,188

Year.	Trade-Guilds.		Friendly Societies.		Independent State Associations.		Total.	
	Number.	Members.	Number.	Members.	Number.	Members.	Number.	Members.
1885	224	24,879	1,805	730,722	474	143,785	18,776	4,294,173
1886	238	32,013	1,843	731,943	479	148,644	19,238	4,570,087
1887	350	41,700	1,838	727,127	466	143,374	19,573	4,842,226
1888	392	55,428	1,822	745,171	461	142,895	19,254	5,398,478
1889	420	63,237	1,848	786,272	463	144,872	20,065	6,144,199
1890	448	74,438	1,836	810,455	461	144,668	20,568	6,579,539
1891	462	78,064	1,804	838,481	446	138,883	20,897	6,879,921
1892	469	76,411	1,697	796,840	433	131,494	20,981	6,955,049
1893	472	90,528	1,838	662,860	264	63,007	20,681	7,106,804

of wage-earning men and women in Germany. The proportion of members who are women has steadily increased. On December 1, 1885, there were 22.2 women for every 100 men, while in 1893 the proportion was 27.9. This increase is probably due, not so much to any change in the policy pursued or in the character of the population to which the insurance law applies, as to the fact that it was difficult at first to reach the women, and they have only gradually been brought under the provisions of the act.

It has been necessary to give the figures for each kind of association separately, since it is a matter of prime importance to determine whether there is any tendency for the work to become centralized in fewer associations, and which kinds of organizations are proving themselves the stronger; or, in other words, toward what form of organization sick insurance is tending.

Concerning the first point, it is seen that the average number of associations has increased from 18,776, in 1885, to 20,681, in 1893. This increase, however, has not been sufficient to counterbalance the increase in membership. The result, therefore, has been that the average membership of associations, with the exception of friendly societies and independent state associations, which are dying out, has steadily increased. The average membership of each kind of association in 1885 and in 1893 was respectively; 83 and 157 for the communal; 415 and 752 for the local; 230 and 280 for the factory; 146 and 335 for the building trades; and 111 and 191 for the trade-guilds associations, or nearly, if not quite, a doubling in each case.

The question as to which kinds of associations are increasing in relative importance is one of still greater interest. Though all the funds are intended to serve a like purpose, there is evidently a wide difference between them. The factory association, for example, is a compact body of workingmen, all employed in the same establishment, while the communal or local association is based on territorial divisions and comprehends heterogeneous classes of laborers. Several important tendencies are clearly discernible. The first of these is the steady, and, in the latter years, rapid decrease in the number and membership of the friendly societies and independent state associations. The first have decreased from 1805, in 1885, representing 9.6 per cent of all associations, to 1338, or 6.5 per cent, in 1893. The second have decreased from 474, or 2.5 per cent, in 1885, to 264, or 1.3 per cent, in 1893. If the relative number of persons insured be taken, — a more important test of development, — this movement is seen to be still more pronounced. The registered friendly societies, which at the end of 1885 contained 17 per cent of all persons insured, at the end of 1893 contained but 9.8 per cent: the independent state associations, which at the end of 1885 contained 3.3 per cent, at the end of 1893 contained but 0.9 per cent. The significance of the elimination of these two kinds of associations lies in the fact that these are the two forms of voluntary insurance that the government was unwillingly forced to recognize, and that their place is being taken by the state-created institutions.

The factory associations, while increasing in both

number and membership, have declined slightly in relative importance, having but 26.1 per cent of the total membership of all associations at the end of 1893, as against 29.4 at the end of 1885. This is due to the rapid increase in importance of the communal and local associations. The membership of the first increased from 13.7 per cent of all persons insured in 1885, to 17.1 in 1893; and the second from 35.7 to 44.7 per cent. This increase resulted from the fact that when the law went into effect there was already organized a great many factory relief funds, and their constitution under the new plan was an easy matter. The organization of insurance in the rural districts, or among the workingmen employed in small industrial establishments, where the local and communal form of association had to be resorted to, was a more difficult matter and required time. The later years, therefore, show a rapid increase in these kinds of associations.

The information concerning the number and duration of cases of sickness contained in the reports of the German insurance associations constitutes perhaps the most important collection of statistics in existence in relation to sickness among workingmen. The three elements involved in the rate of sickness consist of the number of cases of sickness per member, the average duration of cases of sickness, and the average number of days of sickness per member. The latter constitutes what is called the "coefficient of morbidity." With these data, it is an easy matter to calculate the probable cost of sick insurance under any scheme. These facts are therefore shown in a table that follows. The information is not given for the years prior to 1888, as during those years only the number of persons insured at the end of the year was given, instead of the average number, as is done for the later years. It should also be stated that the figures here given do not represent the total number of days of sickness, but only those of which cognizance was taken by the insurance institutions. Thus, by days of sickness, there should be understood the number of days during which relief was granted. Such relief does not in general begin until after the third day, and cannot be prolonged beyond a fixed period. The number of cases of sickness also signifies exactly the number of interruptions of labor caused by sickness lasting more than three days, and the average duration of sickness expresses the average duration of such interruptions.

		1888.	1889.	1890.	1891.	1892.	1893.
Cases of sickness per 100 insured	men	33.5	34.8	38.1	35.9	36.8	40.7
	women	28.8	28.9	31.6	30.8	31.1	34.5
	both sexes	32.6	33.2	36.8	34.9	35.6	39.3
Average duration (days) of cases of sickness	men	16.6	16.1	16.0	16.8	17.0	16.2
	women	17.7	17.5	17.2	19.2	18.3	17.8
	both sexes	16.8	16.4	16.2	17.0	17.3	16.5
Days of sickness per 100 insured	men	555.6	553.0	608.4	601.5	626.6	659.8
	women	508.3	507.0	543.4	559.9	569.7	615.1
	both sexes	547.0	544.1	595.4	593.0	614.7	650.1
Deaths per 100 insured	men	1.0	1.0	1.0	1.0	1.0	1.0
	women	0.8	0.7	0.8	0.7	0.7	0.8
	both sexes	1.0	0.9	1.0	0.9	1.0	1.0

The two questions of importance that arise in connection with a table such as the one just given, are as to the amount of sickness that the insurance institutions must count upon, and whether sickness is becoming more or less prevalent.

As regards the first point, it will be seen, that, if the last year be taken as a basis, the insurance institutions must count upon an average of 39.3 cases of sickness per 100 members, or a little over one case for each three members insured. The average duration of cases of sickness being 16.5 days, it results that each member will on an average require relief during 6.5 days of each year. As would be expected, this coefficient of morbidity varies considerably in the different kinds of associations. The building-trades associations come first, with a coefficient of 8.6 days, and the factory associations second, with 7.2 days. This is quite natural, owing to the fact that these associations comprehend workingmen engaged in the more dangerous occupations, and all but severe accidents are considered as cases of sickness. The friendly societies come third, with 7.1 days, due to their more liberal provision in regard to the length of time that relief is granted; the independent state associations fourth, with 6.9 days; the local fifth, with 6.7; the trade guilds sixth, with 5.5; and the communal last, with 4.7 days.

A comparison of the figures for the two sexes reveals two rather curious facts. In every instance the number of cases of sickness per 100 members is greater for the men than for the women. On the other hand, with almost equal invariability, the average duration of cases of sickness is greater for the women than for the men. The general result, therefore, as shown by the coefficient of morbidity, does not differ greatly for the two sexes. A partial explanation for this may be found in the fact that the men are more exposed to accidents, which swell the number of cases of sickness, but that they either possess greater recuperative powers, or are more anxious to return to work as soon as possible than the women.

Concerning the second point, as to whether sickness has increased or not, the evidence unfortunately is not conclusive. The tables undoubtedly show, during the more recent years, an increase in the number of cases of sickness, and, consequently, in the number of days during which relief was granted. The increase in the number of cases per 100 members has been from 32.6 in 1888 to 39.3 in 1893, and in the number of days of sickness, from 547 to 650. This increase is found in the case of both men and women, and, in general, in all the different kinds of associations, showing conclusively that it is not due to special or local causes. If this represented a real increase in the amount of sickness, a serious showing would be made. The result here brought out has been made the chief support of the vigorous attacks that have been directed against the principles of compulsory insurance. There is little reason to believe, however, that sickness has actually increased. The increased number of cases of sickness is due to the fact that workingmen appeal for aid in a greater number of cases. Did these demands represent real cases requiring aid, there would be no occasion for comment. Unfortunately, a greater or less proportion represent cases of imposition. Simulation and malingering have probably increased, until to-day their detection constitutes the greatest difficulty with which the insurance officials have to deal. The opponents of compulsory insurance allege that this is the necessary concomitant of this form of insurance. On the other hand, those favoring the system claim that the increase shown is largely accounted for by the fact that when the system was new, all cases were not reported, and that the tendency has been to interpret the regulations more and more liberally as regards the right of workingmen to relief. In respect to simulation and imposition, they recognize the evil, but maintain that better supervision and increased experience will enable the associations to keep them in check, and that, furthermore, such imposition is by no means peculiar to a compulsory system, but exists in voluntary organizations as well. With our present knowledge, it is impossible for us to pass final judgment upon the question. We can only recognize that simulation is an evil that has to be encountered in any general system of insurance. The most effective remedy against it would seem to be to make benefits so low that inducements for its practice would be absent.

We now turn to the financial operations of insurance. We have seen the amount of sickness with which the insurance institutions have had to deal. It remains to show how much relief has been granted, and how the necessary funds have been raised. The growth of the system, from the financial standpoint, during the nine years under survey, is shown by the following statement of total receipts and expenditures during each of these years.

Year.	Receipts.	Expenditures.
1885	$15,731,882	$12,479,380
1886	17,366,002	13,819,508
1887	18,784,931	14,444,884
1888	21,875,635	20,353,067
1889	24,402,100	22,700,520
1890	27,264,879	25,668,444
1891	28,542,297	26,830,707
1892	29,512,104	27,805,497
1893	31,311,789	29,837,937

This table is of value only as showing the rapid development of the financial operations of the system. The sums stated do not represent the actual amount of money raised and expended each year, as there are included such terms as cash on hand, the purchase and sale of securities, and the like, which, for official purposes, it is necessary to include in the accounts. Fortunately, we are able to construct from information given in the annual reports the following table, in which account is taken of those items only which are actual receipts and expenditures. We are thus able to determine exactly how much the system of sick insurance costs each year, and how the money is raised and expended.

Actual Net Receipts and Expenditures of Sick Insurance Associations.

RECEIPTS.

Year.	Amount.				Per Cent of Total.			
	Contributions.	Interest.	Other.	Total.	Contributions.	Interest.	Other.	Total.
1885	$ 13,360,149	$ 195,225	$ 500,793	$ 14,056,167	95.0	1.4	3.6	100.0
1886	14,786,593	260,276	484,853	15,531,722	95.2	1.7	3.1	100.0
1887	16,013,353	317,453	508,869	16,839,675	95.1	1.9	3.0	100.0
1888	17,814,090	392,963	656,531	18,863,584	94.4	2.1	3.5	100.0
1889	20,063,849	485,366	654,170	21,203,385	94.6	2.3	3.1	100.0
1890	21,715,261	553,852	766,235	23,035,348	94.3	2.4	3.3	100.0
1891	23,028,315	612,603	761,503	24,402,421	94.4	2.5	3.1	100.0
1892	23,628,138	657,495	793,302	25,078,935	94.2	2.6	3.2	100.0
1893	25,300,874	656,137	867,162	26,824,173	94.3	2.5	3.2	100.0

EXPENDITURES.

Year.	Amount.				Per Cent of Total.			
	Relief.	Administration.	Other.	Total.	Relief.	Administration.	Other.	Total.
1885	$ 11,281,229	$ 805,519	$ 341,832	$ 12,428,580	90.8	6.5	2.7	100.0
1886	12,623,762	845,167	295,883	13,764,832	91.7	6.1	2.2	100.0
1887	13,138,092	910,144	332,999	14,381,235	91.4	6.3	2.3	100.0
1888	14,651,633	1,071,781	344,287	16,067,701	91.2	6.7	2.1	100.0
1889	16,892,096	1,175,968	340,989	18,409,053	91.8	6.4	1.8	100.0
1890	20,001,523	1,283,576	391,456	21,676,555	92.3	5.9	1.8	100.0
1891	21,221,530	1,381,668	410,580	23,013,778	92.2	6.0	1.8	100.0
1892	22,433,493	1,465,123	449,179	24,347,795	92.1	6.0	1.9	100.0
1893	24,269,264	1,632,333	440,862	26,342,459	92.1	6.2	1.7	100.0

The most noticeable fact shown by this table is the invariability from year to year of the relative importance of the items. All have naturally increased with the growth of the system, but all have increased in nearly the same proportion. The actual cost of sick insurance, it will be seen, is now over $26,000,000, or more than twice as much as when the system was first organized.

As regards the manner in which this sum is raised, it may be said that sick insurance is almost entirely supported by the contributions of the employers and employés, that item alone accounting for from 94 to 95 per cent of net receipts. The item of interest accounts for about 2.5 per cent, and other miscellaneous receipts for a little over 3 per cent. Slight differences exist between the different kinds of associations in regard to the relative importance of the different items. Thus, the factory associations show only from 91 to 92 per cent of receipts to be derived from contributions, while trade-guilds associations show from 96 to 97 per cent to be derived from this source.

The information regarding expenditures is of still greater interest. The most important feature is that of the cost of administration. The results as shown in the table are in this respect very favorable. Expenses of administration are accountable for only about 6 per cent of net expenditures, while about 92 per cent goes directly for purposes of relief. Naturally some difference is found in the different kinds of associations. In the case of the communal associations, no expense of administration is returned, since the system is administered by the local government authorities, and no special account is kept of its cost. The effectiveness of the factory association is strikingly evident. Ninety-seven per cent of all expenditures go directly to their members in the form of relief of one kind or another, and the cost of administration is practically nothing. Trade-guilds associations show the greatest cost of administration, about 13 per cent of expenditures being absorbed in this way. Local associations come next, with 10 per cent going for this purpose.

To bring out more fully the significance of statistics of sick insurance, however, it is necessary to bring the total amount expended into relation with the total number of persons insured and the total days of sickness indemnified, so that it will be possible to determine the cost of insurance per member and the average expense per day of sickness. In this way only can it be seen what insurance actually means to the individual. These calculations have been made, and are shown in the table following. The information cannot be given for the years prior to 1888, as the official reports did not return the average number of persons insured.

This table shows in the most direct way the real workings of the insurance system. The actual cost of sick insurance is thus shown to be $3.70 per member during the last year covered by the table, and the expenditures to be 52 cents per day of sickness. In both cases it will be seen that the average expenditure has constantly increased. The net average expenditure per member, which was but $2.97

in 1888, has risen each year, being in 1893 73 cents more than that amount. That this is due to the greater liberality shown in granting relief, is seen from the fact that the average expenditure per day of sickness has likewise increased.

Net Expenditure per Member and per Day of Sickness of Sick Insurance Associations.

	Year.	Communal.	Local.	Factory.	Building Trades.	Trade Guilds.	Friendly Societies.	Independent State Associations.	Total.
Net expenditure per member.	1888	$1.67	$2.87	$3.63	$4.23	$2.37	$3.31	$3.36	$2.97
	1889	1.67	2.94	3.67	4.96	2.43	8.42	8.41	2.99
	1890	1.80	3.20	4.11	4.86	2.66	3.85	3.83	3.29
	1891	1.79	3.29	4.14	4.58	2.84	3.95	3.78	3.34
	1892	1.89	3.41	4.31	4.95	3.07	4.32	4.26	3.50
	1893	2.01	3.65	4.71	5.44	3.24	4.34	4.63	3.70
Expenditure per day of sickness.	1888	0.41	0.47	0.59	0.47	0.48	0.45	0.45	0.49
	1889	0.42	0.48	0.61	0.56	0.50	0.46	0.47	0.50
	1890	0.42	0.47	0.61	0.59	0.50	0.48	0.48	0.51
	1891	0.42	0.48	0.64	0.61	0.49	0.49	0.48	0.52
	1892	0.42	0.48	0.65	0.59	0.50	0.49	0.52	0.52
	1893	0.42	0.48	0.63	0.60	0.50	0.54	0.54	0.52

A considerable variation in the amount of relief given and the cost of insurance in the different kinds of institutions will be noticed. It will be remembered that each association is given considerable freedom in regard to the amount of relief that it may grant. In the factory associations, which are the strongest organizations, the average expenditure per person was, in 1893, $4.71½, and in the building-trades associations $5.44½, while in the communal associations the average expenditure was but $2.01. In all, however, there is found a steady augmentation during the later years.

Another showing of interest is that whereby the amount paid by members themselves is contrasted with the amount that they receive in the way of aid when sick. This is best done by showing the average amount paid by each member in dues and entrance fees, the average expenditure per member for actual relief, omitting all other expenditures, and the excess of the latter over the former. It will be remembered that in all the obligatory associations the dues are paid by the workingmen and their employers, in the proportion of two-thirds by the former and one-third by the latter. Entrance fees are entirely paid by the workingmen. Taking all of the associations together, the average amount paid by each member was, in 1889, $2.38. Each year has shown a slight increase, and in 1893 the average amount was $2.53. The average value of the relief given has during the same time increased from $2.75 in 1889 to $3.41 in 1893. Each year the position of the insured has become more advantageous. In 1889 he received 37 cents more than he paid in; in 1890, 64 cents; in 1891, 66 cents; in 1892, 77 cents; and in 1893, 88 cents. A considerable difference will be found in this respect in the different kinds of associations. The factory and building-trades associations occupy one extreme, where the members received, in 1893, $1.65 and $1.80 respectively more than they contributed, and the registered friendly societies and independent state associations the other extreme, with an actual excess of contributions over relief afforded.

Insurance against Accidents. — The insurance of workingmen against accidents was the second branch of workingmen's insurance introduced by Germany.

The system, as it exists to-day, is the result of a steady growth. At the time of its introduction, Germany pursued the policy of, first including under its provisions only the more important classes of workingmen, and then, after the system was in good running order, extending them, by subsequent legislation, to other classes. The first law, that of July 6, 1884, provided for the obligatory insurance of workingmen employed in the manufacturing and mechanical industries. By the law of May 28, 1885, the system was extended so as to embrace employés of companies engaged in inland transportation by land or water, including the administration of the postal and telegraphic services, the railways, the army, and the navy. This extension, which is essentially based upon the law of July 6, 1884, placed the insurance, as far as the government institutions above named were concerned, directly in the hands of the empire or the respective federated states. The next law, that of March 15, 1886, provided for the insurance of state officials, military officers, and soldiers. In the same year, a law of May 5 extended the provisions of the fundamental law of 1884 to persons engaged in agriculture and forestry. In the next year, the two laws of July 11 and July 13, 1887, respectively, extended the system to persons employed in construction work and to seamen, not including fishermen. At the present time, therefore, there are included under the system of compulsory insurance against accidents practically all workingmen, except fishermen, domestic servants, and certain artisans and other laborers working on their own account. This steady extension explains the rapid growth in the number of persons insured, as shown by the tables hereafter given.

The insurance provided for by these laws is made compulsory only for workmen and officials whose salaries do not equal or exceed 2000 marks ($476) per annum. This maximum may be raised by statutory regulation, and the privilege of becoming insured may be granted to employers.

The object of the insurance is to secure compensation for bodily injury or for death in consequence of an accident to a workingman while working for his employer, injuries sustained on other occasions being excluded. As a matter of course, the injured man must not have brought about the accident purposely. The compensation includes the cost of the cure, and, in addition, a fixed allowance during the period of his incapacity for work, or, in fatal cases, burial money and an allowance to the surviving widow, children, or parents from the day of death. When the injured person is totally disabled, the compensation amounts to two-thirds of his average year's earnings; if only partially incapacitated, a fraction of this amount. For the first 13 weeks after the accident (the so-called waiting time), the sick association, or, in its absence, the employers, take care of the injured.

The system of insurance is that of trade associations, organized under the guarantee of the empire. Owing to the different character of the workingmen insured, it was found desirable to group them into the three distinct categories of employés engaged in manufacturing and mechanical industries, in agriculture and forestry, and in public administration, and to establish for each a somewhat different system of organization. That for the first class, which is by far the most important of the three, constitutes the fundamental basis for the whole scheme, and has been departed from only when special conditions have made it advisable.

For this group, employers in the same lines of industry are organized into trade associations, or corporations, including all of their number in certain districts or in the whole empire. These trade associations enjoy the character of legal persons and a perfect self-administration, which they may decentralize by forming "sections" or appointing "confidential agents." They are in a way independent insurance societies. The insured workingmen themselves are neither members of the association nor do they bear any of the corporate burdens. They have, however, as will be seen, a voice in fixing the indemnity, in cases where the amount to be awarded is in dispute. The entire burden of the insurance is borne by the employers in proportion to the risks to which each one exposes his association. These risks for each establishment are determined by a distribution of the various occupations over the several classes of a danger tariff drawn up by the association.

As it is evident that both the trade associations and their individual members have a strong interest in diminishing the number of accidents, the law confers on associations the right to prescribe regulations for the prevention of accidents. Through these regulations, the employers can be compelled, under penalty of higher assessments, to adopt the necessary measures for safety, and the workmen be forced to follow these rules by fines. Nearly, if not all, of the associations have adopted such regulations.

The amount of compensation is fixed for each accident, after a police investigation, by the organs of that trade association in whose jurisdiction the accident happens. Against this decision an appeal may be made to an arbitration court, composed of two members of the trade association, two representatives of the injured workman, and a presiding magistrate. This tribunal is invested with the character of a special court of law. In more complicated cases, an appeal from its verdict may be made to the imperial insurance department. This latter body is the supreme court for all that has reference to the organization and administration of the system. It is composed of permanent members, consisting of a president appointed for life by the Emperor, on the recommendation of the federal council, and several higher officers similarly appointed, and temporary members consisting of four delegates from the federal council and representatives of the employers and employed, in equal numbers. Two judicial officers are added to assist in the decision of the more important cases, such as appeals to the imperial insurance department and the settlements and adjustments of claims in the case of changes in the composition of trades associations. For some of the federated states, special state insurance officers have been established.

The actual operation of the payment of indemnities is made through the post-offices, upon orders of the directing board of the associations. These advances have to be refunded by the associations at the end of each year.

In the case of the agriculture and forestry group, certain deviations from the fundamental system, more particularly with regard to organization and management, were found necessary. Thus, in consequence of the uniformity in agricultural pursuits, the districts of the insurance association adjust themselves to the political boundaries of county, province, or state; and the current administration, as far as it belongs to the directing board, may be entrusted to organs of the political administration. The average rate of wages for agricultural laborers, as fixed by the higher administrative officers after consultation with the local authorities, moreover, is taken as the basis for determining the amount of the benefits, instead of the actual earnings of the injured. The contributions, too, may be assessed, not according to the number of hands employed, but on the basis of direct taxes, and small proprietors may be partially or totally exempted.

As regards the third group, that of public administration, the important difference is that the expense of insurance is made a charge upon the budget of each particular service. There is, therefore, no special levying of contributions, no apportionment of expenses, etc. The imperial insurance department has really, therefore, but little concern with this class of insurance.

This system has now been in operation twelve years. Unfortunately, owing to the delay in issuing annual reports, we will be able to study the results of only the first nine years.

As in the case of insurance against sickness, it is preferable to consider independently the results of the system so far as they throw light upon the extent of the insurance operations and the frequency of accidents, and the actual financial operations of insurance. There is, therefore, first given a table showing the number of insurance associations and the number of persons insured in each of the three groups for the first nine years that the system has been in operation. Employés engaged in agriculture and forestry were not brought under the provisions of the law until the year 1888. Public works include state railways, telegraphs, etc. This table is of importance merely as showing the constant growth of the system. By far the most interesting class of information is that concerning the number and severity of accidents. The information here afforded is of unique value. Heretofore statistics have been obtainable concerning accidents to special classes of workingmen, as railway employés or miners. For the first time, however, there is here afforded information concerning accidents to laborers in practically all industrial pursuits. This information is given in the official reports separately for each of the 64 groups of industries, or insurance associations, into which the employés of manufacturing and mechanical industries are organized. Limitation of space, however, prevents us from giving more than the most general results.

NUMBER OF ACCIDENT INSURANCE ASSOCIATIONS AND PERSONS INSURED, 1886–1894.

Year.	Manufacturing and Mechanical Industries.		Agriculture and Forestry.		Public Works.	
	Associations.	Persons Insured.	Associations.	Persons Insured.	Associations.	Persons Insured.
1886	62	3,478,435	..	...	47	251,878
1887	62	3,861,560	..	...	48	259,977
1888	64	4,320,663	22	5,576,765	178	446,250
1889	64	4,742,548	48	8,088,698	285	543,320
1890	64	4,926,672	48	8,088,698	316	604,380
1891	64	5,093,412	48	12,289,415	352	632,459
1892	64	5,078,132	48	12,289,415	348	646,733
1893	64	5,168,973	48	12,289,415	372	660,462
1894	64	5,243,965	48	12,289,415	385	658,307

Under the German system, accidents are classified into those fatal, those causing total and partial permanent disability, and those causing only a temporary incapacity for labor. This is the system that is almost universally employed where any effort is made to collect statistics of accidents. The only class in which a serious difference between different systems is made, is that of the last, or accidents resulting in temporary disability. There are, of course, a great number of accidents resulting in so slight an injury that no account should be taken of them. The test for their inclusion is usually the establishment of a minimum number of days of incapacity, and only those accidents resulting in an inability to work of longer duration than this period entitle the victims to an indemnity, and consequently figure in the statistical returns of the number of accidents indemnified. In Germany this minimum, as has been shown, is very high, 13 weeks, owing to the provision that lesser accidents shall be cared for through the sick-insurance system.

The following table shows the number of accidents declared and the number for which indemnities were granted during each year since the organization of the system.

NUMBER OF ACCIDENTS DECLARED AND INDEMNIFIED, 1886–1894.

Year.	Manufacturing and Mechanical Industries.		Agriculture and Forestry.		Public Works.	
	Declared.	Indemnified.	Declared.	Indemnified.	Declared.	Indemnified.
1886	92,319	9,723	. . .	. . .	7,840	817
1887	105,897	15,970	. . .	. . .	9,578	1,132
1888	121,164	18,809	5,102	808	11,181	1,440
1889	139,549	22,340	19,542	6,631	14,694	2,048
1890	149,188	26,403	32,186	12,573	17,332	2,444
1891	162,674	28,289	42,296	19,559	19,087	2,859
1892	165,003	28,619	50,186	23,231	19,567	2,977
1893	182,120	31,171	59,006	27,553	21,213	3,150
1894	190,744	32,797	68,751	32,491	21,347	3,389

This table serves to bring out the great extent to which the working classes in all industries suffer from accidents. The reason for the great difference between the number of accidents declared and those indemnified lies in the fact that all accidents causing the sufferer to be unable to work during three days must be reported, while only those causing disability during 13 weeks are indemnified.

A more important point, however, than the absolute number of accidents is the risk that each employé runs of being injured. To show this, it is necessary to make a calculation of the number of accidents in proportion to the number of persons insured. It is only in this way, also, that the results of different years can be compared. In the accompanying table, therefore, there is shown the number of accidents per 1000 workingmen insured for each group of insurance institutions and for each year.

Without a doubt the most important feature of this table is the information which it presents concerning the question as to whether the number of accidents is increasing or not. The class of manufacturing and mechanical industries is the really important group, and it will be sufficient to make an examination of the figures concerning it. For this group, it will be seen that there is shown a steady augmentation in the number of accidents in proportion to the number of persons insured. From a proportion of 2.80 accidents indemnified per 1000 workingmen in 1886, the number has increased to 6.25 in 1894.

At first inspection, this represents a startling increase, and the figures have been made the basis for

Number of Accidents per 1000 Persons Insured, 1886–1894.

Industry.	Year.	Accidents Declared.	Accidents Indemnified.				
			Fatal.	Total Permanent Disability.	Partial Permanent Disability.	Temporary Disability.	Total.
Manufacturing and mechanical industries.	1886	23.78	0.70	0.44	1.09	0.57	2.80
	1887	27.42	0.77	0.73	2.11	0.53	4.14
	1888	28.04	0.68	0.43	2.38	0.86	4.35
	1889	29.42	0.71	0.49	2.70	0.81	4.71
	1890	30.28	0.73	0.38	3.27	0.98	5.36
	1891	31.94	0.71	0.31	3.43	1.10	5.55
	1892	32.49	0.65	0.30	3.55	1.14	5.64
	1893	35.23	0.69	0.27	3.82	1.25	6.03
	1894	36.37	0.65	0.16	3.82	1.62	6.25
Agriculture and forestry.	1888	0.91	0.06	0.01	0.03	0.04	0.14
	1889	2.42	0.17	0.03	0.33	0.29	0.82
	1890	3.98	0.23	0.05	0.67	0.60	1.55
	1891	3.44	0.18	0.05	0.72	0.63	1.58
	1892	4.08	0.16	0.06	0.90	0.77	1.89
	1893	4.80	0.18	0.06	1.21	0.79	2.24
	1894	5.59	0.18	0.04	1.40	1.02	2.64
Public works.	1886	31.13	1.17	0.91	0.72	0.44	3.24
	1887	36.84	1.21	1.30	1.29	0.55	4.35
	1888	25.06	0.78	0.61	1.29	0.55	3.23
	1889	27.04	0.80	0.54	1.63	0.80	3.77
	1890	28.68	0.80	0.62	1.82	0.80	4.04
	1891	30.18	0.88	0.55	2.27	0.82	4.52
	1892	30.29	0.78	0.54	2.33	0.95	4.60
	1893	32.12	0.78	0.51	2.42	1.06	4.77
	1894	32.42	0.84	0.51	2.65	1.15	5.15

an adverse criticism of the system of compulsory insurance, similar to that directed against the scheme for sick insurance. It is claimed that it is thus statistically demonstrated, what before had been merely alleged, that compulsory insurance tends to lessen the carefulness of workingmen; that, certain of assistance, they take fewer precautions to avoid danger. A further analysis of these returns, however, in order to see which classes of accidents have contributed the most to this increase, goes a long way toward the refutation of this assumption. It will be seen that in the classes of serious accidents, or those resulting in death or total disability, there has been an actual decrease of from 0.70 per 1000 workingmen in 1886, to 0.65 in 1894, in the first case, and from 0.44 to 0.16 in the second case. The entire increase has therefore been in the class of minor accidents, the increase being from 1.09 in 1886 to 3.82 in 1894, in the case of accidents causing partial permanent disability, and from 0.57 to 1.62 for accidents causing temporary disability only. Now it happens that it is in the classes of serious accidents that little room is left for a variation in practice from year to year in determining what accidents shall be indemnified. In the case of lesser injuries, the same cannot be alleged. The increases shown in the tables are easily susceptible of explanation upon the ground that, as the system became more developed and better known by the workingmen, slight accidents were made the basis for a claim for an indemnity that in the early years were not believed to be of sufficient severity to warrant the recipients making them known. The conclusion of the French Labor Bureau, which made an investigation of this question, can probably, therefore, be safely adopted. "It is thus not proven," it says, "that obligatory insurance has increased the number of accidents as the result of negligence it has induced on the part of employer or employé. If this cause had acted, it ought to have made itself manifest in all the categories of accidents. But that which can be affirmed is, that injured workingmen have not shown the same energy to recommence work after an injury giving a right to an indemnity, and that this tendency has materially increased the number of accidents which give a right to an indemnity without causing an absolute incapacity for labor."

Before passing now to an examination of the financial operations of the system, or the insurance feature proper, it will be necessary to describe briefly the system according to which provision is made for the payment of indemnities which extend over a number of years. An accident causing death or total disability gives a right to a pension that may run for a number of years. In making provision for the payment of such pensions, a choice lies between two systems Under the first, provision is made only for the payment of the money due during the current year, leaving to the receipts of subsequent years the payment of the sums falling due those years. Under the second system, as soon as the amount of the pension is determined, there is carried to a special fund a sum estimated to be sufficient on the average to meet all payments that will be required on account of that pension.

Germany has adopted the first of these, or the *Umlageverfahren* system, as it is called, while Austria, as will be seen, has adopted the second, or *Deckungsverfahren* system. The selection of one or the other of these systems materially determines the character of the financial organization of the scheme. Under the German method, the amount paid for indemnities must increase rapidly, as during each succeeding year there will have to be met, not only the indemnities due on account of accidents occurring during its course, but payments on all pensions still running as the result of accidents received during previous years. Theoretically, it is estimated that the charges will not become constant for a period of twenty-four years. To meet this certain increase in expenditure, therefore, each insurance institution in Germany is required to make heavy payments into a reserve fund during the first few years. During the first year this payment must be equal to 300 per cent of the amount paid out in indemnities; during the second year, a sum equal to 200 per cent; during the third, 150 per cent; during the fourth, 100 per cent; during the fifth, 80 per cent; during the sixth, 60 per cent; and 10 per cent less each year until the eleventh year. After the first eleven years, the interest of the reserve fund is to be added to the principal until the fund reaches twice the sum annually needed, and thereafter, so long as this standard is maintained, the interest of the reserve fund may be used for meeting current obligations.

The foregoing explanations have been necessary in order that the statement of receipts and expenditures that will now be given may be understood, and especially that the figures may be used intelligently for purposes of comparison with the results obtained under the Austrian and other systems of insurance. In this table it has been necessary to make separate state-

RECEIPTS AND EXPENDITURES OF ACCIDENT INSURANCE ASSOCIATIONS. MANUFACTURING AND MECHANICAL INDUSTRIES.

	1886.	1888.	1890.	1892.	1894.
Receipts.					
Funds on hand	....	$739,963	$1,471,985	$2,331,849	$2,519,475
Contributions	$2,911,054	6,160,082	8,145,919	9,876,076	11,040,848
Fines	4,491	33,857	33,392	38,940	38,836
Interest	5,632	17,064	38,777	69,804	94,023
Other	25,729	28,786	41,245	88,508	166,914
Total	$2,946,906	$6,979,752	$9,731,268	$12,405,177	$13,859,596
Expenditures.					
Aid and indemnities	$407,384	$2,061,744	$3,886,631	$5,705,685	$7,404,254
Preventive measures	16,644	78,156	81,283	104,421	147,410
Investigation	20,608	63,556	118,920	153,958	199,075
Arbitration	28,733	56,484	74,223	92,363	109,416
Administration proper	553,182	779,978	908,135	1,025,793	1,159,437
Organization	140,452	27,046	3,673	887	84
Reserve fund	1,285,647	2,930,243	2,881,005	2,805,899	2,232,131
Total	$2,452,650	$5,997,207	$7,948,870	$9,889,006	$11,251,807
Funds on hand	$739,422	$980,545	$1,782,398	$2,516,171	$2,664,328
Amount of reserve fund	$1,300,218	$6,737,446	$13,169,422	$19,815,456	$26,081,830

AGRICULTURE AND FORESTRY.

	1888.	1890.	1892.	1894.
Receipts.				
Funds on hand	....	$116,874	$255,730	$418,204
Contributions	$108,623	735,837	1,652,846	2,730,076
Fines	38	996	2,036	2,207
Interest	16	1,126	3,779	6,989
Other	1,570	7,501	4,877	7,484
Total	$110,247	$862,334	$1,918,768	$3,164,960
Expenditures.				
Aid and indemnities	$10,201	$447,073	$1,197,854	$2,048,700
Preventive measures	31	917	1,693	4,588
Investigation	1,965	38,266	86,499	129,894
Arbitration	951	13,787	27,690	43,082
Administration proper	64,114	204,553	273,499	376,583
Organization	29,449	4,675	1	....
Reserve fund	3,197	98,212	190,601	224,786
Total	$109,908	$807,483	$1,777,837	$2,827,633
Funds on hand	$42,321	$163,335	$356,557	$474,175
Amount of reserve fund	$3,197	$135,546	$516,053	$965,327

PUBLIC WORKS.

	1886.	1888.	1890.	1892.	1894.
Expenditures.					
Aid and indemnities	$48,473	$227,626	$444,275	$688,528	$933,743
Preventive measures	5	1,718	5,179	4,408	4,329
Investigation	112	495	1,867	3,089	6,646
Arbitration	1,424	2,712	4,540	6,332	8,462
Administration proper	466	846	1,320	1,562	1,767
Organization	7	332	588	71	151
Total	$50,487	$233,229	$457,769	$703,990	$955,098

ments for each of the three groups of industries, as conditions are so dissimilar in each. In the case of public work, only a statement of expenditures is given, as there were, properly speaking, no receipts. The expense of the payment of the indemnities constitutes an annual charge upon the regular budgets of the different public works.

These tables show a rapid increase from year to year in almost every particular. In the case of manufacturing and mechanical industries, receipts have increased from $2,946,906 in 1886, to $13,859,596 in 1894. The greater part of receipts comes from contributions required of employers, though, with the accumulation of interest-bearing funds on hand, the item of interest figures to an increasing extent. Expenditures in the meantime increased from $2,452,650 in 1886, to $11,251,807 in 1894, which augmentation has been almost entirely due to the increase in the amount paid for aid and indemnities. It will be remembered that this increase is the necessary result of the financial system adopted.

Owing to the fact that the indemnification of an accident may not be completed for a good many years, it is impossible to show what has been the cost of insurance, either per accident, or per person insured. If we take the total expenditures for the nine years, and the total number of accidents indemnified during that period, it will be found that each accident has cost, on an average, $322.06. This average amount, however, will continue to increase as the pension list becomes longer. The average expenditure per person insured was, in 1894, $2.16, a sum that will also increase yearly, until a period of equilibrium is reached As yet, therefore, it is impossible to tell what is the normal cost of insurance under the German system.

Insurance against Old Age and Invalidity. — The insurance of workingmen against invalidity and old age constituted an integral part of the general scheme of workingmen's insurance, as outlined in the imperial message transmitted to the Reichstag in 1881, and on which a first beginning was made by the creation of the sick-insurance system in 1883. It was not, however, until June 22, 1889, that the government was able to secure the enactment of a law putting this intention into execution.

Previous to this date, however, a large number of organizations, such as mutual-aid societies, miners' relief societies, railway-employés relief associations, and certain other industrial societies, had long had in operation systems of invalidity and old-age insurance in connection with insurance against sickness. But with the exception of the miners' societies (*Knappschaftsvereine*), which in Prussia were regulated by law since 1854, and the regulations adopted for the railway employés' funds, this insurance was left entirely to individual initiative and management.

The law of 1889, therefore, completed and rounded out the work of organizing compulsory insurance in Germany. By the three systems together, — those of insurance against accidents, sickness, and invalidity and old age, — the workingmen are rendered secure against want as the result of inability to work consequent upon physical disability due to no matter what cause.

The enactment of this law was preceded by an elaborate study of the basis upon which such a system should rest. Following a custom frequently followed in Germany, the government first published, November 17, 1887, a draft of the bill it proposed to introduce, accompanied by a report explaining its provisions and the reasons for its introduction, and two elaborate memoirs prepared by expert accountants and specialists, explaining the mathematical basis of the scheme and the probable expenditures that its operation would entail. In his speech from the throne, November 24, 1887, the Emperor invited the study of this proposition by all competent bodies, and soon after the Prussian government convened the Volkswirthschaftrath, a sort of superior council of labor, composed of government officials, manufacturers, and laboring men, to deliberate on the subject. The opinions expressed by this and other bodies caused the modification of the proposition in some respects. The final bill was introduced in the Reichstag, November 22, 1888, and, after still further modification, became a law, June 22, 1889.

In general, the law renders insurance against invalidity and old age, compulsory upon all persons working for wages in every branch of trade, apprentices and servants included, and managing officials and commercial clerks, 16 years of age or over, whose annual wages do not exceed 2000 marks ($476). This obligation can also be extended, by order of the federal council, to small employers with only one assistant workman, and to so-called home industrials, irrespective of the number of persons employed. The opportunity, moreover, is given to small employers and independent workingmen voluntarily to participate in the system, if they desire to do so.

The purpose of the system here created is to provide for the payment of an annuity to each person insured, after he has become incapacitated for work as the result of physical disability, or has reached the age of 70 years. The pension for invalidity is granted, irrespective of age, to every insured person who is permanently disabled, that is to say, who is no longer able to earn one-third of his average wages, reckoned according to certain fixed principles; and also to persons not permanently disabled, but who for an entire year have been unfit to work, during the remaining period of their disability. The right to such a pension, however, does not accrue until the workingman has paid the dues required of him, during a period of 5 years of 47 contributory weeks, or, in other words, has made contributions for at least 235 weeks.

The pension for old age is granted without proof of disability to all who have completed their seventieth year. It forms an addition to the earnings of old, but not necessarily incapacitated, working people, and makes some amends for the diminished vigor of age. Here, however, a condition precedent for a pension is that the member has paid dues during 30 years of 47 weeks each. In other words, 1410 weeks' contributions must be paid before the insured can enter upon the enjoyment of a pension. Provision is also made whereby widows, and orphans less than 15 years of age, of workingmen dying before becoming entitled to a pension, will have restored to them the money which has been contributed by the deceased. Finally, a sick benefit may be granted to sick persons not covered by the sick-insurance law, in so far as, in consequence of the illness, a claim for an invalid pension, by reason of incapacity for employment, is to be apprehended.

The amount of the pension is determined according to the average wages that the one having a right to it has been earning. The original project of the government provided for a fixed pension to be paid in all cases. While conducive to simplicity, this provision was evidently a vicious one. Not only the dues demanded of workingmen, but the amount of the pension, should bear a certain correspondence to the latter's economic condition. The law as passed, therefore, divided workingmen into the following four classes, distinguished from each other according to the wages earned by the members of each. Class I. includes all persons earning 350 marks ($83.30), or under; Class II., those earning over 350 ($83.30), but less than 550 marks ($130.90); Class III., those earning over 550 ($130.90), but less than 850 marks ($202.30); and Class IV., all those earning 850 marks ($202.30) or over.

The amount of an invalidity pension, then, consists of: first, an annual subsidy of 50 marks ($11.90) paid by the state towards each pension; and second, a fixed sum of 60 marks ($14.28), increased by a variable sum according to the number of weeks that the pensioner had made contributions. This increase is at the rate of 2 pfennigs ($0.005) for each week, in case of members in Class I.; 6 pfennigs ($0.014) for those in Class II.; 9 pfennigs ($0.021) for Class III.; and 13 pfennigs ($0.031) for Class IV. It amounts, therefore, after the required five years of contribution payments, to at least 115.20 marks ($23.85) for Class I., 124.20 marks ($29.56) for Class II., 131.40 marks ($31.27) for Class III., and 141.00 marks ($33.56) for Class IV.

The amount of the old-age pension consists of a like state subsidy of 50 marks ($11.90), increased by a certain sum for each week for which contributions are made, as follows: In Class I., 4 pfennigs ($0.01) for each week; in Class II., 6 pfennigs ($0.014); in Class III., 8 pfennigs ($0.019); and in Class IV., 10 pfennigs ($0.024). Hence the old-age annuity, after payments have been made the required 30 years, amounts to 106.40 marks ($25.23) for the first class, 134.60 marks ($32.04) for the second, 162.80 marks ($38.75) for the third, and 191.00 marks ($45.46) for the fourth class.

All pensions are paid monthly in advance. Should the insured be already in possession of an accident annuity or a state pension, his claim to the old-age or invalidity annuity will remain in abeyance so long and so far as the annuity in question, when added to the other pension, exceeds the sum of 415 marks ($98.77), that is, the highest amount of the invalidity annuity after 50 years of contributions.

The expense of maintaining this system of insurance is borne jointly by the state, the employer, and the employés. The state contributes to each annuity the fixed amount of 50 marks ($11.90) per annum, pays the contributions of the workingmen while serving in the army or navy, defrays the expenses of the imperial insurance department, and effects gratuitously the payment of pensions through the post-offices. All other expenses are borne in equal shares by the insured and their employers. It is evident that the amount of the contributions of these latter should be such that receipts would but little more than balance expenditures. As wages, according to which the amount of the contributions is determined, vary according to localities and occupation, it is impossible to fix a uniform rate. It is for this reason that the law created, as will be seen, special insurance institutions, to which is entrusted the task of determining the rate for its members. As it is impossible, in spite of all statistical calculations that can be made, to estimate accurately probable charges, it is provided that such rates shall be subject to revision after the first ten years, and thereafter at the end of each five-year period. For the first period of ten years, however, the weekly contributions have been fixed by law at 14 pfennigs ($0.033) for the members of Class I.; 20 pfennigs ($0.048) for Class II.; 24 pfennigs ($0.057) for Class III.; and 30 pfennigs ($0.071) for Class IV. Any surplus or deficiency is to be balanced during the next five-year period.

As a rule, the contributions are paid by the employers by means of stamps similar to postage stamps, which are affixed each week to a personal card with which each insured workingman is provided. The payment of the contributions is thus interrupted in no way by the workingman changing his employer.

The machinery provided for the carrying out of this system of insurance consists of special insurance institutions, each having charge of the insurance of workingmen in a particular district, the boundaries of which coincide with the communal or state divisions. Each of these institutions constitutes an autonomous insurance society. Each has its own constitution, drawn up by a managing committee. This committee is composed of at least five representatives of both employers and employés, the latter chosen by the directing boards of the sick-relief societies and similarly constituted bodies. The real management of the institutions, however, is vested in a directing board composed of communal or state officials, to which may be joined representatives of the employers and the insured. Should this not be done, a supervising council may be elected, in which the representatives of both employers and employed take an equal share. This council has the supervision of the directing board, and is required to attend to such other business as the statute may prescribe.

When a claim to a pension has been made to the lower administrative authorities, and transmitted to the competent insurance institution, it devolves on the directing board of the latter to approve or reject it in writing. If rejected, an appeal lies to an arbitration court similarly composed as those for accident insurance. Against its verdict, both parties may appeal to the imperial insurance department. The members of the directing board, other than the government officers, the council of supervision, the confidential agents, and the members of the arbitration courts, are honorary, and receive no compensation other than actual expenses. A state commissioner is attached to each insurance institution, in order to distribute the liabilities among the different institutions consequent upon the moving about of the insured, and to regulate the participation of the empire in the pecuniary burden.

Finally, the law allows certain old-age and invalidity pension funds already in existence, such as those in connection with the mining and railway industries, to continue in operation, and to be treated as separate insurance institutions on the same footing as those created by the law, which correspond to administration districts.

The scheme of insurance as outlined above relates to the definitive form of the organization. In order that it might enter into immediate operation, and workingmen already at an advanced age be provided for, it was necessary to make certain temporary provisions. It was thus provided that such of the insured as had already completed their fortieth year when the law went into effect (January 1, 1891), and could show that in the preceding three years they were so employed as to have been subject to insurance, would have the number of years that they were required to make contributions shortened by the number of years that their age was in excess of 40. Hence, on January 1, 1891, septuagenarians could claim the old-age pension without having made a single payment on their part.

This system commenced operations January 1, 1891. It will be many years before its workings become normal. The tables that will be given to show results thus far must therefore be interpreted with the fact in mind that the period covered is one during which the system has been just entering into operation.

The official reports of the imperial insurance department do not give the number of persons insured against old age and invalidity, as it is impossible to get at this number accurately. Dr. Bödiker, the president of the department, however, estimated the total number in 1894 to be 11,510,000, of which 11,000,000 were insured through the regular, and 510,000 through the nine special institutions.[1]

The number of pensions granted during the year, and the total number of pensioners on the rolls at the end of each year, from 1891 to 1894, are shown in the statement on the following page.

The number of persons insured each year, and the total number of pensioners carried on the rolls, show the influence of the fact that the system has not yet reached its normal condition. Thus, under the influence of the transitory provisions of the law, 132,667 pensions for old age were granted during the first year, and but 44 on account of invalidity, while in subsequent years the number of pensions granted for invalidity has increased rapidly, being 17,638 in 1892, 35,064 in 1893, and 44,397 in 1894; and the number

---

[1] *Die Arbeiterversicherung in den Europäischen Staaten*, von Dr. T. Bödiker, Präsident des Reichs-Versicherungsamts. Leipzig, Duncker und Humblot, 1895.

of pensions granted for old age has declined, being 42,028 in 1892, 31,045 in 1893, but slightly increased in 1894 to 33,442. The total number of pensioners on the rolls has naturally increased rapidly, and will continue to increase until the period when the number of pensions lapsing on account of death or other causes

NUMBER OF PENSIONS GRANTED AND PENSIONERS ON THE ROLLS, DECEMBER 31, 1891–1894.

Year.	OLD AGE.		INVALIDITY.		TOTAL.	
	Pensions granted during year.	Pensioners Dec. 31.	Pensions granted during year.	Pensioners Dec. 31.	Pensions granted during year.	Pensioners Dec. 31.
1891	132,667	(1)	44	(1)	132,711	118,997
1892	42,028	150,403	17,638	11,999	59,666	162,402
1893	31,045	166,976	35,064	37,815	66,109	204,791
1894	33,442	183,168	44,397	71,755	77,839	254,923

(1) Not reported.

will equal the number of new pensions granted. It is estimated by the insurance department that this time will not be reached before the year 1921.

The average value of pensions granted has shown a tendency to increase slightly. That for old age was, in 1891, $29.36, in 1892, $30.41, in 1893, $30.96, and in 1894, $30.24. The average invalidity pension was for each of these years, $26.98, $27.29, $28.08, and $28.79 respectively.

It will be seen that the average value of the pensions granted is by no means an extravagant one.

The amount of money required to pay these pensions has necessarily risen rapidly. The following table is intended to show in detail the receipts and expenditures of the thirty-one regular insurance institutions since the beginning of their operations. The nature of the reports of the nine special institutions does not permit a similar showing in their case. In this statement all participation on the part of the government is excluded. The latter only intervenes after the pension has been determined by the insurance institutions, when it increases it by 50 marks, or $11.90.

RECEIPTS AND EXPENDITURES OF THE REGULAR OLD-AGE AND INVALIDITY INSURANCE INSTITUTIONS.

	1891.	1892.	1893.	1894.
Receipts.				
Contributions	$21,155,099	$21,070,288	$21,394,345	$22,069,842
Other	180,956	842,541	1,390,766	2,046,543
Total	$21,336,055	$21,912,829	$22,785,111	$24,116,385
Expenditures.				
Invalidity pensions	$ 2	$169,837	$665,828	$1,282,460
Old age pensions	2,153,527	2,931,870	3,174,007	3,421,865
Medical attendance	72	7,577	25,508	86,340
Other relief	81	15	229	216
Administration	900,580	1,095,139	1,133,727	1,199,851
Reserve fund	818,822	2,207,877	1,516,425	1,747,119
Total	$3,873,084	$6,412,315	$6,515,724	$7,737,851
Excess of receipts	$17,462,971	$15,500,514	$16,269,387	$16,378,534
Cash on hand and invested	....	17,462,971	32,963,486	49,232,878
Reserve fund	815.961	3,061,023	4,694,953	6,638,483
Total assets	$18,278,932	$36,024,508	$53,927,826	$72,249,890

The receipts of the institutions consist almost entirely of equal contributions by the employers and employés. The item of other receipts, however, shows a rapid increase from year to year on account of interest, which becomes of increasing importance, due to the augmenting interest-bearing funds in the possession of the institutions.

The items of expenditures have to be interpreted in the light of the financial system adopted. As in the case of insurance against accidents, instead of setting aside for each pension, when determined, a sum sufficient to meet all the payments until it becomes extinguished, there was adopted the system of including in each year's account the payments actually made that year. Under this system, as the number of pensioners on the rolls must increase for a good many years, the total expenditures will increase in proportion. Contributions, therefore, are made heavy enough more than to meet expenses during the first few years, and thus to provide for a reserve fund to meet future augmented charges. This calculation seems to have been made on a liberal basis; for the reserve fund, as shown by the table, has increased from $815,961 in 1891 to $6,638,483 in 1894, while total assets have increased from $18,278,932 in 1891 to $72,249,890 in 1894. These sums are invested in approved securities. The insurance department reports that the average rate of interest earned has been 3.67 per cent in 1891; 3.67 in 1892; 3.66 in 1893; and 3.65 in 1894.

The relation of the cost of administration to receipts and expenditures and to the total number of persons insured is always an important point. In the present case the relation of expenses of administration to receipts is of more value than its relation to expenditures, as the former is a normal item, while the latter increases yearly. The percentage of cost of administration of total receipts was 4.13 in 1891; 4.93 in 1892; 4.88 in 1893; and 4.91 in 1894, a rate which would seem to be a very favorable one. The average cost per person insured was, in 1891, 9¼ cents; in 1892, 11½ cents; in 1893, 12 cents; and, in 1894, 12¼ cents, the tendency thus being for the cost per person insured to increase slightly. With a growing pension roll this is but natural.

It will be remembered that the state contributes an annual subsidy of $11.90 towards each pension. It is of interest, therefore, to know how great a financial burden this entails upon the state. In 1891 the amount of its contribution was $1,439,863.92; in 1892, $2,135,115.15; in 1893, $2,680,273.42; and in 1894, $3,297,465.38. It is estimated by the government that this sum will continue to increase until the year 1900, after which it will remain nearly constant at between $5,236,000 and $5,474,000, except as the population of the empire may increase.

CHAPTER III.

WORKINGMEN'S INSURANCE IN AUSTRIA.

Introduction. — Austria has followed resolutely in the footsteps of Germany in the introduction of systems for the compulsory insurance of workingmen. She has now in practical operation general systems for the insurance of workingmen against accidents and sickness; and measures looking to the organization of the third branch, that against old age and invalidity, are now pending before the imperial parliament. No more than in Germany was either the regulation of insurance by the state, or the introduction of the principle of compulsion, a sudden innovation. Previous to the passage of the law of March 30, 1888, creating the present system of insurance against sickness, such insurance had been made the subject of regulation by various laws. The imperial decree of February 18, 1837, first subjected sick-aid societies to legal regulation. According to it, employers were ordered to furnish to their workingmen, when sick, free hospital treatment during four weeks. The principle of compulsion was thus fifty years old. Following this, a series of laws relating to the same subject were enacted. The law of November 26, 1852, subjected mutual-aid societies to certain conditions. The law of May 23, 1854, provided for the creation of sick funds for the benefit of mining employés. The law of December 20, 1859 (*Gewerbeordnung*), made it compulsory upon employers of large industrial establishments to create sick funds. This law was amended by the law of March 15, 1883, which provided for the creation of corporations among small industrial establishments, and made it compulsory upon them to provide for the insurance, through aid societies, of their employés against sickness.

In spite of the principle of compulsion contained in these laws, but a small proportion of the workingmen were actually insured. The majority of the large employers failed to comply with the law. The Minister of Commerce stated in his report for 1886, that of 3810 corporations, only 188 had created insurance funds. It was, therefore, not so much to introduce a new system, as to complete one already inaugurated, that a bill was introduced in 1885. This measure, after various legislative experiences, during which it suffered slight modifications, became the law of March 30, 1888, and organized the present system of insurance.

In the meantime, the whole question of workingmen's insurance was receiving an earnest attention; and it was the system of insurance against accidents that was first actually established. A bill introduced into the Reichstag in 1884, after receiving several modifications, became the law of December 27, 1887, thus antedating that for insurance against sickness by a few months. The insurance of workingmen in Austria, therefore, rests upon three series of fundamental laws: that of March 30, 1888, afterwards modified by the law of April 4, 1889, providing for insurance against sickness; that of December 27, 1887, supplemented by the law of July 20, 1894, providing for insurance against accidents; and that of July 28, 1889, in relation to the insurance of miners, who were exempted from the provisions of the general insurance laws.

Regarding the general attitude of the people toward these laws, Mr. Julius Kaan, chief inspector of the insurance department at Vienna, in an address at the international congress in relation to workingmen's insurance, at Milan, in 1894, said: —

"The fact that legislation in relation to insurance has taken a longer time to develop in Austria than in Germany is not due to any opposition to the principles upon which it is based. There is no opposition to the development of the system of compulsory insurance. On the contrary, it can be stated that all political parties, as well as all social classes, without any difference of opinion, are unanimous in the recognition of the necessity for its extension. The principal object that to-day retards its development is the difficulty of devising a plan by which the necessary financial burden can be made supportable by the smaller employers and farmers, who, as is well known, are at the present time in an unsatisfactory economic condition."

Insurance against Sickness. — The law of March 30, 1888, as slightly modified by the law of April 4, 1889, provides for the compulsory insurance of all workingmen of both sexes coming under the provisions of the accident-insurance law, and, in addition, of workingmen employed in all kinds of industrial enterprises, including railroads and inland transportation. Agricultural and forestry employés, however, are not included, even in cases where mechanical motors are employed. The obligation of insurance, therefore, extends to the small industry without the restrictions imposed in the case of insurance against accidents.

In creating institutions for the administration of insurance, account had to be taken of the sick-insurance funds already in existence. Of these, the most important were the miners' relief funds, organized in virtue of the law of 1854. These had reached such a degree of development that it was deemed desirable to make of them a special system for the insurance of miners. Other institutions were the trade-unions funds, regulated by the law of 1883, and the friendly societies. Though these institutions could be utilized, it was necessary to supplement them with others. The law, therefore, provides for the following six types of funds: —

1. District Associations (*Bezirkskrankenkassen*).
2. Factory Associations (*Betriebskrankenkassen*).
3. Building-trades Associations (*Baukrankenkassen*).
4. Trade-guilds Associations (*Genossenschaftskrankenkassen*).
5. Friendly Societies (*Vereinskrankenkassen*).
6. Miners' Associations (*Bruderladen*).

This classification, it will be seen, is very similar to that adopted by Germany. The district associations, like the communal and local associations of Germany, are the fundamental organs of the system, and correspond to geographical and administrative districts. The factory, the building-trades, and the trade-guilds associations, are almost identical in character with the similarly named institutions in Germany, and include, the first, employés working in the same industrial establishments; the second, those employed by a contractor in construction work; and the third, the members of trade-guilds of smaller industrial enterprises. Finally, the friendly societies are either the old sick-benefit societies which were in existence prior to the enactment of the present law, and were allowed to continue in operation, or other societies subsequently organized along the same lines. The insurance funds of the railway companies, both public and private, as well as those of the state manufacturing establishments, are included among the factory associations. Miners' associations are institutions which were in existence prior to the adoption of the new act, and are organized into an independent system by a special law. Their operations, therefore, cannot be here considered.

The insurance comprehended by the general system provides for the granting of various kinds of relief in cases of sickness. The law determines in each case the minimum amount of relief that must be afforded. Provided that this amount is given, the various voluntary associations permitted by the law are given great freedom in regard to their methods of organization and administration, and the extent to which they may give relief above that required by the law. It will be scarcely practicable to attempt to describe their various systems. Concerning the district associations, which constitute the fundamental insurance organization of the system, and generally concerning the new kinds of associations provided for by the law of 1888, it was necessary to make more detailed and stringent regulations. For these associations, a maximum, as well as a minimum, amount of relief is established.

The minimum of relief applicable to all associations consists of: (1) Free medical attendance and supplies; (2) an indemnity in case of sickness causing inability to work for more than three days, from the first day of sickness, equal to 60 per cent of the average daily wages of laborers in the district in which the patient lives, during a period, if necessary, of 20 weeks; (3) the same indemnity to women for four weeks after child-birth; and (4) in case of death, an indemnity to the wife or heirs for funeral expenses, equal to 20 times the average daily wages paid in the district.

In the place of medical attendance, hospital treatment can be substituted, if the circumstances are such as to make it desirable. For the associations created by the law, the maximum amount of relief that can be granted is limited to free medical attendance and supplies, cash indemnities in cases of sickness, equal to three-fourths of average wages, for a period not to exceed one year, and an indemnity for funeral expenses not to exceed 50 florins ($24.11).

In principle, the resources of these associations, excepting the miners' associations and the friendly societies, are obtained from contributions of the members, two-thirds of which represent the payments of the workingmen, and one-third that of their employers. The latter can, if they choose, assume a larger portion, or even the whole burden of the support of the insurance. In the case of the voluntarily organized friendly societies, the employers are not required to contribute at all. The maximum amount of dues required of members cannot exceed three per cent of their wages. If this rate of dues is not sufficient to pay the indemnities, the amount of the latter must be decreased.

The principal provision regarding the financial operations of the district associations, is that requiring each to set aside 20 per cent of the dues collected, for the constitution of a reserve fund, until such fund amounts to double the annual expenditures, and of a general reserve fund for the association of district associations to which it belongs.

The general association of district funds constitutes a distinct departure from the German system of organization. While the German communal and local associations are intended to operate as independent organizations, the Austrian district associations occupying contiguous territory are grouped into associations for the accomplishment of certain administrative ends. The purposes of this grouping are: (1) to constitute a common reserve fund; (2) to co-operate in the investment of funds; (3) the organization of a statistical service; (4) the making of common contracts with physicians, druggists, and hospitals; (5) better organization, inspection, and supervision; and (6) the creation of a higher tribunal for the adjudication of disputed points.

In tracing the history of the operations of this system, the effort will be made, as far as possible, to follow the scheme of presentation adopted for the German system. There is, therefore, first given a table showing the number of each kind of insurance institution and the number of persons insured for each year since the system has been in operation. The delay in the publication of the official reports prevents us from bringing our record down to a later date than the year 1892.

NUMBER AND MEMBERSHIP OF SICK INSURANCE ASSOCIATIONS, 1890–1892.

	Year.	District.	Factory.	Building Trades.	Trade-Guilds.	Friendly Societies.	Total.
Number of Associations.	1890	545	1,427	3	632	53	2,660
	1891	552	1,450	5	699	75	2,781
	1892	549	1,428	8	737	88	2,805
Number of members.	1890	550,606	505,642	663	230,578	261,336	1,548,825
	1891	592,042	531,438	489	255,909	286,912	1,666,790
	1892	641,300	529,000	773	273,046	296,955	1,741,074

These figures show that the number of persons insured has increased each year, and in the last year was 1,741,074 persons. Of these, 1,359,584 were men, and 381,490 were women. But little readjustment has taken place in the relative number and size of the different associations. While the number of district associations has decreased, their membership has increased both absolutely and relatively. It is interesting to note that the average size of the associations has steadily increased, the average membership each year being 582, 599, and 621 respectively. The experience has not been sufficiently long to enable us to determine toward which form of organization the system is tending.

The facts relating to the number and duration of cases of sickness are, however, of the most interest. As has been pointed out in the case of Germany, the important feature is not so much the absolute number of cases of sickness, as the proportion that they bear to the total number of persons insured. A table similar to the one given for Germany, therefore, shows this information for each of the three years.

		1890.	1891.	1892.
Cases of sickness per 100 insured	men	50.	44.	46.
	women	50.	41.	43.
	both sexes	50.	43.	45.
Average duration (days) of cases of sickness	men	14.7	16.0	16.1
	women	17.1	18.7	18.4
	both sexes	15.2	16.6	16.5
Days of sickness per 100 insured	men	730.	700.	730.
	women	840.	780.	800.
	both sexes	760.	720.	750.
Deaths per 100 insured	men	1.0	0.9	0.9
	women	1.0	1.0	1.0
	both sexes	1.0	1.0	0.9

In interpreting this table, and especially in attempting to compare it with the results in Germany, it should be remembered that in Austria indemnities can be paid for as long a time as 20 weeks, and commence the first day of sickness; while in the latter country, the limit, in general, is 13 weeks, and the indemnities commence only after the third day; and also that in Austria, women, on the occasion of childbirth, have a right to an indemnity during 4 weeks, while in Germany, an indemnity frequently is not paid in such cases. The Austrian is thus the more liberal system in every respect.

Turning now to the table, the shortness of the period covered prevents any attempt to analyze the returns with any great profit. It will be seen that there has been but slight variation, either in the average number of cases of sickness per person insured, or in their duration. During the last year, 1892, the associations gave indemnities for 7.5 days of sickness for each member. There was an average of 0.45 cases of sickness per member, the average duration of each case being 16.5 days. There was little difference between the two sexes as regards the amount of sickness.

The financial operations of the system are shown in the table upon the next page, which gives the actual receipts and disbursements during each year.

This table shows that total receipts and expenditures have increased but slowly. In 1890 the receipts were \$5,960,486, and in 1892, \$6,806,190. Expenses in the first year were \$5,469,066, and in 1892, \$6,226,654. The relative importance of the particular items of the account has scarcely varied. The contributions of the insured amounted to 65.6 per cent of all receipts in 1892, and those of the employers to 28.2 per cent. The item of contributions, therefore,

Receipts and Expenditures of Sick Insurance Associations, 1890–1892.

	1890.	1891.	1892.
Receipts.			
Contributions of members	$3,862,715	$4,199,319	$4,467,366
Contributions of employers	1,678,271	1,814,452	1,916,454
Entrance fees	15,253	15,096	15,787
Fines	46,810	54,626	60,647
Interest	78,457	106,947	123,183
Other	278,980	239,090	222,753
Total	$5,960,486	$6,429,530	$6,806,190
Expenditures.			
Cash benefits	$2,962,999	$2,992,271	$3,222,636
Salaries of physicians, etc.	868,061	934,491	1,012,835
Medical supplies	662,866	665,499	740,663
Hospital service	214,274	284,482	334,394
Funeral expenses	160,953	171,639	178,293
Administration	433,050	468,698	495,973
Reserve fund	20,929	19,625	23,052
Other	145,934	205,057	218,808
Total	$5,469,066	$5,741,762	$6,226,654

forms almost the total income of the associations, accounting for 93.8 per cent of all receipts, as against 1.8 per cent from interest and 4.4 per cent from all other sources.

In expenditures, cash benefits accounted for over half of all disbursements, or 51.7 per cent; salaries of physicians, 16.3 per cent; medical supplies, 11.9 per cent; hospital service, 5.4 per cent; funeral expenses, 2.8 per cent; administration, 8.0 per cent; the reserve fund, 0.4 per cent; and other miscellaneous, 3.5 per cent. The first five items, constituting relief proper, therefore, together absorbed 88.1 per cent of all expenditures.

As in the case of Germany, it is interesting to reduce this information to the basis of the individual and day of sickness. This is done in the following statement: —

EXPENDITURES PER MEMBER AND DAY OF SICKNESS OF SICK INSURANCE ASSOCIATIONS.

	Year.	District.	Factory.	Building Trades.	Trade-Guilds.	Friendly Societies.	Total.
Expenditure per member.	1890	$2.90	$3.79	$5.76	$3.25	$4.58	$3.53
	1891	2.99	3.60	4.93	3.11	4.37	3.44
	1892	3.11	3.90	4.99	3.20	4.50	3.58
Expenditure per day of sickness.	1890	.38	.37	.50	.47	.40	.39
	1891	.38	.37	.55	.48	.41	.39
	1892	.37	.37	.49	.48	.41	.39

This table shows that during the three years there has been but little variation, either in the cost of insurance per member, or the cost of a day's sickness. During the year 1892, the expenditure per person insured was $3.58, of which $3.15 went directly for purposes of relief. The expenditure per day of sickness was 39 cents.

If we now contrast the average amount that each insured person received from the system with the amount that he himself had to pay in the way of dues or entrance fees, we find that, as in Germany, the insured received relief greater in amount than their contributions. To the workingman the cost of sick insurance was, in 1892, $2.57, while the value of the relief that he received in return was $3.15, an excess of 58 cents. The amount of the contributions and of the relief received varies considerably in the different kinds of associations, but, in all, expenditures for sickness exceed the amount of the payments of the insured. Both the contributions and expenditures are the highest in the trade-guilds and factory associations.

Insurance against Accidents. — The compulsory insurance of workingmen against accidents was provided for by the law of December 28, 1887. Prior to its enactment, Austria may be said to have passed no legislation upon the subject. Except in the case of railway employés, workingmen had no legal claim for indemnities from their employers in case of accident, except when they were due to the direct fault of the employer; in which case, the law gave a right of action. As in other European countries, opinion soon became almost unanimous that the best method of reform lay in the development of insurance, rather than in increasing the legal liability of employers. The result was the enactment of the law of 1887. The essential provision of this law can be briefly summarized.

Insurance against accidents is made compulsory upon all employés in factories and workshops, in mining works not included under the provisions of the general mining law under which most miners were already insured, in quarries, in the building trades, in industries making use of explosives, and in agricultural and forestry works, where mechanical motors are employed, and in certain other specified industries. The general theory was to make the law apply to all classes of industry in which the risk of accidents was especially high. It was the declared intention of the legislature, however, to extend the system as rapidly as possible, so as to embrace all industrial workers. But one such extension, however, has been made, that by the law of July 20, 1894, according to which the provisions of the law of 1887 were extended to the transportation industry, theatres, professional firemen, and some other industries. ·It is estimated that this extension added from 150,000 to 200,000 persons to the number insured.

For its execution, the law provides for seven special territorial insurance institutions. When railway employés were included, an eighth institution was created for their special insurance. The management of these institutions is given to committees composed, one-third of members appointed by the minister of the interior, one-third of members chosen by the employers, and one-third of members chosen by the workingmen. The law, however, permits several employers to join together to form a special fund for the mutual insurance of their employés, or enterprises already possessing such funds to fulfil their obligations regarding insurance through them. In both of these cases, however, the authorization of the government must first be obtained, and this has been granted in but few cases. The eight insurance institutions, therefore, include practically all workingmen subjected to compulsory insurance.

In principle, the amount of the indemnity allowed in cases of accidents is made proportional to the amount of the injured person's wages during the preceding year. In case of death there is paid: (1) a sum of $12.06 for funeral expenses, an annuity to the widow, if there is one, equal to 20 per cent of the annual wages of her husband, until her death or remarriage, in which case she receives a lump sum equal to three annual payments, in definite liquidation of her claim; (2) an annuity to each legitimate child, until 15 years of age, equal to 15 per cent, or in case the child has no mother, equal to 20 per cent, of the father's wages; and (3) an annuity to the father or mother, if they were dependent upon their son for support, equal to 20 per cent of the latter's wages. In case of an illegitimate child, an amount equal to 10 per cent is allowed. The total amount of the annuities, however, cannot exceed 50 per cent of the deceased's annual wages.

In case of total incapacity, an annuity is paid to the workingman equal to 60 per cent of his usual wages. In case of partial incapacity to labor, the indemnity varies in amount according to the degree of incapacity, but cannot exceed 50 per cent of the former wages of the recipient. These provisions in regard to indemnities do not come into force until after the fourth week. During the first four weeks the injured workingman is cared for by the sick-insurance institutions.

The funds necessary for the maintenance of this system are raised by contributions, of which nine-tenths are paid by the employers and the remaining one-tenth by the workingmen, through deductions made from their wages. As the risk of accidents varies greatly, not only in different industries, but in different establishments of the same industry, equity demanded that some method be devised whereby the contributions required of each employer could be made as nearly as possible proportional to the probable charges that accidents to his employés would entail upon the insurance institutions. To accomplish this, the law provides for the establishment of twelve classes of risks, to which were afterwards added two sub-classes, to embrace cases where the risk of accidents is very slight. Each class is then made to include a number of coefficients of risks, ranging, for all of the classes combined, from 1 to 100. Thus, for example, Class XII. includes coefficients of risks from 81 to 100 inclusive; Class XI., from 65 to 80, etc. Each industry is first assigned to one of these classes, according to the estimated risk of accidents that obtains in it. Within each class, each industrial establishment has a particular coefficient of risk, higher or lower, within the limit of coefficients assigned to that class, according to whether there have been many or few accidents within its particular branch. The utility of this system of determination of coefficients, lies in the fact that it is to the immediate advantage of each employer to see that as few accidents as possible occur in his establishment, in order that his coefficient of risk, and consequently his contributions to the insurance fund, may be as low as possible.

The amount of contributions required of each employer is therefore determined by the two elements, the total amount paid by him for wages, and the particular trade risk assigned to his establishment. In inaugurating the system, a tariff of risks was applied to the different industrial establishments as dictated by the best statistical information in the possession of the government. The amount of the contribution was fixed at 0.0566 florins per 100 florins of wages paid, supposing the coefficient of risk to be one. Thus, for example, an establishment whose coefficient was 25, would pay a contribution equal to 0.0566×25, or 1.42 florins per 100 florins paid in wages by it. The law, however, provides that this tariff shall be revised every five years in accordance with the results of the actual operations of the insurance institutions.

Finally, it is necessary to say a few words concerning the system adopted by Austria for the liquidation of the indemnities to which accidents give rise. It will be remembered that, in Germany, each year is made to pay only the sums actually disbursed during the year, without regard to the time when such liabilities were incurred. In Austria, however, the more scientific system was adopted whereby each year is required to provide for the liabilities incurred during its course, though their complete liquidation may not be accomplished for a great many years. Upon an accident occurring, therefore, the amount necessary for the complete payment of the pension to which it gives rise, is calculated according to tables of mortality, and then carried to the special insurance fund for the payment of pensions. The consequences of this system are, that, in the beginning, the payments on account of pensions are much larger than they would be under the German method. On the other hand, these payments should remain fairly constant in amount, instead of constantly increasing, until a period of equilibrium is reached, as occurs under the latter system.

This law, the essential provisions of which have just been given, did not go into operation until November, 1889. The last official report that has been published is that for the year 1893. As the system was in process of organization during the first two months, it is preferable to disregard the operations during the year 1889, and consider only the four years 1890 to 1893, inclusive. The development of the system and its present proportions are shown in the accompanying statement of the number of establishments and the number of persons insured, the

NUMBER OF ESTABLISHMENTS AND NUMBER OF MEMBERS INSURED IN ACCIDENT INSURANCE INSTITUTIONS, 1890-1893.

Year.	Manufacturing and Mechanical Industries.			Agriculture and Forestry.		
	Establishments.	Working-men Insured.	Complete Working-men.	Establishments.	Working-men Insured.	Complete Working-men.
1890	53,193	893,324	795,758	78,133	388,494	27,408
1891	58,386	957,525	832,702	86,923	412,238	24,581
1892	61,645	1,003,806	866,836	88,583	377,575	27,046
1893	64,441	1,070,428	915,063	95,916	395,842	25,860

necessary distinction being made between the two classes of manufacturing and mechanical industries and agriculture and forestry.

In this table especial attention should be directed to the column showing the number of complete workingmen. Each industrial establishment, in making its report to the insurance department, is required to show, not only the total number of persons employed, but the total number of hours of labor performed. With this data, it is possible to calculate the number of workingmen required to perform the same amount of labor if working full time for 300 days in the year. This number of "complete workingmen" is, then, the number used for purposes of comparison with the number of accidents. There is no doubt that this method constitutes a radical improvement over the German practice. It is evident that in this way it is possible to calculate, in a much more scientific and accurate way, trade risks of accidents, than if no account were taken of the time that the establishments were not in operation, or were only running part time. Throughout all the subsequent tables, therefore, the number of workingmen, either expressed or used in any of the calculations, is the number of complete workingmen, and not the total number insured.

As will be seen from this statement, the system as yet applies to only a limited number of workingmen in comparison with the number insured in Germany. The number, however, has increased each year, and, as has been already stated, the law of 1894, extending the system to transportation and other employés, will probably add from 150,000 to 200,000 members.

The number of accidents recorded each year is shown in the accompanying table. The classification is identical with that adopted for Germany, with the exception that the class of accidents causing temporary disability includes all accidents of this character resulting

NUMBER OF ACCIDENTS DECLARED AND INDEMNIFIED, 1890–1893.

				Accidents Indemnified.			
	Year.	Accidents Declared.	Fatal.	Total Permanent Disability.	Partial Permanent Disability.	Temporary Disability.	Total.
Manufacturing and mechanical industries.	1890	15,613	519	83	1,857	4,458	6,417
	1891	20,774	540	92	1,858	5,887	8,377
	1892	25,716	555	106	2,247	6,121	9,029
	1893	32,335	625	112	2,951	6,822	10,510
Agriculture and forestry.	1890	428	29	17	136	142	324
	1891	542	25	13	188	181	407
	1892	582	19	14	163	197	393
	1893	582	24	3	178	186	391
Manufacturing and mechanical industries, per 1000 persons insured.	1890	19.62	0.65	0.11	1.71	5.59	8.06
	1891	24.95	0.65	0.11	2.23	7.07	10.06
	1892	29.67	0.64	0.12	2.59	7.06	10.41
	1893	35.34	0.68	0.12	3.23	7.46	11.49
Agriculture and forestry, per 1000 persons insured.	1890	15.62	1.06	0.62	4.96	5.18	11.82
	1891	22.05	1.02	0.53	7.65	7.36	16.56
	1892	21.52	0.70	0.52	6.03	7.28	14.53
	1893	22.50	0.93	0.12	6.88	7.19	15.12

in an inability to work during 4, instead of 13 weeks, as under the German system. In order to show the degree of intensity of accidents, as well as to permit of the comparison of one year with another, there is also given a statement showing the number of each kind of accidents per 1000 persons insured.

The facts regarding the prevalence and increase of accidents, as shown in these tables, differ in no essential particular from those found in the tables concerning the German system. The number of accidents declared has rapidly increased, being 19.49 per 1000 complete workingmen in 1890, and 34.98 in 1893. This increase falls almost exclusively in the class of manufacturing and mechanical industries. The proportion of accidents indemnified has likewise increased, but not to the same extent as that of accidents declared, the increase in manufacturing and mechanical industries being from 8.06 to 11.49. Fatal accidents, however, have remained almost constant, being for all industries 0.67, 0.66, 0.64, and 0.69, and for the class of manufacturing and mechanical industries 0.65, 0.65, 0.64, and 0.68. The accidents causing total permanent disability have likewise varied but slightly. The whole increase, therefore, as in Germany, falls in the two classes of lesser accidents. The explanation for the increase in these two classes that has been given for Germany applies equally to the figures here given.

The organization of the financial operations of the system provides for the complete liquidation of each accident as it occurs. From the statistical standpoint, this system has the great advantage of rendering it possible to know at all times the exact financial standing of the system, and also to calculate more accurately the average cost of insurance per accident. The receipts and expenditures of the system are shown in the following table for each year, 1889 to 1893:—

RECEIPTS AND EXPENDITURES OF ACCIDENT INSURANCE INSTITUTIONS, 1889-1893.

	Nov. 1, 1889, to Dec. 31, 1890.	1891.	1892.	1893.
Receipts.				
Capital on hand for indemnification of accidents	....	$1,258,861	$2,715,077	$4,278,791
Contributions	$1,825,440	1,844,204	2,059,233	2,198,971
Interest	13,737	63,421	118,783	177,802
Fines	6,273	6,816	10,720	10,638
Other	13,543	145,745	158,345	150,086
Total	$1,858,993	$3,314,047	$5,062,158	$6,816,288
Expenditures.				
Indemnities	$99,150	$282,689	$428,022	$601,973
Capital set aside to meet pensions	669,921	1,775,686	2,808,826	4,050,255
Capital reserved to meet current indemnities	583,940	939,390	1,469,965	2,036,147
Investigation	10,217	16,696	23,339	31,648
Legal expenses	156	1,365	2,801	5,538
Inspection	9,520	8,626	8,632	8,632
Administration	142,822	182,512	209,497	237,283
Organization	20,479	10,860	8,939	24,346
Pension fund for officials	8,777	18,405	18,038	11,005
Other	36,967	44,762	73,860	71,381
Total	$1,581,949	$3,280,991	5,051,919	$7,078,508

These figures show that expenditures have increased much more rapidly than ordinary receipts. A number of the individual insurance institutions have shown an excess of disbursements over receipts during the last three years, and the system as a whole shows a deficit for the year 1893. This state of affairs will render necessary a readjustment of the amount of contributions required, or of the indemnities paid. The change will probably be made by increasing the percentage of the risk of the industries in which accidents have been the most prevalent.

In Austria, the system by which each accident is completely liquidated at one time, renders it possible to obtain accurate information concerning the average cost of each accident. In 1890 an average of $174 was paid for each accident; in 1891, $164; and in 1892, $175. The cost per accident has not, therefore, greatly increased. The French Labor Bureau has carried this calculation still further, and, taking the data furnished by the Austrian government for the three years 1890 to 1892 combined, has shown the average cost of each class of accidents. It found that, on an average, each fatal accident had cost $400; each accident causing total permanent invalidity, $1184; each one causing partial permanent invalidity, $470; and each one causing only a temporary invalidity, $24.

The official reports also carefully indicate for each year the amount of actual expenditure for relief, that is, indemnities and capital set aside for the payment of pensions caused by accidents during the year. These sums were, for 1890, $1,178,230; for 1891,

$1,445,312; and, for 1892, $1,650,563. These figures represent an actual cost per complete workingman of $1.43, $1.69, and $1.85 respectively. It is evident, therefore, that the increase in expenditure is by no means accounted for by the increase in the number of persons insured, but that thus far the system has constantly tended to become more expensive. This does not necessarily mean that the system has worked badly. On the other hand, it may mean that its advantages have proved to be such that it has seemed desirable to increase the liberality with which relief is granted.

CHAPTER IV.

Workingmen's Insurance in France.

Introduction. — Though France offers no such comprehensive and methodical system of workingmen's insurance as is found in Germany and Austria, the study of the problem there is probably, from the standpoint of the consideration of insurance principles, of equal value to that of the experience of her German neighbors. The especial significance of her experience lies in the remarkable collection of institutions, public and private, that have been voluntarily organized for the insurance of workingmen; and, from the American standpoint, voluntary insurance is of far greater importance than compulsory insurance, which rests upon principles of state action foreign to American thought. Finally, the study of French conditions is of especial interest at the present time, as nowhere else is the struggle between the principles of obligatory and voluntary insurance being so thoroughly fought out in the legislative chambers and in the press.

The study of insurance in a country under a voluntary régime, is necessarily a much more difficult task than that of the same problem in Germany and Austria. In the latter, there exist general schemes under the auspices of the state, and information concerning their operations is easily obtainable in the annual reports of their operations. In France, the student is confronted with no single harmonious scheme, but, instead, with a great variety of institutions, concerning which complete information is often very difficult to obtain. Fortunately, for ease of study, these institutions can be classified into several distinct categories.

There are, first of all, the state insurance institutions, three in number, — the *Caisse Nationale des Retraites pour la Vieillesse*, established in 1850, for the provision of old-age pensions, and the *Caisse Nationale d'assurance en cas de Décès* and *Caisse Nationale d'assurance en cas d'accidents*, both created by the same law in 1868, the especial object of which is the insurance of the working classes against death and accidents. These, though state institutions, are purely voluntary in operation. No one, with the exception of coal miners, the insurance of whom was made obligatory by a recent law, is required to make use of these institutions unless he desires to do so.

Secondly, there has developed in France an extensive system of mutual-aid societies, — *sociétés de secours mutuels*, — institutions which, originally for the most part relief organizations, have, by a process of evolution, become very satisfactory organizations for insurance against sickness. Their utilization for other kinds of insurance is also being attempted. In 1850 these societies had reached such a development that their regulation by the government was deemed advisable. The law of July 15, 1850, therefore, by requiring from them annual reports, and by the creation of a special bureau for the regulation of all matters relating to them, organized them in a regular system, which subsequent legislation tends to make more and more systematic. As these societies are also subsidized to some extent by the government, and make use of the government insurance institutions for certain purposes, they may be considered as standing half way between state and private institutions.

Finally, there are in France private insurance funds, organized for the most part by the heads of large industrial concerns, either with or without the coöperation of their employés, for the benefit of the latter, to an extent, and of an excellence, that is found in no other country in the world. It is almost impossible to overestimate the importance of these institutions from the standpoint of this study. They constitute a type of insurance the exact antithesis of the compulsory insurance system, and afford the best examples obtainable for the study of purely voluntary insurance. Through their means, a large proportion of the employés of the large industries, such as railway transportation and mining, as well as of a great many other industrial establishments, have been insured without the intervention of the state.

Among these voluntary institutions, it is desired to direct particular attention to the system lately developed, whereby employers in the same trades have joined forces to form general funds for the common insurance of their employés. This represents the most important step that has yet been taken in the development of voluntary insurance. The organization of insurance funds in connection with large industrial establishments, is, as has been shown in the introductory chapter, a comparatively simple matter, and represents a very efficient form of workingmen's insurance. With small establishments it is quite a different matter, and voluntary insurance has in the past failed to reach the employés of these establishments. In France, however, plans have been started which bid fair to fill this gap. Employers in certain industries have, through their national organizations, formed central insurance funds for their employés. Typical, and most important of these, is the *Caisse Syndicale d'Assurance Mutuelle des Forges de France*. This institution was created in 1891 by the *Comité des Forges de France*, an organization exactly corresponding to the Iron and Steel Association in this country, and, therefore, including all of the important manufacturers of iron and steel in France. The voluntary creation of such an institution, representing the united action of employers in such an important industry, is of the greatest significance for voluntary insurance. It represents the avowed purpose of the employers to provide as far as possible for the insurance of their employés. Furthermore, it represents the centralizing tendency which is observable in all insurance work; the substitution of one strong fund for a number of smaller ones.

To recapitulate, then, the study of workingmen's insurance in France, involves the study; first, of state insurance institutions; secondly, mutual-aid societies; and, thirdly, employers' insurance funds, voluntarily organized. To this must be added an account of the present condition of the problem of workingmen's insurance, the lines along which reform is being attempted, and, particularly, a consideration of the efforts to create national systems of compulsory insurance, and to modify the existing laws in relation to employers' liability for accidents to their employés.

State Insurance Institutions. — Though the question of the insurance of workingmen against old age and invalidity in France, has of late years sprung into greatly increased importance, it is by no means a new one there. For thirty years previous to this latter movement, which may be said to date from about the year 1880, France has had in operation a national institution, the *Caisse Nationale des Retraites pour la Vieillesse*, the sole purpose of which is to provide for the insurance of workingmen against old age and invalidity. The history of old-age insurance in France during this period is practically that of this institution. Its study is of value for this reason, and because it constitutes the most important example of the effort to provide insurance by the state without introducing the principle of compulsion.

The National Old-Age Insurance Bank was created by the law of June 18, 1850. It is interesting to note that in the discussion prior to its adoption, the proposition to make the insurance obligatory was raised and rejected. At the same time, all propositions looking toward the aid of the bank by the resources of the state were also voted down, and it was determined to make of the bank a perfectly independent and voluntary institution.

This original law has been modified a number of times during the forty-five years of its existence.

WORKINGMEN'S INSURANCE IN FRANCE. 117

The general character and principles of the bank, however, have been left untouched, the changes introduced relating for the most part to the rate of interest according to which pensions were calculated, the minimum and maximum pensions that could be acquired, or of amounts of single and annual deposits that could be made. These successive modifications can be concisely shown in the following table:—

	LAWS OF									
	June 18, 1850.	May 28, 1853.	July 7, 1856.	June 12, 1861.	May 4, 1864.	July 27, 1870.	Dec. 20, 1872.	Dec. 29, 1882.	July 20, 1886.	July 26, 1893.
Rate of interest for calculating pension.	5	..	..	4½	..	..	5	4½	4	3½
Minimum single deposit. fr.	5	5	5	5	5	5	5	5	1	1
Maximum annual deposits.	none	2000	2000	3000	4000	4000	4000	4000	1000	500
Minimum pension that could be acquired. fr.	none	5	5	5	5	3	3	3	2	2
Maximum pension that could be acquired. fr.	600	600	750	1000	1500	1500	1500	1500	1200	1200

This table enables us readily to see the history of the phases through which the bank has passed, and the difficulties that it has encountered. The great defect of early legislation was that a too high rate of interest was allowed, and, at the same time, a sufficient restriction was not placed on the amount of deposits that could be made by a single member. This led to the use of the bank for purposes of investment, and, as the interest offered by the bank was greater than it could earn, it was necessary that the government should make good the deficiency.

Recent legislation, and especially the last two laws, has attempted to remedy these defects, and restore to it its original character as a workingmen's insurance institution. They have in fact provided for its practical reorganization. The rate of interest, which in 1882 had been reduced from 5 to $4\frac{1}{2}$ per cent, was still further reduced, first to 4 and then to $3\frac{1}{2}$ per cent. The minimum deposit that could be made was reduced to one franc and the maximum annual deposit to 500 francs, while the maximum pension that could be acquired was reduced to 1200 francs.

There are two other important changes introduced by the law of 1886 that should be noticed. Previous to its enactment, the rate of interest according to which pensions were calculated could only be changed through an act of the legislature. This lack of elasticity menaced on several occasions the prosperity of the bank. By this act, the manifest improvement was introduced, whereby the administration of the bank was directed during the December of each year to fix the rate that should be applicable during the succeeding year. This rate is determined according to the average rate earned by the securities in the possession of the bank, without taking account of the expenses of administration. It is of course understood that these changes of rate do not apply retroactively.

· The second change had for its object to increase the independence of the bank. Prior to 1884, the law had been, that, as soon as a depositor reached the age at which he was entitled to a pension, the bank transferred to the *Caisse des Dépots et Consignations* (an office of the government the duty of which is to manage the government funds) securities sufficient in amount to secure the payment of the annuity according to its calculations. For all practical purposes, therefore, the bank terminated its relations with the pensioner as soon as it had completed this transaction. In 1884 this was changed, and complete autonomy given to the bank. Henceforth its duties did not cease with the collection of deposits and their investment, but included, as well, the actual payment of the pensions. This provision was a vast improvement in that it put the bank upon a more scientific basis, by allowing it to calculate more accurately the relationship between receipts and expenditures.

Having thus traced the general changes through which this institution has passed, we now turn to a description of it as it exists at the present day. It was the intention of the government to create a thoroughly self-supporting institution, through which workingmen could provide for modest old-age pensions. All sums paid in are invested in government securities. The amount of the pension is then calculated according to a determined rate of interest, and the chances of life as shown by accepted mortality tables.

Provision is made for two kinds of insurance, individual and collective. The latter is where a number of persons are insured at the same time, as, for instance, where a railroad or mining company desires to insure all of its employés. In practice it will be seen that this latter kind of insurance has been much the more important of the two.

The plan of individual insurance is, in general, such as would be constituted by a private insurance company. The radical difference lies in the provision that depositors are not required to contract for a certain fixed pension which would thus necessitate the regular payments of certain premiums. Participation in the benefits of the bank is not only entirely voluntary, but each depositor is left practically free as to the amount of his payments. The method of operation in this respect is that of the ordinary savings bank. A separate account is opened with each depositor. The latter then makes deposits as he is able. Each single deposit, no matter how small, gives a right to a pension the value of which is determined by the age of the depositor. The sum of these pensions constitutes the amount of the annuity to which he will ultimately be entitled. Each depositor thus knows at all times, by consulting the tables of the bank and his account book, the exact amount of the pension to which his payments entitle him.

The minimum age at which pensions begin to run is fixed at 50 years, but can be deferred until the depositor is 65 years of age, in which case, of course, the amount of the pension is proportionately increased. In case of invalidity, resulting in inability to work, before the depositor reaches the age of 50 years, a pension is paid, the value of which is determined according to the amount of the payments that have been made and the age of the depositor.

In both individual and collective insurance a choice is offered of two kinds of insurance: that obtained where the depositor desires his deposits to be considered as alienated (*capital aliéné*), and that where he desires it to be considered as reserved (*capital réservé*). In the first case, provision is made simply for the constitution of an annuity after the depositor has reached the required age. In the second, the additional provision is made, that, on the death of the depositor, all deposits that he may have made will be repaid, without interest, to his heirs, the principle of life insurance thus being combined with that of old-age pensions. It is needless to say, that the same amount of deposits will give a right to a much larger pension in the former than in the latter case.

The table on the following page shows the value of the pension of each kind that a depositor will be entitled to for a payment of $100 according to his age at the time of making the deposit, and the years at which he elects to have his pension begin.

It will thus be seen from this table, that any one making a payment of $100, when 20 years of age, is guaranteed an annuity of $26.18 for the remainder of his life, after he is 50 years of age, or of $97.27 after he is 65 years old. Or, if he desires at the same time to ensure that his children will receive the amount of his savings, upon his death, the value of the annuity is reduced to $18.99 and $70.58 respectively. If he should make a deposit of $100 at each age, as indicated by the table, the amount of the pension would then be the sum of these columns. The tables as published by the government of course give the calculation of annuities in much greater detail. They show in fact the value of pensions for each year between 50 and 65 and according to age of depositors reckoned by quarter-years.

Age of Depositors.	Alienated Capital.				Reserved Capital.			
	Age at which Pension begins.				Age at which Pension begins.			
	50	55	60	65	50	55	60	65
3 years	$51.22	$74.66	$114.77	$190.32	$41.15	$59.98	$92.21	$152.91
5 years	47.15	68.78	105.66	175.22	87.72	54.99	84.53	140.17
10 years	38.95	56.77	87.27	144.72	80.25	44.09	67.79	112.41
15 years	32.15	46.86	72.05	119.47	24.07	85.08	53.98	89.43
20 years	26.18	38.16	58.66	97.27	18.99	27.68	42.56	70.58
25 years	21.16	30.84	47.41	78.62	14.88	21.69	33.35	55.80
30 years	17.15	24.99	38.42	63.71	11.55	16.84	25.89	42.93
35 years	13.89	20.24	31.12	51.61	8.86	12.91	19.85	32.91
40 years	11.22	16.85	25.18	41.67	6.68	9.73	14.96	24.80
45 years	9.00	13.11	20.16	33.42	4.92	7.17	11.02	18.28
50 years	7.18	10.40	15.98	26.50	3.52	5.12	7.88	13.06
55 years	....	8.05	12.37	20.51	....	3.52	5.41	8.97
60 years	....	....	9.31	15.43	....	....	3.53	5.85
65 years	....	....	....	11.13	....	....	....	3.53

The introduction of the principle of collective insurance undoubtedly gives to this institution its most important feature. The object of this device is to afford employers of labor facilities for the insurance *en bloc* of their employés in their old age. This is usually done in the following way. The employers enter into a contract with their employés whereby it is agreed that the employer shall retain a certain percentage, usually two per cent, of the wages of the employés, to which they agree to add a contribution of an equal amount, or, in some cases, the employer agrees to assume the whole burden. These sums are then paid into the national old-age insurance bank, under special arrangements, which enable them to insure all of their employés at one time and by a single payment covering them all. The particular right of each workingman to a pension is exactly proportionate to the amount of his wages.

It is impossible to overestimate the importance of this kind of insurance. It is safe to say, that, if it were not for collective insurance, the results accomplished by the national institution would have been insignificant. It has been repeatedly shown that the great proportion of those insured individually cannot properly be classed as workingmen, while those insured collectively belong strictly to the laboring classes. The real service of the National Bank, therefore, has been to encourage both employer and employés to make sacrifices to provide pensions for the latter in their old age. For doing this a state institution offers great advantages over private funds organized by the employer or the employés. In addition to a perfect security, the insured are relieved from the trouble and expense of book-keeping and administration; tables of mortality are furnished; the exact amount of payments required is always known; and, above all, the changing of employer or employment can in no way affect rights already acquired.

A special law allows mutual-aid societies to make a similar employment of that portion of their funds which they wish to devote to the creation of pensions for their members.

Finally, it should be mentioned, that the state accords to the bank various advantages, such as the use of the postal system for the receipt of deposits and the payment of pensions, the remission of certain taxes, and the grant of certain cash indemnities carried on each annual budget for the increase of pensions secured through mutual-aid societies. This last is given in order to encourage these societies to enter the field of old-age insurance.

The complicated nature of the transactions of this institution, the fact that for a long time it did not itself pay the pensions, but only purchased annuities, which remained a charge upon the national debt, and that the system of accounts has been changed a number of times, renders it impossible to present a complete statement of receipts and expenditures, without entering into an intricate statistical study. In the table on the opposite page, taken from the last annual report of the bank, enough information, however, is given to show the general progress and character of the insurance work performed by it.

From this it will be seen that since its organization in 1852, 987,696 persons have opened accounts, and have paid in a total of $163,345,967.46, of which $90,203,307.45 was under the system of reserved capital (and thus either has been or will be returned to the depositors, upon their death), and $73,142,660.01 to the account of alienated capital (or definitely abandoned).

The most important distinction, however, is that

OPERATIONS OF THE NATIONAL OLD-AGE PENSION BANK OF FRANCE, 1852–1893.

Year.	Number of New Accounts.	Payments of Members.		
		Individual Insurance.	Collective Insurance.	Total.
1852–83	640,338	$64,931,791.09	$34,235,244.23	$90,167,035.32
1884	27,997	4,491,106.53	2,792,078.58	7,283,185.11
1885	26,581	5,007,379.23	2,872,996.93	7,880,376.16
1886	80,488	6,312,517.01	3,185,498,20	9,498,015.21
1887	31,431	1,475,203.96	3,065,173.96	4,540,377.92
1888	80,209	1,594,424.13	3,075,853.25	4,670,277.38
1889	29,284	1,844,408.35	3,196,201.10	5,040,609.45
1890	31,585	2,466,932.61	3,333,242,62	5,800,175.23
1891	44,479	2,851,880.84	3,764,429.22	6,616,310.06
1892	35,786	2,512,341.27	3,818,055.72	6,330,396.99
1893	59,523	2,385,188.37	4,184,020.26	6,519,208.63
Total	987,696	$95,823,173.39	$67,522,794.07	$163,345,967.46

Year.	Pensions Granted during Year.		Pensioners on Rolls End of Year.	
	Number.	Amount.	Number.	Amount of Pensions.
1852–83	234,227	$5,083,650.53	138,154	$4,540,234.68
1884	30,181	1,154,649.13	144,868	4,904,743.55
1885	33,106	1,355,888.88	147,696	5,248,154.24
1886	32,494	1,300,470.28	154,416	5,610,738.51
1887	36,884	1,441,420.50	156,501	5,873,842.09
1888	29,606	857,119.56	161,907	5,950,715.92
1889	29,166	861,080.89	165,719	5,992,495.02
1890	31,657	895,764.53	173,388	6,122,478.59
1891	34,478	965,216.16	180,470	6,221,791.95
1892	35,994	979,888.86	187,846	6,324,921.89
1893	32,753	942,015.63	189,498	6,351,293.79

between the amount paid directly for individual, and that for collective insurance, or the insurance of a body of men through an intermediary, either a mutual-aid society, a large employer of labor, or a government service. There can be no doubt that the individual payments have been made only in very small part by the laboring classes. The official reports say that the majority of these accounts consist of single deposits large enough in amount to purchase pensions. This branch of the work of the bank, from the standpoint of workingmen's insurance, may therefore be said to have been almost a total failure. The bank has been used as a means of investment, rather than of insurance through small dues paid in from year to year. The repeated limitation in the amount that can be deposited during any one year, or that can be credited to any one account, has, however, more and more restricted the operations of the bank to its legitimate purpose, and individual deposits now being made probably represent contributions of workingmen to a larger extent than ever before.

From every point of view, the collective insurance of workingmen is of the greatest importance. It is interesting to note, therefore, that here a steady increase is found. Each year shows the adhesion of a number of new firms to the list of those insuring their employés. The provision of such insurance is now almost universal on the part of the railway and larger mining companies, while the list of other large industrial concerns that do the same is a very extended one. The amounts thus paid for insurance represent enormous sums. Thus, in 1893, the four principal railway systems, the Orleans, the Western, the Paris, Lyons, and Mediterranean, and the Northern paid in, respectively, in this way, $588,254.35, $351,385.94, $343,455.66, $216,863.18; the great coal mining company of Anzin paid $74,134.77; the Creuzot Iron Works, $123,990.53; the General Omnibus Company of Paris $54,378.52; the Glass Works of Saint-Gobain, $22,784.42; the apartment store of the Louvre at Paris, $65,127.85; and scores of other concerns from $2000 to $30,000. The government, moreover, has made use of this bank for the insurance of a great many of its employés, such as road laborers, employés in the state tobacco and other factories, telegraph employés, etc. Payments for the insurance of the road employés, in 1893, amounted to $294,478.63; for forestry employés, $25,587.55; for government factory employés, $137,560.17; for telegraph employés, $10,847.37; and for certain workingmen under the war department, $7,060.13. Under the head of collective insurance is also included the large number of persons insured through mutual-aid societies. Payments on account of these societies amounted, in 1893, to $1,536,303.35. The especial significance of this kind of insurance is, as has been stated, that practically all of it represents the insurance of workingmen proper.

As regards the number of pensions that have been acquired, it is seen that between 30,000 and 35,000 persons are now granted pensions every year, and that the total number of pensioners on the rolls at the end of 1893 was 189,498. As these pensions called for a total expenditure of $6,351,294, the average value of the pensions then running can be stated as $33.58. The average value of the pensions granted in 1893 was only $28.76. This is a very small sum, but it should be remembered that in the majority of cases deposits are returned upon the death of the pensioners. There was thus repaid in 1893 the sum of $2,657,645.

In conclusion, then, it may be said that the National Old-Age Pension Bank of France, as originally organized and managed during the earlier years of its existence, by no means represented a good type of a state institution for the insurance of workingmen. Its financial basis was exceedingly faulty. It did not adjust pensions according to the amount that deposits would earn, and was thus not self-supporting. It has utterly failed directly to reach the individual workingman. Indirectly, however, it has accomplished a great deal through collective insurance. Even here, however, it should be recognized, that but certain classes of laborers have been provided for. The railroad and coal mine employés have been reached to a very large extent. The state has insured a large number of its employés, and the mutual-aid societies have secured the insurance of a considerable number of persons, but this is almost entirely due to the great financial aid granted to them by the government, as will be explained when the work of these societies is more particularly considered. The great mass of laborers, employed on their own account, or in small establishments, have scarcely been reached.

This institution, however, should not be judged from its past alone. Scientific workingmen's insurance is scarcely ten years old. In obedience to now well-established principles, the bank has been repeatedly reorganized, especially by the law of 1886, and, as at present organized, represents a fairly good type of a state institution operating under a régime of purely voluntary insurance. As regards collective insurance, few changes could be desired. The proposed modification of the law regulating mutual-aid societies, which has every chance of a speedy enactment, according to which these societies, instead of providing simply for collective insurance, will act as intermediaries for individual insurance, will go a long way toward putting the system of individual insurance upon a proper foundation.

The two other national insurance banks are much less interesting institutions. Their operations, owing to their defective organization, have been on a very limited scale. A very brief statement concerning them will therefore be sufficient.

By law of July 11, 1868, the French Parliament created two independent insurance banks, the *Caisse d'Assurance en Cas d'Accidents,* for the insurance of workingmen against accidents, and the *Caisse d'Assurance en Cas de Décès,* for the provision of life insurance. Both of these institutions differ but little in principle from private insurance societies, except that in each there is fixed a low maximum amount of insurance that can be contracted, and no provision is made for a medical examination. The only safeguard in this respect, is that no life insurance is paid on death occurring within two years after the policy is taken out.

The organization of the accident insurance bank provides for three grades of insurance, according to whether three, five, or eight francs ($0.58, $0.96, or $1.54) a year are paid as premiums. Applicants for insurance must be at least 12 years of age. In case of an accident causing an absolute incapacity for physical work, a pension is purchased for the victim from the National Old-Age Pension Bank with a capital equal to 640 times the amount of annual dues paid by him. For permanent incapacity to follow his special occupation the insurance is one-half this amount. In case of death the heirs receive a lump sum in two annual payments equal to twice the annual pension allowed for total incapacity.

How little has been the usefulness of this institution, is seen from the fact, that in 1892 but 1601 persons contracted insurance, involving the payment of $2,027.85, and that, from the origin of the bank in 1868, to the end of the year 1892, but 33,112 persons had taken out insurance policies. On these they had paid $39,817.53 in premiums. But $27,645.41 were paid during this time in the way of indemnities.

The constitution of the national bank for life insurance provides for two kinds of insurance, individual and collective. The latter exists on account of a special provision which permits any mutual-aid society to insure all of its members together. In the case of insurance individually contracted, the applicant must be at least 16 and not more than 60 years of age, and the value of the policy cannot exceed 3000 francs ($579). For collective insurance, the mutual-aid society pays a certain sum which insures all of its members, provided they are not under 3 or over 94 years of age. In this case the insurance is for but one year, and may or may not be continued the next year. For individual insurance, the rate for a 1000 franc ($193) policy, is 17.60 francs ($3.40) for applicants between the ages of 20 and 21; 21.75 francs ($4.20) for those between 30 and 31; 28.75 francs ($5.55) for those between 40 and 45; and 42.30 francs ($8.16) for those between 50 and 51 years of age. Collective insurance is calculated according to a different method.

The operations of this bank have been but little greater than those of the bank for insurance against accidents. During the year 1892, but 181 persons contracted individual insurance, the amount of which was $60,250.13, and but 62 mutual-aid societies, representing 13,607 members, contracted insurance to the amount of $15,976.92. Since its organization in 1868, but 2097 individual policies, and but 1382 collective policies, representing 336,272 persons, have been taken out.

In view of the meagreness of these results it is unnecessary to comment further upon the organization or operations of these institutions.

Mutual-Aid Societies. — The mutual-aid society is the simplest and most primitive method resorted to by men collectively to assume the burden entailed by sickness or other eventualities. What distinguishes these societies in Europe from kindred organizations in America, is that in each country of the former continent the government has taken cognizance of their existence, and by the enactment of laws regulating their operations, has attempted to organize all such societies into a general system which shall, in a way, provide voluntary insurance against sickness and even old age and invalidity. It is thus possible to speak of a system of mutual-aid societies of France, Belgium, Italy, or Switzerland in a way that cannot be done for the United States.

Great similarity exists between these societies and the policies that have been pursued in regard to them in the various countries. It will be quite unnecessary, therefore, to give an account of their workings in more than one country. France, being the one in which these societies have reached their greatest development, offers the best opportunity for such a study. The account that follows, therefore, is of importance, not only as showing the workings of these institutions in this one country, but of mutual-aid societies generally in Europe.

The date of the organization of the first mutual-aid society of France cannot be stated. The real history of the modern society, however, begins with the year 1852, when the French government, by its act of March 16, first recognized and attempted to organize them into a regular system operating under government supervision. The important feature of this act was that whereby all mutual-aid societies were divided into the two classes of authorized societies (*sociétés autorisées*) and approved societies (*sociétés approuvées*). This distinction is maintained to the present day. Societies of the first class are left subject to Articles 291 and 292 of the penal code, which simply provide that associations of twenty or more persons organized for certain purposes must receive the authorization of the government. Societies of the second class are now subject to the provisions of the organic law of March 16, 1852, the decree of April 26, 1856, concerning old-age pensions, the law of July 11, 1868, and the decree of November 28, 1890, relative to collective life insurance by the National Life Insurance Bank. This distinction means that any society can be organized under the general provisions of the penal code, but that in order to profit by certain subsidies and other advantages offered by the government, it must be approved by the government, and be therefore subject to certain conditions regarding its constitution and management. The government attempts to make the advantages sufficient to induce all societies to become approved, and thus to be brought under its supervisory powers. This result it would seem is being gradually accomplished. As approved societies constitute the most important and well-developed organizations, and present the form toward which all the societies are tending, it is with them that we are chiefly concerned.

According to the laws and decrees cited above, the purposes of approved mutual-aid societies are declared to be, the care of their members and the payment to them of cash benefits when sick, the payment of funeral expenses on their death, the payment of pensions to members in their old age or when invalidated, and the insurance of their lives for the benefit of their widows and children. Practically all of the societies provide for the insurance of their members against sickness. This constitutes their great work. It is optional with each society to determine whether it will provide old-age or life insurance. Sick insurance is entirely taken care of by the societies themselves. For old-age or life insurance, however, use must be made of the national insurance institutions.

In order to encourage the development of old-age insurance, the government, in the act of 1852, granted a subsidy of 10,000,000 francs ($1,930,000) as a permanent endowment, the interest on which should be used for the increase of pensions provided for by mutual-aid societies. Since then the government has granted various other subsidies. In 1882, Parliament commenced the policy of granting yearly a sum for the purpose of aiding mutual-aid societies to provide pensions for their old members. During the years 1882 to 1888, this sum was 160,000 francs ($30,880). In 1889 the subsidy was increased to 400,000 francs ($77,200), and each year since has been still further augmented, being 450,000 ($86,850) in 1890; 475,000 ($91,675) in 1891; 675,000 ($130,275) in 1892, and 775,000 ($149,575) in 1893. The interest on the original endowment amounts to 51,000 francs ($98,430). The amount of the government subsidy in 1893, therefore, amounted to 1,285,000 francs ($248,005).

The method employed for determining what members are entitled to pensions is a very peculiar one. The government *Caisse des Dépots et Consignations*, is made the banker for all the mutual-aid societies. The latter are required to deposit all of their funds in excess of 3000 francs in this institution. The deposits are invested in government securities, but the government pays to the societies four and one-half per cent interest regardless of what the securities themselves realize. In practice this amounts to a still further government assistance of no small amount. That portion of these deposits which the societies wish to devote to old-age pensions is kept in a separate fund which can be drawn upon by the societies for no other purpose. The amount of this fund is then increased by the subsidies annually granted by the government, or realized from the 10,000,000 francs endowment. As soon as the amount credited to any society amounts to a sufficient sum to purchase an annuity, the society designates one of its members, who must be at least 50 years old and have paid dues during 10 years, as the person to whom such annuity shall be paid. The *Caisse des Dépots et Consignations* then purchases such an annuity from the National Old-Age Pension Bank according to the tables in use by that institution, and the transaction is closed as far as the mutual-aid society is concerned.

It is scarcely necessary to call attention to the crudeness of this method. There is no engagement entered into by the members of the societies, by which they will receive a pension in proportion to the amount of their dues; indeed, they may never receive a pension. It is also by no means certain that it is desirable to encourage societies to devote a portion of their funds to creating old-age pensions, when, to do so, requires that they should diminish their general funds, which are already insufficient to provide for sick insurance. The principal advantage of the system is that it has prevented societies from making engagements to pay pensions beyond their resources.

When a society desires to insure its members against death, it pays a lump sum to the National Life Insurance Bank for the collective insurance of all of its members during the ensuing year. The amount of the policy cannot exceed 1000 francs.

From the foregoing, it is seen that though nominally, and, for many purposes actually, each society is an independent organization, the government has, by a series of laws, bound them together into a national insurance system. Not only are all of the societies required to make annual reports to the government, but they are required to deposit all but a small proportion of their funds in the national *Caisse des Dépots et Consignations*, by which they are invested, and the national insurance institutions are placed at their disposal. This, however, far from means a system of state insurance. Not only is there not the slightest compulsion upon the people to become members of mutual-aid societies, but these latter, when constituted, are left perfectly free as regards the determination of the amount of dues to be paid, and the character and extent of the relief to be granted. In other words, there is presented a pure type of voluntary but state-aided insurance.

Every mutual-aid society is required by law to make an annual report to the Minister of the Interior. On the basis of these reports the government issues an annual report concerning the operations of all mutual-aid societies during the year. From these reports it is possible to trace the history of these societies from their first recognition in 1852. In the brief sketch that follows it is not necessary, however, to go back of the year 1871. During the years preceding this date the same steady growth took place that is shown for the years 1871 to 1892.

In order to show the development of the system from year to year there is first given a table (p. 138) showing the number of societies, the number of members, honorary and participating, the total receipts during the year, and the total amount of the funds of the societies on deposit with the *Caisse des Dépots et Consignations*. The distinction between honorary and participating members lies in the fact that the former contribute as regular members, but do not claim any of the benefits offered by the societies. Their large number is due to the fact that employers, or the more well-to-do portion of a community, take this mode of encouraging the organization of such societies among their employés or fellow-citizens. Only the participating members, therefore, represent the number of persons insured.

These figures show the extent to which the working people have connected themselves with mutual-aid societies, and the growth of these societies from year to year. On the 31st of December, 1892, there were 9662 societies in operation, with a total of 1,503,397 members, of whom 1,383,021 were participating members. This represents by no means all of the laboring men and women which would be insured under a system of compulsory insurance. Nevertheless it is no slight achievement that over a million and a quarter of men are insured under a purely voluntary system. The tables show not only a steady increase each year, but an increase which is much greater in the later than in the earlier years.

NUMBER, MEMBERSHIP, ETC., OF MUTUAL-AID SOCIETIES OF FRANCE, 1872–1892.

APPROVED SOCIETIES.

Year.	Societies.	Members.			Receipts.	Capital Invested.
		Honorary.	Participating.	Total.		
1872	4,237	95,731	494,198	589,929	$1,879,052.24	$8,054,096.04
1874	4,152	103,502	517,268	620,770	2,009,974.92	9,222,737.67
1876	4,273	110,798	550,909	661,707	2,233,458.69	10,798,246.78
1878	4,474	119,312	590,852	710,164	2,404,082.14	12,348,711.08
1880	4,790	129,857	661,382	791,239	2,622,432.74	13,850,962.77
1882	5,188	141,988	729,046	871,034	2,958,922.56	15,982,614.99
1884	5,570	153,039	775,749	928,788	3,338,227.22	18,661,636.58
1886	5,969	161,046	808,176	969,222	3,454,729.91	21,552,532.35
1888	6,279	170,216	868,178	1,038,394	3,720,616.17	24,321,919.58
1890	6,674	179,197	911,955	1,091,152	4,047,535.27	27,344,034.76
1892	7,070	194,859	952,490	1,147,349	4,292,641.85	31,109,397.84

AUTHORIZED SOCIETIES.

1872	1,556	11,839	197,043	208,882	$882,803.71	$3,138,145.72
1874	1,596	12,259	213,405	225,664	998,188.77	3,466,444.43
1876	1,650	14,521	225,679	240,200	1,153,931.13	3,860,671.11
1878	1,819	16,263	251,325	267,588	1,250,923.95	4,197,639.98
1880	1,987	18,179	279,045	297,224	1,350,984.13	4,398,417.05
1882	2,091	21,528	288,185	309,713	1,445,097.14	4,739,089.72
1884	2,173	22,564	296,559	319,123	1,513,574.06	5,065,182.49
1886	2,264	23,902	299,231	323,133	1,487,601.93	5,823,948.09
1888	2,410	25,293	301,781	327,074	1,484,819.25	5,650,908.84
1890	2,470	25,102	320,112	345,214	1,600,571.33	6,136,140.66
1892	2,592	25,517	330,531	356,048	1,759,878.71	6,706,658.83

The receipts of the societies increased nearly a million of francs each year, and in 1892 amounted to $6,052,520.56. The amount of capital deposited in the *Caisse des Dépots et Consignations* shows an even more gratifying increase, being, at the end of the year 1892, $31,109,397.84 for approved societies, an increase during the two years of $3,765,363.08, and for authorized societies $6,706,658.83, an increase of $570,518.17.

It is the desire of those interested in the development of mutual-aid societies that as far as possible all societies should become approved, and thus brought into one system and subjected to the general regulations regarding the use of the national insurance institutions. The comparatively slow increase in the number of authorized societies, their increase during the last year being but 41, while their membership actually declined, while the increase of approved societies, which was in number 207 and in membership 32,790, would indicate that this is taking place. The proposed changes in the laws regulating their operations will tend still further to hasten this result.

Receipts of mutual-aid societies are derived from the dues of members, entrance fees, fines, interest on funds invested, subsidies, gifts, etc., and other miscellaneous receipts. Expenditures consist of payments made for cash benefits to sick members, the salaries of physicians, medical supplies, payments for the aid of those suffering from incurable diseases, the aid of widows and orphans, the constitution of old-age pensions, funeral expenses, expenses of administration, and other. The following table, in which are given the receipts and expenditures of all approved societies during the year 1892, with an additional column showing the relative importance of each item, indicates fully the nature of their financial operations.

RECEIPTS AND EXPENDITURES OF APPROVED MUTUAL-AID SOCIETIES OF FRANCE, 1892.

	Amount.	Percent.
Receipts.		
Dues of honorary members	$427,785.34	9.97
Dues of participating members	2,693,891.81	62.74
Entrance fees	64,067.72	1.49
Fines	73,517.20	1.71
Interest	463,615.20	10.80
Subsidies, gifts, etc.	268,218.78	6.25
Other	302,046.30	7.04
Total	$4,292,641.85	100.00
Expenditures.		
Cash benefits to sick	$1,016,172.07	25.71
Salaries of physicians	516,457.40	13.07
Medical supplies	645,487.07	16.33
Aid to old members and those suffering from incurable disease	283,555.73	7.17
Aid to widows and orphans	79,191.86	2.00
Old-age pensions	701,678.67	17.75
Funeral expenses	171,505.27	4.34
Administration	175,210.73	4.43
Other	363,636.41	9.20
Total	$3,952,895.21	100.00

This table shows the nature of the operations of mutual-aid societies better than could be done by any amount of description. As regards receipts, the most important feature is the large extent to which the contributions of participating members are supplemented by other sources of income. The dues of participating members and entrance fees account for but 64.23 per cent of all receipts. From interest, 10.80 per cent is derived, and from fines and other sources, 8.75 per cent, while subsidies, gifts, etc., and indirect assistance through the dues of honorary members account for 16.22 per cent.

As regards expenditures, the greatest item is that for direct assistance in cases of ordinary sickness. The total of the first three items, which represents this relief, accounts for 55.11 per cent of all expenditures. The item of expenditures for old-age pensions comes next in importance with 17.75 per cent. The most interesting information to be gained from this showing is that of the extremely low cost of administration, or 4.43 per cent. Practically all the money that is raised is thus expended directly in one way or another for the relief of members or their families. From the standpoint of administration, no form of organization has been found to be so effective as that of the voluntary organization of individuals for mutual assistance. Motives of honor prevent men from imposing upon their fellow-members, and most of the work is willingly done without remuneration.

The extent of relief afforded is shown by the fact that during this year relief was granted in 280,893 cases, representing 4,346,619 days of sickness, an average of 15.47 days sickness per case, and 5.16 days for each participating member.

A clear apprehension of the character and work of mutual-aid societies can be obtained by showing the results for the last year reduced to the basis of the individual society and member. It is thus found that the average membership of approved societies is 165 and of authorized societies 147, and the average amount of their invested capital $4566.85 and $2916.84, respectively. The average receipts of the first, excluding societies organized for old-age insurance only, of which there are a few, were $5609.89, and of the second, $6488.20.

The statement of average receipts and expenditures per member is of especial interest, for only in this way is it possible to determine what sick insurance means to the individual. The number of participating members, excluding children who are under a special régime as regards dues and benefits, being 925,581, and the amount of their dues $2,673,885.03, the average dues paid by each was $2.88. The average dues of women was $2.32, and that of men, $3.00. If those societies which are devoted exclusively to the constitution of old-age pensions be omitted, the average contribution of men was $2.88, of women $2.07, and of both combined $2.76. In return for these payments, each member received, on an average, assistance to the amount of $3.78, not including his participation in that portion of receipts that is covered into the fund for old-age pensions. Of this amount, $1.21 was received in the way of cash benefits; $0.61 in the payment of salaries of physicians; $0.77 for medical supplies; $0.32 as aid to old members, not pensioners, and those suffering from an incurable disease; $0.10 to their widows and children; $0.20 for funeral expenses; $0.19 expenses of administration, and $0.38 general expenses; or, deducting the last two items, a total of $3.21 in the way of actual assistance. Considering the fact that this sum is $0.45 more than that he paid in, it is evident that, from the individual standpoint, membership in a mutual-aid society offers substantial inducements.

That portion of the activities of mutual aid societies that relates to the constitution of old-age pensions is of increasing importance. The following is the method employed in providing for this kind of insurance. The societies determine what proportion of their funds on deposit with the *Caisse des Dépôts et Consignations* shall be devoted to the purpose of acquiring old-age pensions. These sums are then set apart as a special fund, and to it are added the subsidies annually granted by the government, the interest on the original endowment of 10,000,000, francs made by the government in 1852, and the gifts of individuals. The whole of this sum then bears interest at the rate of $4\frac{1}{2}$ per cent. With this fund the society purchases annuities from the National Old-Age Insurance Bank, as their means permit, and designates the members to receive them. The cost of annuities has changed from time to time owing to the change in rate of interest according to which policies were calculated. In order to purchase an annuity of 100 francs for a man 50 years of age, there was required during the years 1861 to 1873, 2222 francs; from 1873 to 1883, 2000 francs; from 1883 to 1886, 2222 francs; from 1886 to 1892, 2500 francs; and since January 1, 1892, 2857 francs. This is the rate for pensions where the capital is returned to the society upon the death of the pensioner, the system almost invariably adopted by the societies. It is evident that under this plan a society does not permanently alienate any of its capital. The serious objection to this system is that it makes the present members pay for benefits to be derived by future members, and places the interest of the society above that of the individual members.

In the table on the opposite page are given, for the years since 1871, all those facts which are necessary to show the extent and character of the old-age insurance work of mutual-aid societies.

This table shows that there has been a steady growth in the fund devoted to purchasing old-age pensions, and, consequently, in the number of pensions given each year, and the number of pensioners carried on the rolls. On the whole, the showing can scarcely be called satisfactory. The increase is not in proportion to the increase in the number of mutual-aid societies. It is doubtful if there would have been even an absolute increase but for the fact that the societies are anxious to participate in the subsidies of the government, which are entirely devoted to the assistance of those societies having old-age pension funds. The growth of the pension fund is largely due to the assistance of the government or other benefactions. Of the $18,873,608.72 which now constitutes this fund, but $9,535,115.52 was derived from the contributions of members. The remainder was derived, $3,528,428.64 from subsidies of the government, $349,982.17 from gifts, and $5,462,880.20 from interest. From this sum should be deducted $2797.80 refunded for one reason or another, leaving the total amount of the fund as stated.

THE PROVISION OF OLD-AGE INSURANCE BY MUTUAL-AID SOCIETIES OF FRANCE, 1871-1892.

Year.	Societies having Old-Age Pension Funds.	Amount of Funds.	Pensions Granted during Year.	Pensioners on Rolls.	Amount Paid in Pensions.	Average Value of Pensions.
1871	2,622	$ 3,681,254.26	356	2,957	$ 36,528.63	$ 12.55
1872	2,575	3,894,436.59	1,289	3,927	49,836.27	12.69
1873	2,582	4,212,397.30	1,207	4,720	59,752.99	12.74
1874	2,603	4,573,083.88	1,285	5,577	71,851.58	12.88
1875	2,629	4,954,329.05	1,539	6,589	86,340.87	13.10
1876	2,652	5,359,079.53	1,474	7,442	97,239.56	13.07
1877	2,667	5,797,771.62	1,551	8,406	111,078.06	13.21
1878	2,697	6,274,409.25	1,744	9,888	125,740.46	13.39
1879	2,749	6,782,238.94	2,022	10,700	143,944.42	13.45
1880	2,809	7,355,817.38	2,351	12,075	163,597.61	13.55
1881	2,871	7,998,673.08	2,390	13,400	183,874.77	13.72
1882	2,958	8,784,915.51	2,646	14,963	206,521.97	13.80
1883	3,055	9,562,698.30	3,579	16,557	229,734.27	13.88
1884	3,155	10,470,868.62	2,940	18,183	253,824.30	13.96
1885	3,247	11,451,431.69	3,182	19,904	278,099.49	13.97
1886	3,334	12,446,888.27	3,329	21,651	305,443.15	14.11
1887	3,420	13,424,488.19	3,360	23,271	329,350.06	14.15
1888	3,504	14,467,083.28	3,369	24,663	348,579.23	14.13
1889	3,589	15,529,887.81	3,566	26,311	372,158.43	14.14
1890	3,677	16,578,860.26	3,745	29,787	393,345.77	14.16
1891	3,742	17,606,952.47	4,584	29,907	420,431.97	14.06
1892	3,829	18,873,608.72	3,999	31,310	437,426.39	13.97

That greater results have not been accomplished is due to the faulty system pursued. Each society, as a whole, has a certain interest in the funds for the purchase of annuities. From time to time it is able to purchase an annuity for one of its members. A few thus receive pensions while the great majority receive nothing. The preferable system would be that whereby a separate account is opened with each member. Each individual could thus make payments as he was able, and would be encouraged to do so by the knowledge that he would certainly participate in the government subsidy in proportion to the extent of his own efforts. In other words, there should be introduced the principle of individual, instead of collective, insurance. The scheme of reorganization of mutual-aid societies now pending before Parliament, comprehends all of these changes, and it is expected that a great increase in the amount of old-age insurance will result from its adoption.

These figures which have been given, it should be added, do not show the total extent to which mutual-aid societies provide for old-age insurance. As has been shown in the statement of receipts and expenditures, $283,555.73 was given as aid to old or invalidated members. A total of 17,681 members participated in this relief, each of whom, therefore, received a pension equal, on an average, to $16.04. Approved mutual-aid societies, therefore, in reality provided for a total of 48,991 old-age pensions to the amount of $720,982.12, or an average of $14.72 per pension. In addition to this, the authorized societies paid $83,506.89 to aid 4700 old and invalidated members, and $213,686.19 in the way of regular old-age pensions. The number of persons receiving this latter sum is not stated.

Reference has been made to the fact that the mutual-aid societies can insure their members collectively against death. Actually but little is done in this way. In 1892 but 62 societies took out life insurance for the year 1893. This insurance related to 13,577 members, and the average value of the policies was but $166.58.

From the foregoing statement of results, it can be seen, that the mutual-aid societies have accomplished notable results in the way of providing for the insurance of the working classes against sickness, and somewhat less extensive results as regards old-age and life insurance. As has been intimated, however, the system, as it now exists, far from corresponds to the requirements of a scientifically organized insurance system. The fundamental error has been made of attempting to utilize societies not originally created for that purpose for a general system of insurance. Insurance against sickness, old age, and death constitute quite distinct problems, and should be organized on quite different bases. The original purpose of mutual-aid societies was that of merely binding together a certain number of persons into an organization by which they could assist each other in cases of sickness. Their plan of organization is well adapted to that end. Their utilization for other kinds of insurance has complicated matters greatly. The societies now perform two distinct functions, that of direct sick insurance, and that of serving as intermediaries for the provision of old-age and life insurance through the national insurance institutions.

The measures of reform now before the Assembly recognize the essential differences between these two services. The societies will still be allowed to provide for all the different kinds of insurance, but they will be required to keep the accounts of the operations of each rigorously distinct. The direct work of the societies will be limited to that of granting relief in cases of sickness, and the payment of funeral expenses, operations not requiring complicated accounts, or the constitution of reserve funds to meet future charges. This will be their principal work. As the eminent authority on insurance matters, M. Lafitte, has pointed out in one of his reports, life and old-age insurance can be provided by the state institutions, but mutual-aid societies alone are able to provide insurance against sickness, because they alone can exercise the necessary oversight and furnish guarantees against simulation and fraud. These societies, therefore, should constitute the fundamental organization for sick insurance, and everything should be subordinated to their development as such institutions. The hold which these societies have upon the people, however, gives to them peculiar opportunities for encouraging the other kinds of insurance. The societies will, therefore, be utilized as agents for insuring their members in the national banks. In so doing, however, they will act strictly as intermediaries. This will necessitate radical changes. The chief of these will be the introduction of individual accounts as regards payments made for old-age insurance. According to this method, the payments of each member will be carried to his special account, and the amount of his pension will depend upon his individual efforts. The state will continue to supplement the efforts of members by an annual subsidy, which will be apportioned among the different accounts in proportion to their amounts.

There remains to be considered but one other feature in the history of these societies. In a way, however, it furnishes the key to the most important changes through which they have passed. In mutual-aid societies, as originally constituted, no clear distinction was made between what was granted in the way of guaranteed relief, and that which was given in the way of charitable assistance. To such an extent was this true, that it was a matter of doubt whether they should be classed as charitable or provident societies. There is no such doubt now. There has been a steady evolution away from the idea of relief, until now these societies are real insurance institutions. To be sure they still receive assistance in the way of contributions of honorary members, subsidies of the government, gifts, etc. Assistance given in this way, however, does not imply charity. For that matter, the German system of insurance calls for still larger contributions from the government and employers. The essential feature is that relief is given according to prescribed rules in return for contributions.

Employers' Insurance Funds. — The work of state institutions and mutual-aid societies by no means represents the sum of the efforts made in France for the insurance of workingmen. By far the most important and the most interesting work, is that done by the insurance funds organized by employers, either alone, or in conjunction with their employés. In no other country in the world has so much been done in this way by employers. In certain industries, such as railway transportation and coal mining, the maintenance of old-age and accident pension funds, and the liberal assistance of mutual-aid societies for sick insurance, is almost universal on the part of the larger concerns; and the same is true to a great extent for other large employers of labor. We have obtained some idea of the extent of this work in our consideration of the National Old-Age Pension Bank. It is entirely optional, however, with employers to make use of this institution, and the number so doing, therefore, represents but a portion of the employers maintaining insurance funds. In any case, moreover, each fund is left entirely independent in regard to the important features of insurance, such as the determination of how receipts shall be raised, the amount of the pensions, and the conditions under which they are granted.

In France, as in all countries, the problem of the insurance of workingmen through purely voluntarily organized employers' funds has to meet two conditions of employment: that where the workingmen are gathered together in large bodies of a permanent nature, found chiefly in connection with the large industries, and where they are employed in small industrial establishments, with less stability as regards employment, or continuous employment with the same concern. The organization of insurance in the first case is comparatively simple, and has long been in existence. Insurance in the second case involves a number of special problems, and it is in France alone, and that within very recent years, that an apparently successful scheme of organization has been devised. Each of these two special branches of insurance will be considered separately, especial attention being paid to the latter, as it represents the most important step in the extension of voluntary insurance that has been made in recent years in any country.

It would be impossible even to make a list of the large concerns in France which maintain insurance funds for their employés. Their number would probably run into the thousands. The most important of these are those organized by the railway and mining companies. A study of the character of the insurance funds in these industries will therefore serve to show the nature and operations of employers' insurance funds in France generally.

For various reasons, which will be apparent, the funds organized by the railway companies admirably serve our purpose. In France there are seven great railway corporations, the Paris, Lyon, and Méditerranée, Nord, Est, Ouest, Midi, Orléans, and État, whose systems embrace practically all the railway lines of the country. Each of these companies maintains a system of aiding its employés in cases of sickness, usually through liberal grants to their mutual-aid societies and the maintenance of a medical service, and a system of providing for its old and incapacitated employés, through a pension fund. Mutual-aid societies we have already considered. It is therefore with the old-age pension schemes that we are here chiefly interested.

The organization of all of these funds is, in general, along the same lines. They are usually maintained by the companies retaining a certain portion of the wages of their employés, to which they add an equal or greater sum. The following table shows the extent of the contributions made by the employés and by the companies for this purpose. This statement relates to the year 1887, the latest for which the information for all of the roads could be obtained. Since then most of the companies have found it necessary to raise the amount of their contributions in order to meet increasing charges.

Companies.	Contributions Measured in Per Cent of Wages.		
	Employés.	Company.	Total.
P. L. M.	4	4	8
Nord	3	variable	..
Est	3	8	11
Ouest	4	5	9
Midi	3	6.3	9.3
État	5	5	10
Orléans	..	10	10

As regards the application of the funds thus raised, different methods are used. A usual method is to pay that portion represented by the contributions of the employés to the National Old-Age Pension Bank, the contribution of each employé being placed to his special account, which remains his personal property regardless of how or when he may leave the service of the company. The contributions of the companies themselves are paid into a special fund from which pensions are paid according to a fixed schedule. This system has the very desirable feature that at least the contributions of the employés themselves are independent in every way of their connection with the companies. Other methods are where all the contributions are paid into one company fund, or all are paid to the National Bank.

The following table (p. 154) shows the extent of the old-age insurance work of these companies during the year 1894.

This table, it should be remarked, does not show the full extent to which railroad employés are insured against old age. Thus, the contributions of the employés which are paid into the national insurance bank are not included, and there is more or less old-age insurance provided in other relief funds maintained in whole or in part by the companies. The Orléans company has, properly speaking, no fund. The sum of $1,124,224.42, which is for the most part raised by the company, consists of payments made to the National Old-Age Pension Bank.

The following brief description of the fund of the Western Railway Company will serve to show the essential character of the work of all. This company, which in 1893 employed 41,964 men, maintains two old-age insurance funds, one for its classified force, numbering 30,762, and the other for its unclassified employés, numbering 11,202 men. It will be neces-

Operations of Old-Age Pension Funds of Railway Companies of France, 1894.

Companies.	Persons Insured.	Receipts.			
		From Workingmen.	From Company.	Interest and Other.	Total.
P. L. M.	56,760	$949,349.24	$1,890,804.72	$907,420.77	$3,747,074.73
Nord	22,919	....	774,002.57	271,482.48	1,045,485.05
Est	20,010	224,846.48	897,670.60	564,912.16	1,686,929.24
Ouest	28,309	....	706,633.60	367,251.40	1,073,885.00
Midi	15,521	160,980.91	692,118.46	366,753.65	1,219,853.02
État	6,830	104,728.94	143,586.21	102,133.67	350,448.82
Orléans	....	20,661.61	1,103,562.81	....	1,124,224.42
Total	149,849	1,460,067.18	6,207,878.97	2,579,954.13	10,247,900.28

Companies.	Expenditures.			Assets at End of Year.	Persons Receiving Pensions.
	Aid.	Administration and Other.	Total.		
P. L. M.	$2,477,559.53	$99,046.06	$2,576,605.59	$22,096,667.08	11,089
Nord	....	....	592,169.74	4,462,457.61	8,294
Est	992,041.62	28,473.87	1,020,515.49	12,782,057.72	6,605
Ouest	533,284.67	3,082.40	536,367.07	9,052,065.98	5,774
Midi	406,145.73	24,357.18	430,502.91	5,074,801.88	3,642
État	4,922.46	34,180.30	39,102.76	2,208,874.00	124
Orléans	....	....	....	....	....
Total	4,413,954.01	189,139.81	5,195,263.56	55,676,923.67	35,528

sary to consider the first fund only, as the second differs little from a general aid fund for its casual employés, such as day laborers, section hands, etc.

The fund for the pensioning of classified employés was created in 1850. According to the scheme then devised, receipts were obtained by retaining three per cent of the wages of the employés, the company itself contributing a like amount; and pensions, varying from $48.25 to $115.80 a year, were paid after workingmen had reached the age of 60 years. The insufficiency of these provisions becoming evident, the fund was reorganized in 1869 on a much more comprehensive basis. Further modifications were introduced in 1875, 1878, 1884, and 1891, the purport of all of which was to make still more liberal the provisions of the fund as regards the right of employés to pensions. As at present constituted, receipts consist of contributions by the employés of four per cent of their wages and one-twelfth part of any increase in their wages, and contributions by the company of an amount equal to eight per cent of the wages of the employés and one-twelfth of all increases in wages. These sums are paid into two different funds. The first is deposited in the National Old-Age Pension Bank, according to the system previously described, while the latter goes to constitute a special company fund. As regards the contributions of the employés, therefore, the company does nothing but collect them, by retaining them from wages, and pay them to the national institution.

The company's fund provides for the following scheme of pensions:

1. Full Pension; the right to which is acquired when an employé has been employed by the company 25 years and has reached the age of 55 years. The amount of the pension is as many sixteenths of the average sum he has received in wages during the last six years as the pensioner has been years plus five in the service of the company, but must be at least 500 francs ($96.50).

2. Anticipated Pension; acquired by one 50 years of age after 20 years of service in the company. It cannot exceed 30 sixteenths of the pensioner's wages, but must be equal to 500 francs ($96.50).

3. Pension for Premature Invalidity or Incapacity Resulting from an Accident; which is paid without regard to the age or length of service of the applicant. The amount is equal to as many sixteenths of the workingman's wages as he has been years in the employ of the company.

In addition, it is provided that the widows of workingmen having been employed by the company 15 years will receive a pension equal to that which their husbands had or would have received; and that the children of such employés, if they have no mother, or upon the death of their mother, will be entitled to a pension until 18 years of age.

The importance of the operations of this service is seen from the following figures. In 1893, the total number of employés of the company in the classified service was 30,762. Of this number 27,584 came under the provisions of the fund. The total receipts of the fund during the year were $1,036,893.06, of which $687,489.69 was contributed by the company;

$348,185.50 was derived from interest and $1217.87 from other sources. The assets of the fund at the end of the year were $8,514,548.22. During the year there were granted 677 pensions, of which 403 were to employés, 243 to widows, and 31 to children of deceased employés. The average age of the employés pensioned was 56 years and 5 months, and their average length of service 27 years and 3 months. The total number of pensioners on the roll December 31, was 5388, of which 3208 were workingmen, 2050 widows, 13 children of former employés, and 12 persons drawing pensions under former regulations.

The total amount paid in pensions during the year was $742,136.72, of which $485,864.18 came from the company's fund and $256,272.54 from the state bank. The average value of the pension granted to employés in 1893 was $183.93, of which $121.78 came from the company's fund and $62.15 from the state bank. The average value of widows' pensions was $78.16, of which $54.43 came from the company's fund and $23.16 from the state bank. That for children was $30.49, the total of which was a charge upon the company's fund. In view of these figures it is scarcely necessary to comment upon the liberality of the company regarding the provision of pensions for employés and their families. Its work is fairly typical of that done by the other companies.

From the standpoint of the study of insurance principles, the experience of the French railway companies affords an excellent example of one of the great dangers that should be guarded against in the organization of any system of old-age insurance; that of the failure adequately to provide for the inevitable augmentation of expenses as the system grows older. Almost without exception the French railways have failed correctly to estimate and provide for future increased charges; and disaster to their funds has only been averted by the fact that their financial resources have enabled them largely to increase the amount of their contributions. The Western Railroad, in order to carry out its engagements, was compelled successively to increase its contributions from three to four per cent, then, in 1884, to five per cent, and, finally, in 1892, to eight per cent of the amount paid by it in wages. This same experience has occurred to quite, if not all, of the other railway funds. The fund of the Eastern Railway Company, for instance, was created in 1853, and revised in 1862 on the basis of a contribution on the part of both the employé and the company of a sum equal to two per cent of the former's wages. In 1879 it was found necessary to revise these rates, and the contribution of the employé was raised to three per cent, while that of the company was raised to eight per cent, and, in 1891, still further to twelve per cent. The Central (Midi) Company has had to go still further. From an original contribution of three per cent, it has had to increase the rate to fifteen per cent, while the contribution of the employés remains at three per cent.

No better object lesson concerning this point could be desired than is here afforded. The ability of the companies to decree these successive advances has prevented any disaster resulting from this miscalculation; but if any less strong enterprise had had a similar experience, failure, with its consequent hardships to the workingmen, would have inevitably resulted.

As regards miners' insurance funds the author has already made a detailed study of the funds of two of the most important mining companies, those of Anzin and Blanzy, in his report to the Department of Labor on Industrial Communities. The Anzin Mining Company is not only the largest mining company of France, employing over 10,000 workingmen, but its fund represents the very best type of employers' insurance funds. The following account of the operations of this fund, condensed from this report, therefore, will show the character of workingmen's insurance against old age as provided in the mining industry.

Previous to 1887 the Anzin Company followed the practice of according to workingmen who had grown old in its service, and had become unable to work, a pension for the remainder of their lives, that constituted a direct charge upon the resources of the company. The employés participated in no way in the regulation of these pensions, nor was any portion of their wages during previous years retained to aid in the constitution of the fund from which they were paid. There were serious objections to this system. The workingmen did not like the feeling that they were pensioners on the bounty of the company; and the pensions being dependent on the financial prosperity of the company, they did not feel the same security that an independent insurance scheme would have afforded. Recognizing this, on January 1, 1887, the company inaugurated a new system of old-age pensions. By this system the company frankly took its workingmen into partnership, and provided for the constitution, through mutual sacrifices, of an insurance fund that should be wholly independent of the company's funds or management. Though the company made sacrifices equal in amount to those under the old system, the pension was no longer a bounty, but a right to which the workingman would acquire a title by years of voluntary sacrifices. This system is the more remarkable, for, in 1894, as we shall see, the government adopted *in toto* its principles in framing its laws regulating the insurance of miners generally throughout France. The regulations then adopted by the company concerning the granting of pensions might almost be said to have formed a model after which the French law was drawn.

The essential provisions of these regulations may be summarized in the following paragraphs: —

Dating from January 1, 1887, the company agreed to deposit in the National Old-Age Pension Bank, in the name of each workingman who should make an equal payment, a sum equal to $1\frac{1}{2}$ per cent of the wages of the workingman. The two deposits were then recorded in an individual account book, which remained the property of the workingman. For workingmen employed below ground the payments of the company commenced from the time of their entering upon such work; for those employed above ground, when the workingmen were at least 18 years of age and had been in the employ of the company three years. The payments of the company cease when the workingman has reached the age of 50 years. The latter, however, can defer the enjoyment of his pension, if he so desires, by continuing his personal payments. Through these payments the workingman was enabled to acquire the right to an annuity from the National Bank for Old-Age Pensions, on reaching the age of 50 years, for the remainder of his life. In case of permanent disability before reaching that age, he entered into the immediate enjoyment of a pension proportionate to his age and the amount of deposits to his credit.

In addition to these provisions whereby the company agreed to contribute toward the acquisition of pensions by workingmen an amount equal to their own payments, the company further provided for the increase of these pensions as a reward for long and faithful service. When a workingman had fulfilled the double condition of being at least 35 years of age and had been 10 years without interruption in the employ of the company, a special account was opened with him for the succeeding years of his connection with the company, or until he had reached the age of 55 years, or had been retired on his pension. For each of these years, which can in no case exceed 15, there is added a special supplement to the pension, when due, of 3 francs (58 cents) for workingmen employed below ground, and $1\frac{1}{2}$ francs (29 cents) for those above ground. The total supplementary pension, except in cases of severe injuries or infirmities contracted during work, is not paid unless the workingman remains with the company until he is 50 years of age. The latter, also, cannot enter upon the enjoyment of his supplementary pension until he ceases to work for the company. For workingmen employed as overseers and for married workingmen living with their wives, the pensions are somewhat higher. Provision is also made in all cases for the payment of pensions to widows of workingmen. Temporary provisions made special arrangements for workingmen already in the employment of the company but whose ages prevented them from acquiring pensions according to the regular rates provided in the new regulations.

Adherence to these regulations was purely optional. Ninety-five per cent of the workingmen, however, at once recognized the great advantages offered to them and signified their approval. The table following shows the results of the efforts of the company for pensioning its employés, both for the years immediately preceding the adoption of the new plan and for the years succeeding, including 1893.

In explanation of this table, it should be noted, that the average amount of the pensions shown indicates only the pensions granted by the company as rewards for long service. In addition to this, since 1887, the workingmen have been acquiring pensions through the National Bank for Old-Age Pensions. Thus, in the year 1893, the company paid for this purpose the sum of $56,775.39. In connection with this the workingmen paid an equal amount, the total amount paid into the National Bank being, therefore, $113,550.78.

The year 1893 practically closes the record of voluntary individual efforts on the part of mine-owners to pension their old employés or their widows. Mention has been made of a general law concerning old-age pensions for mine employés. This law was passed June 29, 1894, and by it the insurance of all

OPERATIONS OF THE PENSION SYSTEM OF THE COAL MINING COMPANY OF ANZIN, 1883 TO 1893.

Year.	PENSIONS TO OLD EMPLOYÉS.			PENSIONS TO WIDOWS OF EMPLOYÉS.			Amount Paid by Company to National Bank for Old-Age Pensions.	Total Amount Expended by Company for Pensions.
	Pensioners.	Total Paid in Pensions.	Average Pension.	Pensioners.	Total Paid in Pensions.	Average Pension.		
1883	712	$25,490	$35.80	651	$13,427	$20.62	....	$38,917
1884	794	38,432	35.81	621	13,417	21.62	....	41,849
1885	1,098	39,729	36.18	638	13,688	21.62	....	53,417
1886	1,131	41,734	36.90	664	14,468	21.79	....	56,202
1887	1,168	43,840	37.10	684	14,714	21.51	$5,800	63,954
1888	1,253	47,923	38.24	686	14,858	21.66	20,927	83,708
1889	1,279	49,091	38.38	725	15,655	21.59	26,024	90,770
1890	1,295	49,571	38.27	740	15,962	21.57	31,437	96,970
1891	1,302	50,746	38.97	787	16,616	21.11	55,939	123,301
1892	1,368	53,453	39.07	804	17,072	21.23	55,737	126,262
1893	1,379	54,740	39.69	827	17,400	21.04	56,775	128,915

mine employés was made obligatory. The provisions of this law are considered in the section relating to the present condition of the question of workingmen's insurance in France, as its enactment constitutes an essential part of the modern movement.

The size and stability of firms in such industries as railway transportation and mining renders it possible for each company to maintain an independent insurance fund. Wherever possible, this is the desirable form of organization, for under it each company bears its own burdens of insurance. In the case of small industrial establishments, however, the maintenance of such funds is difficult if not impossible. The problem of reaching workingmen employed in this latter class of industries by means of voluntary insurance institutions is, therefore, a special one. The solution evidently lies in some form of co-operation between the employers of labor in the same industries or localities. This, however, involves so many difficulties, the chief of which is the adjustment of the burdens among the different firms, that it is only recently that efforts in this direction have had any substantial results.

In 1891 the *Comité des Forges de France*, an organization similar to the American Iron and Steel Association, and including all of the important iron and steel manufacturers of the country, decided upon the creation of a central fund for the general insurance of all employés of iron and steel works in France. It was decided to limit the operations of the fund, during the first few years, to insurance against accidents. An organization was definitely effected in that year, under the title of *Caisse Syndicale d' Assurance Mutuelle des Forges de France*. Though organized under the auspices of the Association of Iron Manufacturers, it was left entirely optional with the particular employers whether or not they would become members of the fund. A number of the larger employers of labor had taken the lead, and it was hoped that in time the other employers would join, and thus ensure that practically all iron and steel workers would be insured against accidents.

The scheme of organization comprehends the joining together of the employers to insure all of their employés earning not more than 3000 francs ($597) a year. The accidents insured against are those causing either death, a total or partial permanent disability, or a temporary incapacity for labor of a duration of 90 days or more. In addition, the employers can insure themselves against any judgments for damages that may be obtained against them for injuries received by their workingmen. The following schedule of benefits is provided for: —

1. In case of temporary incapacity for work lasting more than 90 days, a sum equal to one-half of the workingman's wages, with a maximum of two francs ($0.39) per day until the workingman is able to return to work.

2. In case of partial permanent incapacity, a pension varying between 5 and 25 per cent of the workingman's former wages according to the extent of the incapacity and the number of persons dependent upon him for support, with a maximum of 365 francs ($70.44) per year.

3. In case of total permanent incapacity, a pension or annuity varying between 20 and 33 per cent of the workingman's wages according to the number of persons dependent upon him for support. The minimum of 20 per cent is paid to an unmarried workingman having no parents to support, and 5 per cent is added to this for each person dependent upon him

until the maximum of 33 per cent or 600 francs ($115.80) a year is reached.

4. In case of death, the widow to receive one-third of the amount that her husband would have received if totally incapacitated, and the children, for division among them, one-third, provided that no child can receive more than one-sixth. In case one of the parts apportioned to the widow or children is not required, it will be granted to the parents of the deceased, if they were supported by their son at the time of the accident. In certain cases these annuities can be converted into a single cash payment if both parties are mutually agreed.

The method for the determination of the amount to be paid in by each member of the fund is of especial interest, as this is the point of difficulty in funds embracing a number of establishments. The total amount paid by each in wages is taken as the general basis. To this is applied one of three coefficients of risk according to which of three classes, into which all works according to their character have been grouped, the particular establishment belongs. The maximum that can be demanded is 1.80, 1.50, and 1.20 francs per 100 francs paid in wages for each class respectively. The determination as to whether this maximum or a lesser rate shall be demanded is fixed each year for the ensuing year according to past experience and the financial condition of the fund. In practice, this maximum was only required the first year. Since then it has been 1.62, 1.35, and 1.08 francs respectively.

A most important provision is that providing a

system of rebates or repayments of dues to each establishment in proportion to the smallness of the expense that it has caused the fund. Each year, at the annual meeting, the administration determines the amount that the condition of the fund will permit to be returned in rebates. This amount is then distributed among the members who have contributed more than the amount which has been paid for the benefit of their employés, in proportion to their net contributions; that is, the difference between the amount of their contributions and the amount paid to their employés in indemnities. In a mutual insurance fund it is evidently of prime importance that each member should have a direct, as well as a general, interest in having as few accidents as possible. This system of rebates serves the double purpose of equitably adjusting the burdens of insurance according to the number of accidents that each establishment is responsible for, and of making it to the direct advantage of each to take every precaution against the occurrence of accidents. It is difficult to see how this most important consideration could be accomplished in a more direct or simple way.

The most abundant precautions are taken for the adjustment of receipts and expenditures, and to ensure that ample provision is made for the increasing charges that must occur in any pension system as it grows older. The experience of the French railways was fresh in mind, and it was determined if possible to avoid their errors. The only correct method by which increasing expenditures can be provided for, is that whereby each year is made to liquidate in full all charges, present or prospective, due to accidents occurring during its course. In every case, therefore, where a pension is granted, the constitution provides that there shall be carried to a special pension fund a sum sufficient to meet all estimated payments on its account, as determined by accepted mortality and actuarial tables. The amount carried to this fund must be such that the latter will always be equal to ten times the amount paid out in pensions during the preceding year. As many accidents occurring during one year cannot be definitely adjusted until the succeeding year, or even later, provision is also made for a special fund for the payment of unadjudicated claims. The amount paid to this fund is dependent upon the number of such claims remaining unsettled. Finally, provision is made for the constitution of a general reserve fund, in order to provide for the contingency of receipts during any year being insufficient to meet claims incurred.

Provision is made for a medical service, which, however, is of but slight importance, and for the prevention of accidents through an inspection service, the object of which is to see that the members of the fund take all needful precautions against accidents.

The main features of the operations of this fund are shown in the table following, which has been compiled from the annual reports furnished by the officers of the fund.

The fund commenced operations July 15, 1891. The first annual report, therefore, relates to but 5½ months, July 15 to December 31, 1891. At this last date it will be seen that 21 establish-

WORKINGMEN'S INSURANCE IN FRANCE.

OPERATIONS OF THE ACCIDENT INSURANCE FUND OF THE COMITÉ DES FORGES DE FRANCE, 1891–1895.

	1891.	1892.	1893.	1894.	1895.
Firms, members of fund	21	31	38	42	46
Employés insured	41,000	51,125	54,815	55,801	56,110
Receipts.					
Dues	$56,982.01	$149,495.08	$164,772.15	$170,260.08	$169,183.68
Interest	564.82	3,256.95	5,734.76	7,849.98	9,492.77
Total receipts	$57,496.83	$152,751.98	$170,506.91	$178,110.06	$178,676.45
Rebates	....	9,124.51	12,603.66	11,207.23	14,889.83
Net receipts	$57,496.83	$143,627.47	$157,903.25	$166,902.83	$163,786.62
Expenditures.					
Administration	$6,284.77	$8,360.05	$8,068.84	$8,664.25	$8,302.19
Medical service	55.00	301.92	598.24	597.56	553.33
Inspection	....	946.97	474.91	149.88	488.53
Cash benefits	8,895.44	36,605.65	65,897.73	88,445.58	100,195.15
Pension fund	7,435.28	28,809.86	38,090.47	59,127.13	51,301.01
Fund for unadjudicated claims	15,154.44	43,205.75	35,123.06	268.48	2,946.41
Total expenditures	$37,824.93	$118,230.20	$148,253.25	$157,252.88	$163,786.62
Surplus carried to reserve fund	$20,171.91	$25,397.27	$9,650.00	$9,650.00	....
Assets.					
Pension fund	$7,435.28	$33,804.23	$67,258.75	$118,076.27	$157,393.27
Fund for unadjudicated claims	15,154.44	58,360.19	93,483.25	93,751.68	96,698.09
Reserve fund	20,171.91	45,569.18	55,219.18	64,869.18	64,869.18
Total	$42,761.63	$137,733.60	$215,961.18	$276,697.13	$318,960.54

ments, representing 41,000 workingmen, had become members of the fund. The latter, therefore, immediately started upon its career as the most important private accident insurance fund then in existence. Each year since then has shown a steady increase in the number of firms participating and the number of persons insured. In 1892 the number of firms had increased to 31, in 1893 to 38, in 1894 to 42, and in 1895 to 46, while the number of persons insured increased, first to 51,125, and then to 54,815, 55,801, and 56,110 persons.

The soundness of the financial basis is shown by the steady increase in the various funds. From a total of $42,761.63 in 1891 they increased to $318,960.54 in 1895. Though the rate of contribution the first year was the very low sum of 1.80, 1.50, and 1.20 per cent of the amount paid in wages for the three classes respectively, it was found that this could be reduced to 1.62, 1.35, and 1.08 and still permit of the return of large sums in the way of rebates, and the increase of the reserve fund, after providing for the other funds, of $25,397.27 in 1892, and $9650.00 in 1893 and 1894. The cost of administration now represents about 5 per cent of total expenditures.

During the period covered by this table indemnities were paid to 1637 workingmen on account of injuries received as the result of accidents. The number indemnified each year and the degree of severity of the injury are shown in the accompanying statement.

In view of the character of this institution, representing as it does the declared determination of the most important organization of iron and steel manufacturers that their employés should be insured against accidents at the expense of their employers, and in consideration of the fact that already it has insured more than fifty thousand workingmen, one can have no hesitation in pronouncing it the most important private institution that has been created for the voluntary insurance of workingmen. The far-reaching

CLASSES OF ACCIDENTS.	NUMBER.					PER CENT OF NUMBER INSURED.				
	1891.	1892.	1893.	1894.	1895.	1891.	1892.	1893.	1894.	1895.
Fatal	20	45	30	41	50	0.49	0.88	0.55	0.73	0.88
Total permanent disability	1	38	41	18	15	0.02	0.74	0.76	0.32	0.27
Partial permanent disability	73	203	268	269	278	1.78	3.97	4.96	4.82	4.95
Temporary disability	19	66	50	53	59	0.46	1.29	0.92	0.94	1.05
Total	113	352	389	381	402	2.75	6.88	7.19	6.81	7.15

effect of its work is already manifest. May 1, 1895, the national association of textile manufacturers of France organized a similar fund under the title of *Caisse Syndicale d'Assurance Mutuelle des Industries Textiles de France.*

This, moreover, is but the beginning of the insurance work of these national associations of manufacturers. Having perfected its accident insurance fund, the *Comité des Forges,* in 1894, created a similar fund for the insurance of iron and steel-workers against old-age and invalidity, under the title of *Caisse Patronale de Retraite en Faveur des Ouvriers des Forges de France.* The recent date at which this fund was created, and the fact that it has been impossible to obtain a report of its operations, will prevent our making any study of its organization or work.[1]

To Americans the study of the insurance funds organized by employers of labor is of greater utility than that of any other branch of workingmen's insurance. In France, the employés in the larger industrial concerns have long been thus insured. The movement has now extended to the employés of smaller establishments. In the work of such funds as those created by the iron manufacturers of France may be said largely to lie the future of voluntary insurance. If its development is not too slow, France may yet escape the necessity of compulsory state insurance.

The Present Problem of Workingmen's Insurance in France. — In the preceding pages we have passed in review all of the principal classes of institutions of France having for their object the insurance of workingmen against want when physically incapacitated for work. Their history, we have seen, extends back a great many years. Beginning with about the year 1880, however, the problem of workingmen's insur-

---

[1] The insurance work of the *Comité des Forges* and of the textile manufacturers of France has been specially commented upon as being the most important examples of the association of employers for the mutual insurance of their employés. There are other cases, however, of a similar union of forces. Such, for instance, are the insurance funds of the masons and plumbers of Paris: *Caisse Syndicale des Entrepreneurs de Maçonnerie du Département de la Seine*, and *Caisse Syndicale d'Assurance Mutuelle des Entrepreneurs de Plomberie et de Couverture de Paris*, both notable institutions.

ance entered upon a new phase. Largely influenced by the example of Germany, which was then framing its radical insurance laws, the question suddenly sprang into one of great prominence. The position was generally assumed that not simply the few who desired to be insured should have suitable institutions in which to do so, but that in some way the advantages of insurance should be extended to the entire laboring population. The great question then necessarily arose, whether this could be accomplished without the adoption of the principle of compulsion, a step which it was almost universally held should not be taken if it could possibly be avoided. For fifteen years the battle of voluntary *versus* obligatory insurance has been fought with the greatest thoroughness. It has been impossible, however, to break with the past; and practically all propositions that have been advanced, no matter which principle has been advocated, have looked to the development of existing institutions in one way or another.

The present problem of workingmen's insurance in France relates, therefore; first, to the modification of the law relating to employers' liability, and the development of insurance against accidents; secondly, to the reform of the mutual-aid societies; thirdly, to the development of old-age and invalidity insurance through the reorganization of the National Old-Age Insurance Bank; and, finally, to that of the insurance of miners, which circumstances have made an independent question.

Opinion in France regarding the best method for the indemnification of workingmen injured during their work has passed through all of the changes, from that whereby a solution was sought by increasing the legal liability of employers, to that of the advocacy of compulsory insurance. In spite of the great transformation in the conditions under which industry is carried on, France still remains, as regards the liability of employers for accidents to their employés, under the provisions of Articles 1382-1384 of the civil code enacted in 1804. Briefly stated, the provisions of this law are that employers are responsible to their employés only for those injuries which are the result of their fault or negligence or of those directly representing them; and that, according to the general principles of law, the burden of proving this negligence or fault rests upon the workingman making claims for damages.

The first efforts to change this condition of affairs were directed to the modification of the provisions of the law regarding the *onus probandi*. It was sought to accomplish what was called the inversion of proof (*renversement de la preuve*); that is, it was desired to so change the law that employers would be presumed to be responsible for all accidents unless they could prove that they had taken all needful precautions. This consideration led to a whole series of proposed laws, the first of which was that of M. Nadaud, May 29, 1880. All of these propositions were referred to a parliamentary commission, which reported, on November 27, 1887, a bill of its own. The presentation of this report marks the beginning of a new period, for by it was introduced the new element, according to which it was sought to substitute the principle of trade risk (*risque professionnel*) in place of Articles 1382-1384 of the code. The meaning of this is, that the fact was recognized that under modern industrial conditions accidents are inevitable; that the greater number of these are inherent in the industry itself, or at least the responsibility for their occurrence cannot be established; and that, therefore, it is upon the industry itself that should fall the reparation of these accidents. In consequence of this theory, the indemnification of victims of all accidents, except those voluntarily induced, was deemed by this proposition to be one of the legitimate items in the cost of production, and therefore a charge that should be borne exclusively by the employers.

A second important innovation of this report was that whereby it was sought to lessen litigation between employers and their employés by determining in advance the indemnities to which workingmen would be entitled in case of injury. The logical result of this effort was evidently the introduction of the principle of insurance. It recommended, therefore, that employers should make provision against these payments by the insurance of their employés in the National Accidents Insurance Bank, which was to be reorganized on a more effective basis, or should group themselves into syndicates for mutual insurance. In short, insurance was deemed desirable by the chamber, though it was not yet converted to the principle of compulsion.

This and similar bills occupied the attention of Parliament for several years. June 28, 1890, however, the government introduced a new measure which marks the beginning of the third and last period, that wherein, not only the principle of trade risk is fully recognized, but that of compulsory insurance as its logical sequence. Other propositions followed. All, however, agreed in making the indemnification of accidents, according to a predetermined scale of benefits, obligatory. It is interesting to note that the system of insurance provided for by the majority of these bills is substantially that voluntarily organized by the iron and steel and textile manufacturers' associations. The creation of these funds, indeed, gave a new turn to the whole question of workingmen's insurance in France.

Practically, the history of workingmen's insurance against sickness in France is contained, as we have seen, in that of her mutual-aid societies. In them France seems to have found the most practicable form of purely voluntary insurance against sickness. There seems little reason to doubt, therefore, that in the future as well, the extension of insurance against sickness will come through the development of these organizations. It is our present task to consider the means now proposed for bringing this about.

The whole trend of these efforts is toward completing the transformation of these societies, from their original character of partly mutual-aid and partly charitable relief organizations, into a true system of voluntary insurance. The two great lines along which reform is needed are: first, the elimination, as far as possible, of the granting of charitable aid; and, secondly, the reorganization of the societies upon a scientific basis as determined by mortality and morbidity tables and mathematical calculations of probable receipts and expenditures. This latter consideration is of especial importance, inasmuch as within later years these societies have more and more entered the field of old-age insurance, the provision of which requires particularly careful mathematical and actuarial calculations.

It will be thoroughly impracticable to attempt to follow in detail all the steps in this evolution from the date of the first legislative recognition of these societies down to the present time. Moreover, it is only within the last two decades that the changes introduced or proposed are of great importance. If we concern ourselves, therefore, with the modern movement only, it will be unnecessary to go back of the year 1881.

In that year there was introduced a measure which, though repeatedly modified, still forms the basis for the measure at present before the French Parliament. The legislative history of this proposition is simply that of its alternate modification and passage by the two houses. The result of these years of consideration is that the Senate and Chamber of Deputies are agreed that further legislation is desirable. The difference of opinion between the two now relates but to matters of detail, and it is but a question of a short time before a complete agreement will be reached and a bill, substantially similar to the one now before the legislature, become a law. It is worth our while therefore to examine, with some degree of care, the provisions of this measure, for by it it is intended to determine the future organization of sick and old-age insurance in France. Greater clearness will be obtained by taking up some of its most essential features *seriatim*.

1. The existing division of societies into those approved and those authorized is maintained. The utility of this distinction rests on the fact that though it is deemed best that societies should be subjected to a certain amount of governmental regulation as regards their actuarial basis, their accounts, etc., nevertheless the greatest liberty should be left to the people to form societies of whatever character they may wish. It is desired, however, that all societies should belong to the first class. To encourage them to become such, therefore, certain important advantages are accorded to them. They are given the right to make use of the National Old-Age Pension Bank under specially advantageous terms for the provision of old-age pensions, the right of investing their funds either in the National Savings Bank, in government bonds or other government guaranteed securities through the *Caisse des Dépôts et Consignations*, the right to form syndicates among themselves for the mutual provision of insurance, and, finally, a participation in the annual subsidy given to mutual-aid societies.

2. The government makes various provisions obligatory upon the societies, the object of which is to make certain that the relation between receipts and expenditures is established upon a proper basis. Before a society can be recognized, and therefore entitled to the privileges which its official *status* confers, it must satisfy the government that its resources are so calculated as to enable it to meet, in all pos-

sible contingencies, the engagements which it assumes towards its members.

3. Every effort is made by this bill to encourage the societies to enter, or rather to extend, their operations in the field of old-age insurance, and at the same time to ensure that when they do so, an adequate financial basis is provided. The great defects in existing conditions lie in the fact that the services of sick and old-age insurance are not kept separate, and that each year is not made to provide for the burdens which are really incurred in that year. A number of important provisions are therefore made obligatory upon all societies which desire to enter the field of old-age insurance. Whenever such insurance is offered, a special service must be created entirely independent as regards receipts and expenditures of the sick benefit work. Without such a separation scientific old-age insurance is impossible. A condition necessarily accompanying this is that special contributions must be required of all members contracting old-age insurance proportionate in amount to their ages.

4. The important power is given to societies to insure their members individually in the National Old-Age Pension Bank as well as collectively, as was done in the past. Under this system each member will receive an individual account book in which his payments will be entered. The amount of his pension will thus be determined according to his personal effort, and will be in no way dependent upon his remaining a member of the society. The latter, in fact, acts only as an intermediary between the state bank and the workingmen.

5. Finally, the question of a subsidy by the state is left open to be determined by the finance committee. While the authors of the present measure of reform have felt that it was unfortunate that there should be any such question, they recognized that any attempt to abolish the subsidies that have been granted in the past would excite such antagonism as probably to defeat the whole measure. They frankly avow their desire, however, to restrict this subsidy within as narrow limits as possible. So admirably does the reporter of this bill, M. Audriffred, set forth the considerations here involved, and so directly do they apply to all cases of state-aided insurance schemes, that we cannot do better than reproduce his remarks on this point.[1]

"We recognize willingly," he says, "that the payments of honorary members and the subsidies of the state are useful, especially at the present time which forms a transition between the régime of assistance and that of pure mutuality. We are persuaded, however, that though it may be necessary to augment them, the societies should be warned against the false illusions to which they may give rise. The number of persons who are in a position to aid the societies as honorary members is limited. In the early future, when, as we hope, the number of members, which to-day includes 1,250,000 persons, will embrace, as in England, 6,000,000 or exceed that figure, these payments will produce a relatively feeble result.

"The subsidy of the state itself should never

[1] *Premier Rapport sur le Projet de Loi rélatif aux Sociétés de Secours Mutuels*, par M. Audriffred, Député, 1889.

become a constituent element in the budget of mutual-aid societies. It would perhaps be permissible if the state had personal resources outside of taxation, but it has nothing. The state can only distribute that which it has collected by way of taxation; and the tax necessary in order to accord an important subsidy will fall heavily upon the tax-payers or the members of the societies themselves, and will fall in a still more prejudicial manner upon industry, agriculture, and commerce. The subsidy of the state, if it attains large proportions, will only be a fiction. It will not be a gift but a restitution, diminished by the cost of collection and management.

"But, more important still, it would work the gravest injury in that it would enfeeble individual energies so long restrained, so hesitating, so timorous, and so little sure of themselves; energies which rather should be strengthened and encouraged if it is hoped to provide for the country independent social institutions capable of ameliorating the condition of the people without the direct intervention of the state.

"To be truly useful, the subsidy of the state ought to be restricted to certain limits, and its true purposes preserved. This purpose is to provoke saving and providence, to encourage the indifferent to affiliate themselves with mutual-aid societies and to persuade the societies themselves to enter the field of old-age insurance, and, possibly, to come to the aid of the societies at the moment of their organization or in times of emergency or distress as the result of epidemics or other great misfortunes."

To sum up, then, the effort of the bill at present

before Parliament is to leave to the societies all possible independence of action, and, at the same time, to ensure that their financial arrangements and guarantees shall be based upon firm financial foundations and scientific actuarial calculations.

The movement in France for the insurance of workingmen against old age and invalidity has been much weaker than that for their insurance against accidents. The question, nevertheless, is a live one, and the Assembly has constantly before it measures looking toward the extension of this branch of workingmen's insurance. These propositions have in view the extension of old-age insurance in two quite distinct ways. The first has already been considered in our account of recent efforts to reform the mutual-aid societies. The second looks rather toward the reorganization of the old *Caisse Nationale des Retraites pour la Vieillesse*.

The first really serious effort in this direction dates from the year 1873. By a law of April 24, 1872, the National Assembly had created a parliamentary committee to study the general question of the condition of labor in France. The result of its report was the rise of great interest in labor questions, and, among other features, that of providing more fully for the insurance of workingmen against the needs of old age. This interest found expression in various projects, all of which were illy conceived, without scientific basis, largely chimerical in character, and agreed only in imposing heavy financial burdens upon the state. It should be remembered that at this time workingmen's insurance was a new question; and an almost complete ignorance existed in regard to the fundamental principles upon which any scheme should rest.

Nothing of importance was accomplished until the year 1890, when a special commission, of which M. Guieysse was president, was created by the Chamber of Deputies to investigate and report upon all measures having for their object the provision of old-age insurance. Ultimately there came before this commission eleven or more propositions. Of these it is necessary to mention only that of M. Constans, introduced June 6, 1891, on behalf of the government, since the commission in its report practically disregarded the others and reported a bill embodying substantially its provisions. This report was not made until February 11, 1893. It is worth while to understand the essential features of this proposition, for it indicates clearly the present attitude of the French Parliament and people regarding this question.

According to it there is created in place of the existing National Old-Age Pension Bank a new institution under the same name, but having a far wider sphere of activity. Affiliation with this bank, as far as the workingmen are concerned, is left, as before, purely voluntary. Both the number and amount of their payments are purely optional, but the maximum value of the annuity that they can acquire is limited to 600 francs ($115.80). In the acquisition of this pension, however, the workingman will be materially aided both by the state and by his employer. The bill provides that the state shall annually make an addition to each depositor's account of an amount equal to that of his own contributions, with the reservation, however, that it can in no case exceed 30 francs ($5.79) per year, an amount corresponding to a payment on the part of the workingman of 10 centimes ($0.02) per day for 300 working days. In addition to this, a contribution is required from each employer who has made use of his labor of an amount to be determined by a superior central council. For employers engaged in agricultural pursuits this contribution cannot be less than 2 francs ($0.39) nor more than 6 francs ($1.16) per 300 working days; and for other employés not less than 3 francs ($0.58) nor more than 9 francs ($1.74) per 300 working days.

Permission is also given to the depositors to combine ordinary life with old-age pension insurance. In this case, of course, the amount of the pension is somewhat smaller than if no life insurance were contracted. In order to encourage workingmen to take out life insurance, the state agrees to accord in this case a supplemental subsidy equal to one-third the amount of the workingmen's payments devoted to this purpose.

The significant feature of this proposition is, that, while it substantially affirms the principle of voluntary insurance, it in reality introduces the principle of compulsion so far as contributions on the part of the employers are concerned. It also shows the general feeling that the workingmen unaided are unable to lay by a sufficient sum to provide for the constitution of pensions for their old age; and furthermore, as in Germany, it commits the state, not only to the gratuitous maintenance of the insurance institution, but makes it contribute to the extent of at least one-third in the payment of these pensions. The reporter of the bill estimates that when the system is in full operation the number of its members will be about 4,000,000, and the annual subsidy required of the state about 98,000,000 francs.

This was the condition of affairs at the close of the legislative session of 1893. On the opening of the new chamber in the same year a special commission on workingmen's insurance was created. Four old propositions, including the one just considered, and six new ones, have been referred to this body. As yet this commission has not reported. The exact form that old-age insurance will ultimately take in France is, therefore, still uncertain. That some national system will be created, however, there can be but little doubt.

The Insurance of Mine Employés. — In the preceding sections attention has been directed to efforts to establish general schemes of insurance; that is, to systems applicable to all classes of industrial workers alike. None of these various propositions have yet been erected into law. Concurrent with these efforts, however, there has been a strong agitation for the creation of a system of insurance specially applicable to mine employés. This movement has been finally successful in the enactment of the law of June 29, 1894. This law creates a system of compulsory insurance for the single class of mining employés. As an entering wedge of the principle of compulsory insurance into France this law is one of great significance.

The reasons why this particular industry should be selected for legislation can be briefly stated. In the first place the industry is one to which a central system of insurance is peculiarly applicable. It is at the same time one of the most important industries of the country, one which must be carried on on a large scale, and one whose personnel possesses exceptional stability both as regards a change of employment or a change of employer. Again, the employés constitute a body of workingmen exceptionally homogeneous in character, and, in general, earning but moderate wages. Finally, the conditions of labor are such that the miners are exposed to exceptional and seemingly unavoidable risks of accidents and sickness.

In addition to these reasons which are inherent in the nature of the industry itself, is the fact that in no other industry has the practice of voluntary insurance, under the joint action of the employés and employers, reached so high a degree of development. At first inspection it would seem that in an industry where so much had already been done in a purely voluntary way, the demand for a compulsory law would be weaker than in the case of other industries. A closer examination will show that what has actually occurred is not unnatural. Though many of the voluntary insurance funds that had been created were admirable organizations, others again, as might be expected, were established on essentially inequitable or insecure foundations, and their occasional failure to meet obligations gave rise to bitter complaint and much real hardship. Again, those workingmen for whom such funds had not been organized naturally felt that they should be placed in as fortunate position as their brethren.

But, more than anything else, the miners demanded some method by which complete independence should be left to them as regards their right to change employers without forfeiting in any way pension rights already acquired. While adequate provision was made in the better funds to meet this point, the great majority of schemes were in this respect radically defective; and there seemed to be no way by which this most desirable consideration could be accomplished, except by the enactment of a general law which would make the introduction of the individual account system compulsory, and, as a necessary corollary, regulate in some way the nature of the insurance benefits offered, and the conditions under which they could be obtained.

The interference of the state was therefore invoked in order to secure; first, that all mine employés should enjoy the benefit of insurance; secondly, that the insurance funds should possess absolutely safe financial foundations, and be organized and conducted on scientific principles; and, thirdly, that there should be some uniformity in the work of the funds, in order that the deposits of a member might be good wherever he went.

The history of the legislative attempts leading up to this law is of little interest. The first bill having for its specific purpose the insurance of coal miners was introduced in 1880. It was not until June 29, 1894, however, that an agreement could be reached and a law enacted.

The principal features of this law have already been described. In general, its purpose was not so much to create a new system, as to make obligatory upon all mine operators the insurance work already performed by a great many coal-mining concerns; to unify the plans upon which insurance funds could be created, and to require that they would be founded upon adequate financial foundations, and conducted upon approved principles. The radical innovation was the introduction of the principle of compulsion. The details of its provisions may be recapitulated as follows: —

The insurance of all mine employés against both sickness and old age is rendered obligatory upon all mine operators. The two operations of old-age and of sick insurance are kept distinct. To provide for the first, each mine-owner is required to pay into the insurance funds provided by the act a sum equal to four per cent of the total amount paid by him in wages, one half of this amount to be borne by himself and the other half to be deducted from the wages of the employés. This percentage can be increased if mutually agreed upon by the employer and the employés. The sums thus set aside are devoted to the constitution of a fund from which old-age pensions will be paid. The option is given to the mine operators to make these payments directly to the *Caisse Nationale de Retraite pour la Vieillesse,* or to create special independent funds. In the latter case, these funds are subject to rigid oversight on the part of the government, as regards the investment of their funds, the nature of their constitutions, etc. In all cases, however, the value of the pension is determined according to the tables in use by the state bank. The amount of the pension is, therefore, in proportion to the amount of the earnings of each individual workingman. Those employés, however, who earn more than 2400 francs ($463.20) yearly are considered for the purpose of insurance as earning only that amount. Reference to the account of the operations of the National Old-Age Insurance Bank will show the value of the pensions thus provided for. The age at which the right to a pension begins is fixed at 55 years, but can be deferred to a later age if desired, in which case, of course, the value of the pension will be proportionately increased.

For the insurance of workingmen against sickness, it is made obligatory upon each mine-owner to create an aid society, the resources of which are made to consist of: —

1. A deduction from the wages of each employé of an amount to be determined by the administrative council of the society, but which cannot exceed two per cent of his wages.

2. A contribution on the part of the employers of an amount equal to one-half the sum contributed by the employés.

3. Their proportion of the sums allotted by the state as subsidies to mutual-aid societies.

4. Gifts and legacies.

5. The product of fines levied for any purpose upon workingmen.

It is left to the constitution of each society to determine the nature and amount of relief to be granted to members in case of their sickness, or to their families in case of death. The societies are also permitted, if their resources are sufficient, to grant medical aid and furnish medical attendance to the wives and children of members. It is obligatory upon them to make payments to the old-age pension fund for members incapacitated for work as the result of sickness lasting more than four days, of an amount equal to at least five per cent of the indemnity to which they are entitled.

The societies are administered by a joint commission composed of workingmen and representatives of their employers.

It will be seen from this brief statement that the provisions of the law regarding insurance against sickness are far from radical. Practically, the only change introduced is to make the maintenance of mutual-aid societies compulsory, their constitution being altered scarcely at all; and even this innovation has made little difference in practice, for the existence of such societies was already almost universal in the case of mining companies of France.

It is unfortunate that the recent date at which this law went into effect renders it impossible to make any study of the results of its operations.

CHAPTER V.

WORKINGMEN'S INSURANCE IN BELGIUM.

Introduction. — Though the general conditions of the problems of employers' liability and workingmen's insurance in Belgium are similar to those in France, there are there in operation a number of insurance institutions essentially different from any found in the latter country, and presenting features that make them of especial importance to one studying insurance methods. At the present time, Belgium possesses five classes of institutions the purposes of which are the insurance of workingmen against either accidents, sickness, or old age and invalidity, viz.: (1) the National Savings and Old-Age Pensions Bank (*Caisse Générale d'Épargne et de Retraite*); (2) the special Miners' Insurance Funds (*Caisses de Prévoyance en Faveur des Ouvriers Mineurs*); (3) the Mutual-Aid Societies (*Sociétés de Secours Mutuels*); (4) the National Bank for the Assistance of Workingmen Injured by Accidents (*Caisse de Prévoyance et de Secours en Faveur des Victimes des Accidents du Travail*), and (5) Insurance funds organized by the large employers of labor for the benefit of their employés.

The first two of these are of much the greatest interest, the one offering a very successful example of state voluntary insurance, and the other the best example of the insurance of a particular class of workingmen. There has been obtained in this latter class the insurance of all miners with a minimum amount of interference on the part of the state, with the creation of no expensive bureaucratic system, with an extremely low cost of administration, and with a remarkable absence of friction. These features and their fifty years of successful operation make them one of the most fruitful subjects of study of any insurance institutions offered by Europe. In our consideration of workingmen's insurance in Belgium, therefore, chief attention will be given to these two institutions. The others will require but a brief description, not because they are of little importance, but because they possess but few features different from those of kindred French institutions.

Caisse Générale d'Épargne et de Retraite. — The National Savings and Old-Age Pension Bank had its origin in the *Caisse Générale de Retraite* created by the law of May 8, 1850. Fifteen years later, a general savings bank was created, by the law of March 16, 1865, and joined to this institution. Since then these two services have constituted separate branches of a single institution under the name of *Caisse Générale d'Épargne et de Retraite.* By a law promulgated August 9, 1889, this institution was given the further duty of assisting in the provision of workingmen's homes through the loaning of its funds to building societies. The bank has thus become a general public financial institution, the object of which is to assist laboring men in various ways. A study of it in all its operations would furnish a valuable contribution to the subject of workingmen's institutions.

Here, our attention must be strictly confined to that of its insurance work proper. This can be easily done, as each department of the bank's work, as far as accounts are concerned, is managed as an independent service.

The following is an outline of the scheme of insurance offered by it. Any person 10 years of age can provide for the constitution of an old-age pension by making payments of not less than 1 franc ($0.19) at a time. The depositor is entirely free as regards the number and amount of his deposits, with the exception that no pension for more than 1200 francs ($231.60) can be acquired. Pensions begin to run when the depositor has reached the age of 50 years, but can be deferred until he is 65 years old if he so desires. In case of invalidity before reaching the age of 50 years, a right to an immediate pension is acquired proportionate to the age of the invalid and the amount of his payments. There is the same choice between the systems of reserved and alienated capital that is offered by the French bank. The table on the following page shows the pension that will be earned by depositors commencing their payments at various ages in return for a regular monthly payment of $1, according to whether the pension is made to begin when the age of 50, 55, 60, or 65 years is reached.

Thus a person who, from the age of 20 years until 60, makes a regular monthly payment of $1 will acquire an old-age pension of $131.80 if he abandons all right to his capital, or of $70.52 if he desires the amount of his deposits to be returned to his heirs upon his death. If he does not commence his payments until 40 years of age, his pension will be $39.25 and $16.69 respectively.

It is evident from this brief description that there is little or no essential difference between the Belgium and the French systems. The merest statement of the bank's present condition will, therefore, serve every purpose, as the history of the French bank has

Age at First Payment.	Alienated Capital.				Reserved Capital.			
	50 Years.	55 Years.	60 Years.	65 Years.	50 Years.	55 Years.	60 Years.	65 Years.
10	$86.81	$132.89	$213.51	$369.04	$51.94	$78.36	$124.25	$212.35
20	51.07	80.43	131.80	230.50	28.44	43.87	70.52	121.51
30	26.82	44.83	76.33	137.13	13.72	22.26	36.85	64.58
40	10.60	21.01	39.25	74.41	4.90	9.31	$16.69	30.50
50	....	5.46	15.01	33.45	....	2.11	5.48	11.55
60	....	....	....	8.07	....	....	....	2.29
64	....	....	....	1.40	....	....	....	0.37

been given in considerable detail. The following figures were taken from the annual reports of the bank for the years 1893, 1894, and 1895, and serve to give an idea of the extent and character of the strictly old-age insurance work performed by it. The total number of deposits made each year, 1891 to 1895 inclusive, was 30,970, 45,336, 58,882, 69,242, and 85,477 respectively, and the total amount of deposits $215,599.72, $305,001.36, $312,713.85, $340,218.86, $454,337.25. The number of new accounts opened each of these years was 3642, 3874, 3525, 4438, and

5790. Of this last number, 5107 were men and 683 women. The total number of persons receiving pensions December 31 of each year, commencing with 1892, was 1923, 1893, 2120, 2342, and 2608. The total amount of annuities to which this last number was entitled was $169,425.13, an average of $64.96.

It appears from these figures that this institution far from provides a general system of old-age insurance. Nevertheless, as far as it goes, its work is of great value, and the figures just given show a gratifying increase each year in the number of new depositors and the amount of deposits.

Miners' Insurance Funds. — We now pass to the consideration of the most interesting type of insurance institutions in Belgium, that of funds for the insurance of miners. These institutions are interesting because they have had an existence of over fifty years, and have thus proven by long experience the practicability of providing workingmen's insurance without a too great expense or the creation of a very complicated machinery.

In Belgium, as in other countries, the creation of funds for the insurance of miners has preceded that for any other class of workingmen. The first miners' insurance fund was created in 1812. The first permanent institution, however, was that of Liège, founded in 1839 by 25 mining companies joining together for the common insurance of their employés. In the five succeeding years, the other mining centres followed the example of Liège, and created mutual institutions for the insurance of the miners of their districts. A general system for the insurance of miners has therefore been in operation in Belgium since that period.

The scheme of insurance which has been carried out comprehends the division of the country into six districts, in each of which has been created a central institution for the insurance of miners against accidents, and, to a limited extent, their insurance against old age and invalidity; and, secondly, the creation of a special insurance fund by each mining company for sick insurance. Each miner is, therefore, insured in two funds; against accidents in a central fund, and against sickness in the particular fund of his establishment.

The names and dates of creation of the six central funds are: Liège, 1839; Namur, 1839; Mons, 1840; Charleroi, 1840; Centre, 1841; and Luxembourg, 1844. Each of these funds has its own constitution, scheme of dues and benefits, management, etc. The obligation imposed upon the mine-owners is a very slight one, the greatest possible freedom being left to the owners in regard to the organization of their institutions. All, however, are required to report annually to the government, and are subjected to a financial control. In spite of this freedom, the general character of the funds is the same. The main difference lies in the extent to which the burden of insurance is borne by the employers. In the Mons fund receipts are derived by retaining three-fourths of one per cent of the employés' wages and an equal contribution on the part of the employers. In that of Charleroi all the contributions are met by the employers, who pay each year amounts equal to $1\frac{1}{2}$ per cent of their employés' wages.

WORKINGMEN'S INSURANCE IN BELGIUM. 197

In that of the Centre employers and employés each pay an amount equal to 1¼ per cent of wages. In that of Liège the employers pay a sum equal to 2 per cent of their employés' wages. In that of Namur the employers pay about half a franc per person insured per month; and in that of Luxembourg they each pay amounts equal to one-half of one per cent of the employés' wages. In addition to these contributions, the funds have, as other sources of income, subsidies by the state, subsidies by the provinces, interest on funds invested, and gifts and bequests.

The scheme of benefits varies in each fund. That for the Centre is given in detail in the author's report on Industrial Communities, Bulletin of the Department of Labor, November, 1896, and here is more briefly summarized. Monthly indemnities are paid as follows: —

(1) To an employé injured so as to be permanently and totally unable to work, a pension varying from 15.40 to 30 francs ($2.97 to $5.79), according to whether he is married or single, under or over 19 years of age. For women the pension varies from 9.20 to 13.80 francs ($1.78 to $2.66), according to whether they are under or over 16 years of age.

(2) To an employé injured so as to be able to earn not more than 50 per cent of his usual wages, a pension varying from 6.80 to 22 francs ($1.31 to $4.25), according to the recipient's age, sex, and conjugal condition.

(3) To an employé injured so as to be able to earn but from 51 to 70 per cent of his usual wages, a pension varying from 4 to 15 francs ($0.77 to $2.89).

(4) To an employé injured so as to be able to earn

but from 71 to 85 per cent of his usual wages, a pension varying from 2.40 to 8 francs ($0.46 to $1.54).

To persons able to earn more than 85 per cent of their usual wages no benefit is granted.

(5) To a workingman unable to work and 55 years of age or over, and having been employed at least 30 years, or of any age and having been employed 38 years, a pension of 15 francs ($2.89); and to one 60 years of age, whether able to work or not, and having been employed 35 years, a pension of 20 francs ($3.86).

(6) Provision is finally made for the granting of pensions to the widows, orphans, and parents of workingmen who either are killed as the result of an accident, or die while in the receipt of a pension. It will be noticed that provision is here made for old-age pensions. This is exceptional, as the other funds do not make such provision.

The development of this system of insurance, as well as its present extent, can be seen from the table on the opposite page, in which are given the number of persons insured, the total receipts and expenditures, the value of running pensions, and assets at the end of the year of all the six general funds combined for each of a number of years, 1845 to 1894.

The figures there given show that the number of miners insured constantly increased until 1890, after which it has remained nearly stationary, varying with the number of persons engaged in the mining industry. These funds, as has been said, are largely supported by the employers. Of the total receipts in 1894, $407,511.84 was contributed by them, and but $39,836.16 by their employés; $57,910.23 was derived from interest, and the balance, $10,562.32, from subsidies. In regard to expenditures, $460,539.30 went for benefits, and $10,242.51 for administration, the latter item thus representing but slightly over 2 per cent of the total.

The information concerning the number of persons aided during this year is not at hand. In 1893, how-

NUMBER OF PERSONS INSURED, RECEIPTS AND EXPENDITURES, ETC., OF MINERS' GENERAL INSURANCE FUNDS OF BELGIUM, 1845–1894.

Year.	Persons Insured.	Total Receipts.	Total Expenditures.	Value of Running Pensions.	Assets.
1845	22,393	$51,840.76	$32,380.96	$23,120.05	$133,793.89
1850	47,809	71,449.95	61,161.70	39,065.71	202,454.88
1860	80,783	193,398.35	145,085.62	94,894.43	698,606.92
1870	95,809	283,685.30	262,424.03	251,817.91	1,029,890.07
1880	106,633	347,990.77	376,502.28	345,646.21	1,249,756.83
1890	117,396	506,446.66	398,608.29	394,298.04	1,253,495.62
1891	117,265	524,203.44	413,051.84	391,126.85	1,364,721.34
1892	116,420	523,712.25	428,377.20	420,806.01	1,460,056.00
1893	114,697	487,042.83	457,659.94	437,495.68	1,489,436.97
1894	117,359	515,890.54	470,781.81	461,312.27	1,534,216.44

ever, during which the conditions were practically identical with those of 1894, 16,920 persons were aided. The average amount of the relief afforded each was $26.44. During the decennial period 1884–1893, 15.6 per cent of the average number of persons insured received relief annually.

In addition to these central banks for the insurance of miners against accidents, each mine operator, as has been stated, is required to maintain a separate fund for the assistance of his workingmen in cases of sickness and slight accidents. These funds are supported by contributions from the employers and employés measured by a certain percentage of the latter's wages, the former's payments being, however, much the greater. The management of these institutions and the scheme of benefits afforded are similar to the employers' insurance funds that have been described in our consideration of workingmen's insurance in France. It will be sufficient, therefore, merely to indicate the extent of the insurance work performed by showing the receipts and expenditures of these funds during recent years.

RECEIPTS AND EXPENDITURES OF SPECIAL MINERS' INSURANCE FUNDS OF BELGIUM, 1883–1893.

Year.	RECEIPTS.			Total Expenditures.
	From Employés.	From Employers.	Total.	
1883	$68,071.29	$206,005.69	$274,076.98	$277,555.81
1884	57,716.84	222,011.37	289,378.22	284,509.02
1885	52,765.66	228,037.22	280,802.88	284,487.79
1886	52,473.03	229,246.36	281,719.40	283,504.65
1887	52,886.05	233,369.42	286,255.48	288,786.48
1888	53,570.62	286,336.54	339,907.16	285,990.68
1889	54,421.95	244,523.86	298,945.81	293,570.56
1890	68,509.21	287,344.96	355,854.17	348,271.39
1891	68,786.94	301,445.93	370,232.86	366,817.15
1892	61,993.14	326,860.75	388,853.89	392,603.50
1893	49,687.85	299,240.13	348,927.98	356,212.96

The system of insurance here practised possesses several features of unusual merit. In the first place, in making the insurance general, but just enough compulsion has been exercised to ensure compliance with the law. No central or state institution has been created, and almost no government service has been necessary. In the second place, the important distinction has been made between those cases requiring only temporary, but immediate, relief, and those calling for the payment of pensions which may run for years. For the former cases, the mine operators have been contented with seeing that sick insurance societies have been created for the benefit of their employés. For the pension service, a greater permanence and financial stability is required than can be afforded by small independent societies. All mine operators are, therefore, grouped into six central banks corresponding to the mining districts into which the kingdom is divided. The failure of one mine-owner thus will not embarrass greatly a bank, or cause any inability to pay deferred pensions.

The greatest advantage of the Belgium system, however, is the simplicity, and the consequent great economy in the cost of administration, that has been secured. The funds are in all cases administered by officials serving without pay. In 1894, of the total amount expended by the six general funds, $470,781.86, but $10,242.51, or slightly over 2 per cent, was absorbed in the expenses of administration, the remaining 98 per cent going directly to the insured in some form of relief.

This organization by districts, instead of in a central bank, and for a particular industry, simplifies greatly, and, at the same time, makes much more equitable, the apportionment of charges according to risks. Each establishment bears the burden of its own cases of sickness and slight accidents, and, as nearly as possible, that of the more severe accidents.

In concluding, however, it is proper to remark that, though these funds have been able to meet all obligations for so many years, considerable apprehension exists that they will not be able to do so in the future. Payments for pensions are constantly increasing, and an adequate reserve fund has not in all cases been provided. It is quite probable that larger contributions will be required from the mine-owners in order that the engagements of the funds can be met.

Sociétés de Secours Mutuels. — It will be necessary to say but a few words concerning each of the three remaining classes of institutions. The mutual-aid societies differ in no important respect from the mutual-aid societies of France, and a description of their character would entail a needless repetition. The latest available statistics are those for the year 1890. In that year there was a total of 474 societies, of which 369 were societies recognized by the government. The remaining 105 represented only those which voluntarily made reports to the government. The 369 recognized societies embraced 54,347 members. Their total receipts amounted to $171,203.54, their expenses to $148,795.67, and the amount of their assets, on December 31, to $389,526.50.

Caisse de Prévoyance et de Secours en Faveur des Victimes des Accidents du Travail. — The national bank for the assistance of workingmen injured by accidents is of but relatively little importance, since, in spite of the original intention of its founder, it is in no sense an insurance institution. Its creation was due to the generosity of the present king. In 1889 Leopold II., learning that it was the intention of the different provinces to inaugurate fêtes in celebration of the 25th anniversary of his ascent to the throne, requested that, instead, the money be devoted to the establishment of a fund for the benefit of workingmen injured during their work. In compliance with this request, a law was passed, bearing date July 21, 1890, creating a national fund for the relief of injured workingmen, with an original capital of 2,000,000 francs ($386,000). This fund, it was expected, would be constantly augmented through gifts by private individuals or local administrative bodies, and it was stipulated that only the interest from the fund could be used. This expectation has in a measure been realized. At the end of the first year, in 1891, the fund amounted to $425,266.22, and in 1894 to $464,415.90. The original idea was that the fund would be devoted in some way to the encouragement of insurance against accidents. In practice, however, it has been used entirely as a charitable fund for the relief of workingmen and their families in need as the result of accidents. In 1890–1891, 2667 persons were aided to the extent of $18,626.43; in 1891–1892, 3409 persons were given $23,287.38; in 1892–1893, 4863 persons received $31,259.24, and in 1893–1894, 4420 persons received $26,098.23. A special committee of five members, appointed by the king, administers the fund.

Employers' Insurance Funds. — Regarding insurance funds organized by private industrial establishments for the benefit of their employés, it would be impossible to make a complete showing. It can only be said that, as in France, almost all of the larger employers of labor have created such funds. Notable examples are the great zinc works of Vieille Montagne; the iron works of Cockerill & Co.; Solvay & Co.; M. Rey, at Leideberg; and various railway companies.

The Present Problem of Workingmen's Insurance in Belgium. — In Belgium, the modern movement for a general system of workingmen's insurance, either compulsory or voluntary, did not attain importance until within the past year or two. M. Janson, to be sure, introduced a bill in 1890 providing for the compulsory insurance of all workingmen against accidents, and the government a somewhat similar measure in 1891. Owing, however, to the overwhelming importance of the question of constitutional revision, with which the country was then occupied, neither of these propositions received any serious attention. It was not, therefore, until 1895 that the Belgian Parliament began an earnest consideration of the question. The most important of the bills that have recently been introduced are those of M. Defuisseaux, introduced January 17, 1895, relating to the insurance of miners against old age and invalidity; of M. Molander, introduced February 7, 1895, relating to a general old-age and invalidity insurance system; and of M. Guchtenaeri, introduced February 19, of the same year, with a similar purpose in view. These three propositions have been referred to a special commission for investigation. As this commission has not yet reported, it will scarcely be advisable to consider their character.

In the case of Belgium it would seem that the policy to be pursued is along the line of the development of the insurance institutions that have been created for the workingmen in the mining industry.

Instead of making *tabula rasa* of these, their organization should be extended to other industries. These funds have now had an existence of over fifty years. They have entered into the habits and customs of the people, and have proven themselves to conform to the temperament and traditions of the Belgian nation. As regards the small industries, use might be made of the National Savings and Old-Age Pension Bank, or central institutions like that organized by the *Comité des Forges* of France.

The question of employers' liability is also one that is being widely discussed, but offers few points of interest not already commented upon in the case of France.

CHAPTER VI.

Workingmen's Insurance in Italy.

The American is not accustomed to look to Italy as a fruitful field for the study of efforts to improve the condition of the working classes. Yet, in reference to workingmen's insurance, the experience of that country offers several interesting features. The history of the movement for workingmen's insurance there offers not only a typical example of the course through which public opinion has run regarding this question, but affords, in its National Bank for the Insurance of Workingmen against Accidents, an example of the important results that can be achieved by an insurance institution organized under the auspices of, and yet not managed by, the state. In this institution, better than anywhere else, is brought out the essential difference between state encouraged and state managed insurance, of which particular mention was made in the introductory chapter. A study of Italian conditions is also of interest as furnishing an illustration of the fact that a law greatly encouraging insurance can be passed that does not necessarily stifle private initiative, but on the other hand may provoke it.

The question of workingmen's insurance, in its modern aspects, in Italy, may be said to have arisen in the year 1880. Previous to that date the situation of affairs as regards the particular province of accidents to labor was practically that of France, Belgium, and Switzerland, as regulated by the Civil Code of Napoleon; that is, the responsibility of employers for accidents to their employés was limited to those cases where the former were at fault, and the burden of proof in establishing that fault rested upon the victims of the accidents. As regards the existence of institutions for the provision of insurance against sickness, Italy has developed an admirable system of mutual-aid societies. The law regulating them is one of the most liberal in Europe, and permits them to offer insurance against old age and invalidity as well as against sickness.[1] In 1894 these societies numbered over 6000, and counted about 400,000 members. In 1880 there were no national insurance institutions of any kind. Italy had, indeed, passed a law in 1859 creating an old-age pension bank, but political conditions prevented this law from ever entering into effect. In 1877, also, a bill had been introduced proposing practically to re-enact this law. As the result of the agitation thus started, a commission was appointed in 1879 to examine the whole question of workingmen's insurance. The result of this examination was the report and proposition of M. Berti, Minister of Agriculture, Industry, and Commerce, November 30, 1881, for the creation of a national workingmen's insurance bureau. The question of workingmen's insurance as a national question was thus, in 1881, for the first time fairly brought before

[1] Law of April 15, 1886.

the Italian people. Since then it has constituted one of the most prominent measures of social reform before the Italian Parliament.

As regards the problem of insurance against sickness and old age, though numerous propositions of laws looking toward the creation of a state insurance bureau have been made, no positive legislation has resulted. The experience of Italy in the field of accident insurance, however, during this period is worthy of quite a detailed description.

Insurance against Accidents.—In common with the experience of other countries under the Roman Law, the problem of reform first took the legal shape of changing the law of employers' liability by shifting the *onus probandi* upon the employer and of extending his liability to all cases of accidents. Before anything had been accomplished, however, the question of insurance as a remedy for the hardships resulting from accidents began to attract attention in Europe. This solution of the question was eagerly taken up in Italy, and a proposition, introduced by M. Berti, February 19, 1883, contained provisions for the organization of an insurance department by the state.

The traditions of Italy were all strongly against that of state compulsory insurance. The nation was already in possession of the evidences of the success of her privately initiated peoples' savings banks and mutual-aid and other societies. If possible it was desired to avoid state insurance. At the same time it was fully realized that voluntary insurance without some special encouragement was totally unable to furnish adequate relief. The feeling at this time is shown by a quotation from a parliamentary report of the period. "We are persuaded," the reporter says, "that the rôle of the state is not to furnish an insurance institution, but to give to private institutions the securities, guarantees, and facilities for development that necessarily result from wise legislation."

In seeking for the means to encourage workingmen's insurance, it was desired to utilize existing private institutions, such as the savings banks and mutual-aid societies that have already been mentioned. The advantage of making use of these institutions rested on the fact that they were already in close relations with the laboring classes, and had succeeded in gaining their complete confidence and approval.

It was at this point that a federation of the strongest savings banks and other financial institutions for the benefit of the people, led by the Savings Bank of Milan, came forward with a proposition for a national bank for the insurance of workingmen against accidents, to be organized under their auspices, and to be administered by them. This proposition was a purely public-spirited one, as the banks concerned were in no way to profit by its transactions. This proposal met with immediate favor, and was speedily accepted by the law of July 8, 1883. There was created by this law a National Bank for the Insurance of Workingmen against Accidents (*Cassa Nazionale di Assicurazione per gli infortuni degli operai sullaroso*) as the result of a contract between the government and the federation of banks. According to this agreement these institutions were to establish a national insurance bank with a capital of 1,500,000 francs ($289,500), which was to be furnished by them. The Savings Bank of Milan, which was the prime mover in the undertaking, alone furnished 625,000 francs ($120,625) of this amount. The direction of the bank was left entirely to a superior council, composed of a representative from each of the ten institutions co-operating in its establishment, and to an executive committee selected by the Savings Bank of Milan. The entire expense of administration was to be borne by the banks in proportion to their subscription to the capital stock.

The institution thus erected was a national one, inasmuch as the government was given the right of approval, in certain cases, of regulations and tariffs, and because a number of very important concessions were made to the new institution. Thus the bank was exempted from taxation, the franking privilege on mail matter was conferred upon it, and the branch offices of the state postal savings bank were placed at the disposal of the bank as local offices for the payment of premiums and disbursements.

As in France and Belgium, the two kinds of insurance, individual and collective, are offered through this bank. In taking out the second kind the employer can, if he desires, add to this a personal insurance against his civil responsibility, by making a somewhat larger payment. In this case the bank becomes liable for all damages that may be obtained in a court of law against the employer by an employé for injuries he may have received.

The granting of indemnities is regulated as follows:—

In case of death or permanent total disability, a sum according to the policy agreed upon, but not to exceed 10,000 francs ($1930).

In case of permanent partial disability, a sum graduated according to the severity of the injury.

In case of temporary disability, a daily stipend after the fifth day succeeding the accident, for a period varying according to the policy, but not to exceed a maximum of 300 days.

The average indemnity agreed upon in cases of death or total disability has been about 1000 francs ($193); and for temporary disability an average of about one franc ($0.194) per day.

In calculating the premiums, twelve classes of risks, according to occupations, were constituted, and the amount is then calculated according to the risk of accident tables compiled from the result of the German insurance law. In a table on the following page the operations of this institution are shown from its organization in 1884 to December 31, 1893, the latest date for which information was obtained. The figures there given are of more than ordinary interest. They represent the results of a purely voluntary institution for the insurance of workingmen. The government intervenes but slightly in the management of the bank, and only aids it indirectly through the grant of certain privileges. Viewed in this light, the results cannot but be considered as gratifying. The number of persons insured has slowly but steadily increased, there being in 1893 a total of 119,447 persons participating in the benefits conferred by the bank.

In considering these figures, however, a number of points suggest themselves as worthy of comment: The bank once created, the great problem has been to persuade the workingmen to avail themselves of it, or to induce the employers to make use of the bank for the

OPERATIONS OF THE NATIONAL BANK FOR INSURANCE OF WORKINGMEN AGAINST ACCIDENTS, OF ITALY, 1884–1893.

Year.	PERSONS INSURED.			Persons Insured at End of Year.	PAYMENTS MADE ON —		
	Individually.	Collectively.	Total.		Individual Policies.	Collective Policies.	Total.
1884	42	1,621	1,663	443	$ 48.56	$ 925.64	$ 974.20
1885	304	12,220	12,524	13,830	360.52	7,124.25	7,484.76
1886	544	35,134	35,678	31,830	561.64	28,318.29	28,879.93
1887	1,062	44,474	45,536	46,522	1,132.06	29,725.87	30,857.92
1888	1,264	63,102	64,366	65,418	1,366.87	45,775.29	47,142.07
1889	1,283	92,342	93,625	86,645	1,576.61	68,907.73	70,584.34
1890	2,080	101,464	103,544	101,372	3,730.81	83,092.51	86,823.32
1891	1,891	112,811	114,702	107,432	2,619.44	86,100.36	88,720.29
1892	2,009	121,461	123,470	112,485	2,773.01	90,867.71	93,640.72
1893	1,973	129,012	130,985	119,447	2,373.39	98,249.62	100,623.01

purpose of insuring their employés. The accomplishment of this is always the greatest difficulty with which voluntary insurance has to contend. In Italy this propaganda was voluntarily undertaken by a unique species of philanthropic institution called "Patronats," situated in different centres of the country, the most important of which were at Milan and Turin. To these institutions is entirely due the measure of success that has been achieved by the bank. A Patronat is an association of public-spirited individuals, the purpose of which is to encourage all efforts and institutions whose object is the improvement of the condition of the laboring classes. Immediately upon the organization of the National Bank these societies assumed almost the entire burden of spreading information concerning its operations, and of encouraging workingmen and employers of labor to affiliate themselves with it. To do this, they act as business agents of those desiring to take out insurance and gratuitously attend to all the formal steps necessary to securing insurance policies. In worthy cases, moreover, when individual workingmen have taken out insurance, and, owing to sickness or other misfortunes, are unable to continue their payments, temporary, or even permanent, aid is granted by them for the purpose of paying their dues. As a means of bringing to the public attention the importance of accident insurance, elaborate systems for the collection of statistics of accidents have been organized in several localities in co-operation with the hospitals. Their various publications on this and kindred features of the insurance question have been very instrumental in arousing public interest. The importance of these efforts is shown by the fact that during the period 1884–1893, the Patronat of Milan alone procured the insurance of 116,781 workingmen, the great majority of whom were enrolled in the National Bank, the balance being insured in certain private insurance companies, with which it had made a special contract favorable to policy-holders.

The second important point is that progress has been made almost entirely through collective insurance. Individual insurance has played an insignificant part. The experience of the French and Belgian national insurance institutions is thus signally confirmed. Certainly, as far as Europe is concerned, it would seem to be almost conclusively demonstrated that the insurance of workingmen can only be achieved through their employers. It is gratifying to find, however, that there are a great many employers who appreciate the obligation that rests upon them, and are willing to make sacrifices for this purpose. One reason for the success of this institution is that for a long time prior to the creation of the National Bank a number of the large employers of labor had been in the habit of maintaining insurance funds for the benefit of their employés. The opportunity of attaining the same ends through an institution in which they would have none of the care of management was one, therefore, of which they have eagerly availed themselves. The action of these has encouraged others who did not have such funds, so that each year has witnessed important accessions. This provision of means for insurance to those employers who desire to insure their workingmen is the greatest service that a strong central establishment performs, and furnishes the strongest argument for its organization.

The question of the insurance of workingmen against accidents in Italy, however, has by no means been solved by the creation of this institution. Important as have been the results obtained by it, it must be recognized that but a beginning has really been made toward including the whole body of Italian workingmen under an insurance system. The increase in membership, while important in itself, proceeds at such a rate that an indefinitely long period would be required fully to meet the exigencies of the problem.

The failure of the bank to achieve yet more important results is due to the manner in which it has been administered, rather than to any inherent defects in its organization. At Milan, where adequate efforts have been made to extend its operations, a very large proportion of the working population that would naturally come under the scope of an accident insurance system has been included. Thus, out of a total of 119,447 workingmen insured December 31, 1893, 48,990, or between one-third and one-half of the total number insured, were insured through the Milan Bank. In other words, if the same activity had been employed in other centres, five times as great a number, or between 500,000 and 600,000 workingmen, would have been insured, a number that would have gone a long way toward providing insurance to those most in need of its protection.

As the result of this showing, the criticism has been made that the bank has proven itself largely a local institution; that it is almost an adjunct of the Milan Savings Bank, and that the government, after creating the bank, has rested on its oars and has not taken the proper steps to encourage it in its work. These criticisms seem to be just, and the organization of the bank, or rather the spirit in which it is administered, is open to improvement along these lines.

It was undoubtedly the hopes of the founders of the bank that its creation would solve the question of accident insurance, or at least obviate the necessity for any further action on the part of the state. In this, as we have seen, they have been disappointed. In the ten years following the inauguration of the bank, a remarkable change of sentiment has taken place regarding the general principle of obligatory, state, and other insurance. In the beginning of the movement, the principle of obligation was emphatically rejected as contrary to the genius of the people. At the present time, all indications point to at least a partial victory of this principle. This demand for more radical measures has been further increased by the great influence that the legislation of Germany and Austria has exerted over public opinion. Throughout this agitation for further state action, however, nothing but admiration has been expressed for the work accomplished by the bank. What it does, it does well, and in the best way. The only fault found is that it does not do enough. No better demonstration of this could be found than the fact that practically all measures that have been proposed for the introduction of compulsory insurance make this bank the central feature for their scheme, and merely make it obligatory upon employers to insure their employés in it or some other approved institution.

The first official manifestation of this conversion to the principle of compulsory insurance, took place in 1889. In that year M. Miceli, Minister of Agriculture and Commerce, directed M. Carlo Ferraris, Professor at the Royal University of Padua, to make a study of the whole question of accidents to labor, and report to the consultative commission on savings institutions and labor. In this report, which is one of the most important documents relating to the question of accidents to labor in Italy, Professor Ferraris, after showing in detail the futility of attempting a solution of the question by measures directed simply at employers' legal liability, announced himself unreservedly in favor of compulsory insurance. His proposition can be briefly given as follows. Insurance for all accidents, including those caused by the fault of the workingmen themselves, should be obligatory and at the expense of the employers; the latter should also be required to take precautions and introduce appliances to lessen the frequence of accidents as a necessary part of obligatory insurance.

After a prolonged discussion by the commission, these propositions were adopted, with the modification that they were to be made applicable only to certain specified industries in which the risk of accident was especially great. This decision of the commission was incorporated in the proposition introduced by the Minister of Agriculture and Commerce, February 9, 1890. It will be unnecessary to give in detail the history of the legislative experiences of this and other measures. The latest proposition is that presented June 13, 1895, by M. Barazzuoli, Minister of Agriculture, Industry, and Commerce, a measure which is still pending before the Italian Parliament.

The details of all of these measures have differed but little, and consist, practically, of the provisions contained in the report of Professor Ferraris and the first bill. They all make (1) the insurance of workingmen against accidents obligatory upon employers in certain specified dangerous industries; (2) the cost of this insurance is placed entirely upon the employers; (3) all accidents are included, embracing even those due to the fault of the workingmen; (4) no new state insurance bank is provided, the choice being left to the employers to insure their employés in the existing state institution or in private institutions approved by the government; (5) the tariff of premiums and indemnities of the National Bank is in general made the standard to which private institutions must conform; and (6) stringent provisions are demanded for the prevention of accidents. There is little reason to doubt that, in view of the attitude that the Italian Parliament has repeatedly taken on this question, a measure substantially embodying these provisions will sooner or later become a law.

Insurance against Old Age and Invalidity. — At the present time there exists in Italy no national institution for the insurance of workingmen against old age and invalidity. Whatever is done in this direction is performed through private companies, mutual-aid societies, or funds created by large industrial establishments. Nevertheless, the Italian government has occupied itself during a great many years with this question. February 9, 1858, the ministry, presided over by M. de Cavour, presented a proposition for a national bank for old-age pensions that became the law of July 15, 1859. Political events, however, prevented this bank from ever beginning operations. February 3, 1877, an unsuccessful attempt was made for its revival. In 1879 the Minister of the Interior appointed a commission to elaborate a project for the creation of a bank to insure workingmen against accidents and old age. This was the origin of the proposition of M. Berti, of November 30, 1881, which, as we have seen, was the starting-point for modern efforts to provide for the insurance of workingmen against accidents.

Since that date almost every year has seen the introduction of one or more measures having a similar purpose in view. The latest proposition is that of M. Locara, Minister of Agriculture, Industry, and Commerce, in behalf of his ministerial colleagues, introduced November 23, 1893. All of these propositions, in spite of many differences, present common characteristics. An autonomous institution is proposed; the pension is not a gratuity, but the result of regular dues on the part of the beneficiaries; the aid of the state is admitted, but is limited to a subsidy; finally, insurance is not made compulsory.

Insurance against Sickness. — But comparatively little attention is at present paid to that branch of workingmen's insurance which relates to sickness. This is due primarily to the fact that there is not the same necessity for state action in the case of sick insurance, and because Italy already possesses well-organized sick insurance institutions in her mutual-aid societies.

CHAPTER VII.

Workingmen's Insurance in Other Countries of Continental Europe.

Introduction. — In the account of workingmen's insurance which has been given in the preceding chapters, there has been described at least one example of every important type of insurance institution. It will be unnecessary, therefore, to enter into the same details concerning the experience of other European countries. The present chapter, therefore, is limited to a bare sketch of the policy that has been pursued by each country regarding this question, and the probable direction that future action will take.

Switzerland. — A study of the question of workingmen's insurance in Switzerland is chiefly of interest on account of the typical example furnished of the evolution of thought regarding this question, from that of complete *laissez-faire* to the acceptance of the principle that a solution can only be found in obligatory state insurance: and on account of the elaborate studies that have been made by the Swiss government preparatory to the introduction of such a system.

Historically, the movement for the insurance of workingmen in Switzerland took its rise, as in other countries, in the effort to change the law concerning the responsibility of employers for accidents to their employés. Previous to 1875 the law regarding this subject had been that of all European countries subject to the Civil Code. The injustice of this law became apparent first in the case of the business of railway transportation; and this industry was, therefore, made the first point of attack. In 1875 a law was passed establishing, for the transportation industry alone, the principle of inversion of proof that has been described in our account of this question in France. This was but the first of a series of laws tending to extend the civil responsibility of employers. Successive laws were passed in March 27, 1877, June 25, 1881, and April 26, 1887, by which the principle of civil responsibility was extended to all industries and made somewhat stricter.

It was hoped that these laws would afford a solution of the question. The result, though a great improvement over former conditions, failed to realize expectations. In the great majority of cases, the results of accidents had still to be borne by the workingmen. The employer was still absolved from liability in that large class of accidents which were due to unavoidable causes. Even in those cases where the employer could be held, experience showed that it was no easy matter for the workingman to avail himself of the law. The difficulties, uncertainties, and delays of a lawsuit almost counterbalanced the benefits anticipated. Finally, the system of civil responsibility tended to create a kind of hostility between the employer and his employés prejudicial to the interests of both. All of these considerations led public opinion to seek for some other remedy.

In the meantime Germany had embarked upon her course of compulsory insurance; and more and more public attention was turned toward insurance as offering the best solution to the question. This sentiment first found expression in the following motion, adopted March 25, 1885, by the National Council: "The federal council is requested, after having made a study of the question, to report on the advisability of the introduction of a system of general obligatory insurance of workingmen against accidents."

A similar resolution, employing almost the same words, was again passed April 29, 1887. As the result of these last instructions, the federal council took the most vigorous steps for obtaining the necessary information upon which to frame its report. Believing that an investigation ought to precede the discussion of a reform so important and so novel, it organized official inquiries concerning every point involved. Above all things, statistics of accidents were a *sine qua non* for any intelligent action. The council, therefore, in 1887, provided for the organization of a special service to collect and compile statistics of all accidents occurring in Switzerland during the three years, April 1, 1888, to March 31, 1891. To supplement these statistics, the Secretariat Ouvrier[1] was charged with the preparation of a report on statistics of accidents to members of mutual-aid societies during the three years 1886, 1887, and 1888, societies

---

[1] A semi-official labor bureau.

numbering between 1200 and 1300, and counting from 167,000 to 195,000 members. Use was also to be made of similar statistics compiled by M. Schuler, Inspector of Factories, and Dr. A. E. Burkhardt, based on returns from about 150 societies with from 18,000 to 20,000 members, during the years 1880 to 1884. At the same time the date of the general census was advanced two years to December, 1888, in order to furnish a basis for determining the relative frequency of accidents. Special investigations on various other points were also authorized. M. Forrer and M. Kinkelin were requested, in 1889, to prepare memoirs treating of the question of insurance against accidents from the judicial and technical points of view, and in 1890 M. Gaettisheim was directed to prepare a similar memoir regarding insurance against sickness.

In the meantime it became necessary to obtain a modification of the Swiss federal constitution, in order to enable the federal assembly to act upon the information when it should be obtained. November 28, 1889, therefore, the federal council addressed to the federal assembly a message, ordering it to make a study of the question of the desirability of submitting to the referendum a proposition granting to the assembly the power to legislate concerning the compulsory insurance of workingmen against accidents and sickness. This report, which with accompanying appendices makes a volume of 235 pages, is a valuable document. It is of especial importance as showing how strong a hold the policy of compulsory insurance had already taken upon the people. "It is only necessary," it says, "to state that all political parties, employers and employés alike, are of one accord in demanding the introduction of compulsory insurance, and that the solution of the question is considered as a matter of the greatest urgency by all classes of the population." And further, after reciting all the difficulties and inadequacies of optional insurance, the author adds:

"All these inconveniences, all these dangers, can be obviated only by obligatory insurance. Obligatory insurance ought to be substituted for the civil responsibility of employers. Indeed, insurance against sickness ought also to be included."

In pursuance of this report, the following amendment to the constitution was submitted to the referendum: "The Confederation shall provide, by legislative enactment, for insurance against sickness and accidents, account being taken of existing aid societies. It can declare participation in the insurance to be obligatory in general upon all or for certain determined categories of citizens." October 26, 1890, the people, through the referendum, accepted this amendment by the decisive vote of 277,228 to 92,201, thus declaring strongly for the principle of compulsory insurance. It will be noticed that no mention was made of old-age and invalidity insurance. The advisability of incorporating provisions concerning this branch of insurance was discussed, but the consensus of opinion was that action should be postponed until the results of insurance against accidents were at hand.

The introduction of compulsory insurance being

determined upon, the government immediately inaugurated a further series of elaborate investigations in order to determine the exact character that it was desirable to give to the proposed scheme. Dr. Moser, professor of mathematics at Berne, was directed to make a study of the mathematical basis upon which the insurance system should rest. Other officials were ordered to make a thorough study of the German and Austrian systems, and still others to make studies of particular points. As the result of these elaborate investigations M. Forrer was charged, December, 1891, one year after the people had voted for obligatory insurance, and four years after the preliminary investigations were begun, to prepare two bills, one for the insurance of workingmen against accidents, and the other for their insurance against sickness. It had been definitely settled that the insurance of workingmen against accidents and sickness should be considered at the same time. It was believed that, though each should be founded upon quite a different basis, together they should form systems that would complement each other.

M. Forrer's work was completed in December, 1892. The bills proposed by him, after being first considered by a select committee, were referred to a grand committee of experts, consisting of forty members appointed by the federal council. After the most searching examination of every detail, these propositions, somewhat amended, were returned to the Department of the Interior, where they received still another examination, and were then referred to the legislature. As these bills are still before the legislature, and are therefore still subject to a more or less radical alteration, it will not be advisable to attempt to describe their provisions. It will be sufficient to say, that the system of compulsory insurance has been unreservedly accepted; that sick insurance is provided for, as far as possible, through existing institutions, and when such are not sufficient, through specially created local institutions; and that each industrial establishment of sufficient size is allowed to maintain its own independent fund. Insurance against accidents, however, is provided for through a central state-administered institution. The broad theory of insurance as adopted by Switzerland is, therefore, that practised by Germany.

Scandinavian Countries. — The three Scandinavian countries of Norway, Sweden, and Denmark constitute a group of nations the institutions of which can be studied together. In all the influence of the German example is plainly seen. To some extent the principle of compulsory insurance has already been incorporated in the law, and all indications point to the ultimate triumph of the principle.

Norway was the first of the three to follow the example of Germany and pass a compulsory insurance law. After but a comparatively brief preparatory period, a bill was introduced and pushed to its final passage, becoming the law of July 23, 1894. According to this law, a general system of compulsory insurance against accidents is created that differs in no essential particular from the German and Austrian systems. The insurance of their employés against accidents, in a central institution specially created under the guarantee of the state, is made compulsory upon all employers of labor in manufacturing, mining, transportation, and construction work. The benefits provided for include the medical treatment of workingmen after the fourth week of their disability on account of an accident, and the payment to them of cash benefits during such disability, after the first four weeks, equal to 60 per cent of their wages, but not to be less than 50 öre ($0.13) per day or 150 crowns ($40.20) per year in case of total disability, and in case of partial disability an amount proportionate to the disability. In case of death, 50 crowns ($13.40) are paid for burial expenses, and a pension is granted to the widow equal to 20 per cent of her husband's wages plus 15 per cent for each child under 15 years of age; the total, however, in no case to exceed 50 per cent of the workingman's wages. The cost of the insurance is entirely defrayed by the employers, the amount of the contribution of each being determined according to the amount paid by him in wages, and the coefficient of risk which is assigned to his industry. In calculating the amount paid in wages, and in determining the amount of benefits to be paid, that portion of the wages of employés in excess of 1200 crowns ($321.60) per year is not taken into account. The act provides that the first table of trade risks shall be prepared under the authority of the king, and shall be revised after the system has been in operation three years, after which it will be subject to revision at the end of each five-year period. This law did not go into effect until July 1, 1895. It is impossible, therefore, to give any results of its operations.

In Sweden, though as yet no law has been actually enacted, the movement toward compulsory insurance is scarcely less strong. As the result of the German example, and the incentive given to the study of workingmen's insurance by the Berne Congress, Sweden appointed, in 1891, a commission to investigate the subject. This commission terminated its labors in May, 1893, and in its report recommended a bill providing for the compulsory insurance of workingmen against old age and invalidity. This proposition has been before the Swedish Parliament in one shape or another since that time. The latest bill is one introduced by the government January 14, 1895. As there is every chance that this bill, or one substantially similar in character, will finally become a law, the following account of its main provisions will serve to indicate the general feeling of the country regarding workingmen's insurance, and the probable system that will ultimately be adopted.

According to this proposition insurance against old age and invalidity, through a fund organized under the guarantee of the state, is made compulsory upon all workingmen, except those employed by the state, those pursuing an independent trade, and a few other unimportant classes. The insured are divided into three classes: the first, including workingmen whose wages are equal or superior to 10 crowns ($2.68) per week; the second, workingmen earning less than this amount; and the third, workingwomen. The dues of each of these classes are respectively 40, 25, and 15 öre ($0.11, $0.07, $0.04) per week, of which 25, 15, and 10 öre ($0.07, $0.04, $0.03) respectively must be paid by the insured themselves, and the remaining 15, 10, and 5 öre ($0.04, $0.03, $0.01) by their employers. Each insured person is provided with an individual account book, into which the employer each week pastes special stamps to the amount of the required contribution, reimbursing himself for the share that falls upon the workingmen by retaining those amounts from the latter's wages. In return for these payments the workingman is entitled to a pension for the remainder of his life after he has reached the age of 70 years, or when incapacitated for labor, no matter what his age, provided such incapacity has not been contracted voluntarily and he has made payments during at least five years. The value of the pension is 50 crowns ($13.40) plus 10, 5, or 2 öre ($0.03, $0.01, $0.005) for each week that dues have been paid, according to whether the pensioner belongs to the first, second, or third class. As under these provisions pensions will be acquired by a great many persons without their having made sufficient payments for the constitution of pensions, the state assumes the burden of making up the deficit thus caused, as well as undertakes to bear the whole expense of administration. This assistance by the state is calculated to represent from 20 to 25 per cent of the total cost of the insurance.

In Denmark, active steps have been taken within the last few years for the provision of all three kinds of insurance. April 11, 1892, a law was enacted for the regulation of existing mutual-aid societies. All societies are required by this law to limit their operations to a certain district or a particular industry. They are required to supply full medical attendance in cases of sickness, and grant cash benefits not to exceed in amount two-thirds of the average wages of the district, or be less than 40 öre ($0.11) per day. Indemnities cannot be granted for sickness lasting less than three days, nor be continued for more than 13 weeks. It is optional with each society whether it will grant burial expenses or provide for old-age pensions. Membership in these societies is purely voluntary. In order, however, to encourage workingmen to become members, the government makes an annual subsidy of 500,000 crowns ($134,000) for division among the societies. At the present time there are about 500 such societies, with about 120,000 members. In regard to old-age insurance, Denmark passed, April 9, 1891, a general insurance law, which is in almost every way an objectionable measure. According to it, every person 60 years of age, who during the preceding ten years has not received any charitable relief from the public, will, if in need, be entitled to receive assistance in the nature of a pension from the commune in which he resides. Half of the expense of this pension will be borne by the commune and the other half by the central government, a yearly appropriation of 2,000,000 crowns ($536,000) being made for this purpose. This, it will be seen, is not, properly speaking, one for workingmen's insurance, but is rather a measure of poor relief.

Propositions looking toward the creation of a system of compulsory insurance of workingmen against accidents have been before the Danish Parliament for a number of years, but as yet no positive legislation has been enacted.

Other Countries. — Concerning the remaining countries of Europe it will be necessary to say but a few words. In Russia, Spain, and Holland no important system of workingmen's insurance is in operation: nor is there any great likelihood of immediate legislation on this subject. The question is, however, under consideration in each of these countries, and more or less is being done in the way of widening the sphere of private insurance or relief society work, and in modifying existing employers' liability laws.

A recent law of the kingdom of Roumania, however, deserves to be mentioned. By an act passed April 20, 1895, the insurance of all miners against accidents, sickness, and old age is made obligatory; and provision is made for the creation of two insurance funds under the auspices and guarantee of the state. The first is intended to insure miners against cases of sickness and slight accidents, requiring immediate relief. Whenever the number of workingmen in a mine is as high as 120, a special fund is created for that mine. In other cases, the employés of a certain district are grouped into a local fund. These funds furnish free medical attendance, and grant small cash benefits to members when unable to work on account of sickness or accidents. They are supported (1) by the contributions of the workingmen, the amount of which cannot exceed three per cent of their wages; (2) by an equal contribution from their employers, (3) interest on funds invested, (4) fines, etc. The second, or pension fund, is intended for the relief of workingmen in cases where a pension is required, as for old age or permanent incapacity resulting from any cause. For this purpose, all miners are made members of a single central fund. The resources of this fund consist of a payment by the workingmen of a sum equal to two per cent of their wages, an equal contribution by their employers, gifts, interest, etc. It will be seen that the system here created is not dissimilar from that in operation in Belgium.

CHAPTER VIII.

Workingmen's Insurance in England.[1]

Introduction. — Turning now from the continent to England, the problem of workingmen's insurance is presented in quite a new phase. In Europe we have had to deal chiefly with state incorporated or state conducted institutions. In England, chief interest centres around purely voluntary institutions, organized by the workingmen themselves and most jealously guarded against governmental interference. Even that intervention, which is in no way restrictive of their independence, but, on the other hand, is intended to confer upon them certain privileges, or

---

[1] In the preparation of this chapter, particularly that portion relating to friendly societies, the author has not thought it necessary to base his study exclusively upon official and public documents, as was done for the most part in the case of the European countries. The history and operations of the friendly societies of England have been so frequently and so well described that such a study would have been but a useless duplication of the work, and space only permits us giving the general features of this system. Reliance has, therefore, been placed upon a number of the best known and accepted private authorities wherein this subject has been treated. Chief among these must be mentioned the study of Mr. J. M. Baernreither, entitled, *English Associations of Workingmen*, translated by Miss Alice Taylor, and published by Swan Sonnenschein & Co., London, 1889, and several times reprinted, the last edition being that of 1893. Were there no other reason, the existence of this admirable study of friendly societies in England in all of its phases would have made unnecessary a

throw around them certain safeguards, has been steadily antagonized.

A complete treatment of the problem of workingmen's insurance in England involves a consideration of four fairly distinct groups of facts: those relating to (1) voluntary mutual insurance institutions, or friendly societies; (2) the efforts of the government to provide insurance against old age by granting the right to purchase, through the postal savings banks, annuities from the National Debt Office; (3) the legal liability of employers for accidents to their employés; and (4) the recent agitation for the creation of a national old-age pension system. Of these, the consideration of friendly societies will require the greater part of our attention. Indeed, the question of workingmen's insurance in England can almost be said to be the question of friendly societies. The other divisions of our subject need be considered only so far as to give a general idea of all the phases of the problem.

study of English insurance institutions in the same way as has been done for France, Italy, Germany, and other European countries. In the present chapter the author has found it difficult in many places to depart from the language of Mr. Baernreither, though it has not always been practicable to make use of quotation marks. Supplementing this work are: *The Friendly Society Movement*, by Mr. J. F. Wilkinson, London, 1891; the *Guide Book of the Friendly Societies Registry Office*, 1896, an official publication, giving in a very available shape the laws, regulations, model constitutions, and rules, etc., of friendly societies; and the report of Mr. Louis Fontaine on *Sociétés de Secours Mutuels* contained in the report of the Social Economy Section, Universal Exposition of Paris, 1889. Mr. Baernreither's book is rich in bibliographical notes, and reference to it will inform the reader concerning the best sources of information relating to friendly societies and other workingmen's insurance institutions in England.

Friendly Societies. — In the account that follows, we enter upon the study of the most important class of mutual insurance institutions, voluntarily established and wholly free from state control, that has been developed in any country. Not only do the English friendly societies afford an example of the most successful efforts on the part of workingmen to provide for their insurance, but their history exhibits the complete course of evolution of a scientific insurance institution from its germ, as found in the mutual-aid society whose operations were based upon no rule, and partook largely of charitable work. At the same time, in the best types of these societies as they exist to-day, there can be studied all the elements involved in the organization of an independent voluntary mutual insurance society, the affairs of which are conducted upon sound actuarial principles.

An account of friendly societies presents several phases which it will be well to treat separately. We will, therefore, successively consider the character of friendly societies as now organized; the history of their growth in numbers and importance; the relation of the government to them, or laws relating to friendly societies; and, finally, the history of their internal reform, or the movement through which they have been transformed from mutual-aid into insurance institutions.

The English friendly societies are voluntary institutions, organized by the middle and working classes for the purpose of aiding their members in times of distress. The assistance given by them includes relief in almost every possible contingency in which a member is subjected to unusual expense, or is unable to earn his accustomed wages. They thus insure against sickness, accident, unemployment, and, to some extent, against old age. Accidents are insured against, since no distinction is made between disability resulting from sickness and accident. Provision for old-age insurance is made in many cases, since most of the friendly societies identify the notion of sickness with that of disability for work, and accordingly go on paying benefits, though perhaps on a reduced scale, in cases of chronic illness and other infirmity. It has only recently been attempted to constitute provision against old age as an independent branch of friendly society insurance, and to establish separate accident societies for certain trades. Nearly all societies, also, provide for the payment of so-called "death benefits," a sort of life insurance sufficient in amount to pay burial expenses. Other societies provide for "endowments" for the settling of a son or daughter in life, annuities to members' widows, allowances for the education of orphans, and for various other payments. It is, of course, understood that few of the friendly societies provide for all of these different kinds of insurance. The great work performed by them is that of insurance against sickness and accidents, and the payment of death benefits to meet burial expenses.

These institutions are pure workingmen's institutions, for they are not only organized by them, but are managed by officers selected from among their own number, who receive little or no compensation for their services. As far as management and conduct of business is concerned, they offer not a few points of comparison with our own building and loan associations.

The term "friendly society" is frequently used in a broad sense to cover a great many kinds of mutual benefit institutions. The Guide Book of Friendly Societies, issued by the Registrar of Friendly Societies, enumerates fifteen classes of societies concerning which he has jurisdiction. It is only with insurance societies, which constitute a distinct class, that we have to deal, and the term "friendly societies," as used henceforth, will relate to this class alone. But, used even in this limited sense, the term relates to a wide diversity of societies, the practice of insurance lending itself to a great variety of combinations.[1] They all have, nevertheless, the same purpose. The principal distinction, and one that is of fundamental importance from the standpoint of this study, is that between the independent local societies and the great orders, such as the Manchester Unity, the Foresters, the Druids, etc., which, with their thousands of branches, extend their operations over the whole of Great Britain, and even into the Colonies, and number, the strongest of them, over a half a million members each. These orders represent the

---

[1] Mr. Baernreither mentions and describes 12 different kinds of friendly societies: 1, Dividing Societies; 2, Local Village and Country Societies; 3, Local Town Societies; 4, Deposit Friendly Societies; 5, County Societies; 6, Burial Societies; 7, Ordinary Large or General Societies; 8, Particular Trade Societies; 9, Factory Societies and Societies in connection with large establishments; 10, Railway Company Societies; 11, Workingmen's Orders; 12, Societies of Females and Young Persons. Page 169.

highest and most effective type of voluntary insurance in England, and our study, therefore, will largely be the history of their rise and development.

The organization of these orders, and the relation between the branches and the central governing power, are exceedingly simple. Properly speaking, the order itself is an insurance institution to but a slight degree. It merely consists of an aggregation or league of branches, each of which is, in the main, an independent insurance institution, having its own constitution, rules, receipts, and expenditures. These latter are united through a sort of central council, the functions of which are largely those of giving advice, of exercising control and supervision, and of formulating model constitutions and rules. It prepares, at an expense utterly beyond the means of local societies, tables of contributions and benefits, the adoption of which it renders obligatory upon all new branches, and all new members of branches which were in existence before the formation of the tables. It requires annual reports from the branches, and from them compiles a general report showing the condition of each branch and of the whole order. It settles disputes, and, finally, in case of the two strongest orders at least, maintains a central relief fund for the assistance of branches when in distress as the result of unusual or peculiar misfortunes.

The advantages of the orders over the independent societies can be thus summed up. They exercise a supervision which, while leaving the greatest possible independence to the branches, is yet effective in preventing mismanagement, fraud, or unwise action.

Through their annual reports they enable each branch to see how it stands in comparison with the others, and to profit by their experience. They provide a series of tables of contributions and benefits, constructed according to the best actuarial principles, from which new branches can make a choice in organizing their societies. They are able to carry out on a large scale, and therefore at a trifling cost, legal requirements, such as those of valuation. They permit of the transfer of a member from one branch to another. They can supply, with better advantage, the relief of members when travelling in search of work; and, finally, a most important consideration at the present time, they offer the only feasible organization for the establishment of a system of voluntary insurance against old age, the provision of which, as we have seen, requires a large membership in order that the operations may be regular from year to year. There are likewise some disadvantages, the chief of which is that they are somewhat more expensive. Nevertheless, their advantages far outweigh the drawbacks, and there is no doubt that the future of the friendly societies lies in the future of these orders. The whole tendency at the present time is toward concentration, and the orders stand for this principle.

At the same time, there is no danger that the independent societies will disappear or even become absolutely fewer in number. The orders attract to themselves the higher paid artisans, the merchants, clerks, etc.; while the independent societies, with their more modest contributions, simpler constitutions, and strong feeling of fellowship, bring sick insurance at least to the ordinary laborer and mill hand.

The history of these societies is one of continuous growth. To go back to the real origin of the friendly society would carry us into ancient history. Some form of association for mutual assistance in cases of sickness or other distress has existed for many centuries. The important point is, that the friendly society, as found in England to-day, has an historical origin common with the trade unions in the old mediæval trade guilds. Both have mutual aid as their base; and it was but natural that both should meet in the same organization. For a long time the trade guilds were able to perform the services required of both trade unions and friendly societies. In time, however, a separation became inevitable. The reasons for this division are easily apparent. The trade unions are fighting organizations. The friendly societies are essentially peaceful. The former must be organized along trade lines. The latter preferably include persons living in the same town or district.

Mr. Ludlow, the Chief Registrar of Friendly Societies, is of the opinion that the transition to the modern form of friendly society was completed in the first half of the seventeenth century, that the societies increased gradually in importance until the end of the eighteenth century, when they were sufficiently numerous to occupy the attention of Parliament and to be subjected to special legislation. It is only since then, however, or during the nineteenth century, a period contemporaneous with the rise of the factory system and the modern organization of industry, that friendly societies have continuously and rapidly increased. Whatever their historical origin, therefore, it is with their development during the present century that we are concerned.

In tracing the growth of voluntary institutions which for a long time were not required to make any reports to the government, and, indeed, need not do so at the present time, except under certain circumstances, it will be manifestly impossible to give in statistical form their increase in number, membership, or financial operations. We will have to content ourselves with information collected at irregular intervals, which, though it cannot be stated in tabular form, nevertheless clearly shows the growth of the system from period to period. For the years prior to 1874 almost no exact information can be obtained. It is only known generally that the growth of friendly societies was great. The rapid increase in membership of the large orders, for whom the records can be obtained, and which will shortly be given, is conclusive evidence that such was the case.

The first data relating to all friendly societies is that of the estimate contained in the Fourth Report of the Royal Commissioners appointed in 1874 to inquire into friendly benefit societies. At that time the total number of such societies in England and Wales was believed to be at least 32,000, with four or more million members, and disposing of funds placed at £11,000,000. Since then progress has been continuous.

By far the most interesting feature of this development, is that of the growth in importance of the large orders. In the case of these it is possible in many cases to go back of the year 1874. Their relative importance at that date is shown by the fact that the commissioners, in the report already cited, stated that they found in England and Wales 34 orders having over 1000 members each, and together a membership, after making deductions for double memberships, of 1,134,000. The principal orders at the present time are the Independent Order of Odd Fellows, named briefly the Manchester Unity, the Ancient Order of Foresters (these two being far in advance of other orders), the Grand United Order of Odd Fellows, the Loyal Order of Shepherds (Ashton Unity), the National Independent Order of Odd Fellows, after which follow a great many others of scarcely less importance. A brief statement of the growth of several of these will show how rapid has been the movement of insurance through friendly societies.

The Manchester Unity was founded in 1812. In 1832 it had 561 lodges and 31,042 members. Two years later it counted 718 lodges and 47,638 members, and in 1836, 1100 lodges and 70,000 members. In 1839 there were 1600 lodges and 112,000 members. In 1842 it contained (in round numbers) 220,000 members; in 1844, 243,126; in 1857, 229,049; in 1865, 353,556; in 1870, 442,575; in 1883, 593,850, and in 1890, 651,890. Its funds at this last date amounted to the enormous sum of £7,301,186 ($35,531,222).

The Foresters was founded somewhat earlier, exactly when it is not known, but probably some time about the middle of the last century. In 1832 it had 358 lodges or courts, and over 10,000 members. In 1845 its membership was 65,921; in 1850, 80,089; in 1855, 105,753; in 1860, 168,576; in 1865, 301,077; in 1870, 376,663; in 1875, 491,196; in 1880, 555,062; in 1884, 633,288; in 1886, 667,570; and in 1890, 675,-918. Its fund at this last date amounted to £4,392,-662 ($20,375,890). It will thus be seen that though having a greater membership than the Manchester Unity, the latter was financially the stronger.

This growth was not confined to the two large orders. The other important orders increased at an almost equal rate. The Shepherds, for example, counted in 1851 but 13,900 members. Four years later they had 18,000; in 1865, 30,000; in 1867, 35,000; in 1874, 52,000; and in 1890, 88,883. The Grand United Order of Odd Fellows, the third friendly society in importance, had, in 1858, 37,000; in 1869, 67,000; in 1874, 95,000; and in 1890, 171,092 members. The National Independent Order of Odd Fellows had in 1850 only 7000 members; in 1869 this had increased to 31,000; in 1872 to 37,000, and in 1890 to 53,984. The table on the next page, taken from the *Labor Gazette*, published by the Labor Department of the Board of Trade, shows the growth of 10 of the principal societies during the period 1885 to 1895. The membership, as shown in this table, is that only of male adults.

During this period of 10 years, therefore, the number of members of 10 orders alone for which we have a record at hand, increased over half a million, and their reserve capital was augmented by the large sum of $27,740,762.74. Probably the best statement that could be made, showing the real significance of this growth, is to reproduce a short section where Mr. Wilkinson sums up the work done by the two great

CONDITION OF THE TEN LARGEST FRIENDLY SOCIETIES OF GREAT BRITAIN, 1885 AND 1895.

Societies.		Membership.	Income.	Benefits Paid.	Assets.
			$	$	$
Independent Order of Odd Fellows (Manchester Unity).	1885	542,313	4,687,437.18	2,806,228.29	26,767,633.84
	1895	665,233	5,956,829.59	3,538,546.18	37,097,538.76
Ancient Order of Foresters.	1885	582,104	4,206,685.83	3,026,422.82	16,405,594.41
	1895	654,628	5,318,369.12	3,876,386.24	23,567,067.68
Grand United Order of Odd Fellows.	1885	138,971	485,452.84	....	1,339,086.94
	1895	241,104	500,271.88	656,709.84	4,294,408.99
Hearts of Oak Benefit Society.	1885	108,688	1,197,723.51	804,578.44	3,729,442.27
	1895	205,748	2,231,431.38	1,608,704.31	7,826,422.10
Independent Order of Rechabites (Salford Unity).	1885	59,863	372,530.57	158,896.09	1,758,397.85
	1895	108,045	989,072.33	692,566.21	2,184,430.72
National Sick and Burial Association.	1885	54,927	273,706.56	194,066.29	728,539.88
	1895	77,406	514,973.03	383,076.28	1,264,005.24
National Independent Order of Odd Fellows.	1885	50,961	256,975.53	253,418.12	785,725.62
	1895	58,283	268,713.53	218,539.92	1,177,405.88
Loyal Order of Ancient Shepherds (Ashton Unity).	1885	66,941	418,780.36	282,534.89	866,942.64
	1895	109,782	774,620.27	545,048.00	2,276,821.22
National United Order of Free Gardeners.	1885	45,795	304,875.24	231,246.85	610,954.21
	1895	55,515	398,013.67	375,153.62	789,419.30
United Ancient Order of Druids.	1885	26,763	171,626.86	118,830.20	600,608.63
	1895	39,732	251,801.19	192,538.21	856,163.34
Total 10 Societies.	1885	1,672,326	12,370,243.92	7,876,220.99	53,592,905.49
	1895	2,210,476	17,198,595.44	12,082,268.91	81,833,678.28

orders during the decennial period 1874 to 1883. What is true for that period is equally so for later years.[1]

"We take the last decade as a whole, and observe that during the 10 years (1874–1883) there has been received by the Manchester Unity from its members in the United Kingdom, the sum of (in round numbers) £5,438,000 as contributions, and for interest on invested capital £1,670,000, making a grand total of £7,108,000; and that during the same period there has been expended by the Unity, for sickness and funeral allowances to its members, the relative sums of £3,838,000 and £1,075,000, making together £4,913,000. The capital of the Unity was, on December 31, 1873, stated to be £3,412,000, or an average of £7, 2s. 10¾d. per member, while on December 31, 1883, it amounted to £5,519,000, or an average of £9, 13s. 4½d. per member. While, therefore, the society during the past 10 years has expended the large sum above stated in sickness and funeral benefits, it has added to its reserve capital the sum of £2,107,000. These figures do not include what are known as auxiliary funds, such as widow and orphan societies, juvenile branches, benevolent and other funds (shortly to be explained) which in 1878 — the first year of information given — showed a capital of £191,000, and in 1884 increased it to £307,781. The financial year made up gives, including all funds, for the 585,129 members returned out of the full total of members (at home and abroad) of now over 600,000,

---

[1] Pages 111 and 112.

a grand total of £6,034,587 capital; or, exclusive of extraordinary assurances, £9, 15s. 11¼d. per member.

"Passing on to the Order of Foresters, and reckoning up the figures for the same period, we find that the order received from its members in the United Kingdom within the past 10 years a sum of £4,678,000, in the shape of contributions to Sick and Funeral Funds alone, and as interest on invested capital £686,000, or a total of £5,364,000, while the payments have been on the following scale: for sick allowances £3,193,000, and for funeral allowances, not including levies to District Funeral Funds, £851,000. Capital (returns complete to one year later than the Manchester Unity) on December 31, 1874, was put at £2,022,000; and in December, 1884, the worth of the order was £3,584,000, or something over £6 per member. After paying away in 10 years claims to the amount of £4,044,000, the Foresters have added to their reserves £1,320,000. Taking next the relative increase of membership, the increase in Great Britain and Ireland in the 10 years as regards the Manchester Unity has been 97 lodges or branches and 82,837 members, and in the Order of Foresters 625 courts or branches and 164,793 members. But this increase, great as it has been, is relatively less than that of the two previous decades; indeed this present period has not been one, until lately, so much of numerical increase as of financial improvement and consolidation; but the past year witnessed the largest number of initiations into these two orders since their foundation; viz. 56,000 into the Foresters and 42,000 into the Odd Fellows, being at the rate of a thousand per week in the former."

If we compare the mean totals as given for this period with those given in the tables showing the situation of the orders in 1885 and 1895, it will be seen that practically a similar statement could be made for the succeeding period. The Manchester Unity during this decade increased in membership 122,920 and added to its capital $10,329,905.42; and the Foresters increased 72,524 in membership and increased their funds by $7,161,473.27.

The subject of legislation regarding friendly societies is of secondary importance. The essentially voluntary character of the whole movement has been one of its most characteristic features. It was inevitable, however, that the government should be forced to intervene in some way. While some of the societies were doing everything possible in the way of putting their affairs upon a firm financial footing, there were others, the members of which were subjected to great loss and hardships as the result of either faulty financial systems, mismanagement, or even fraud on the part of their officers. Under these circumstances the state could not remain inactive. So great has been the aversion to government interference, however, that this action has always been of the most timid and restricted kind.

The first need of legislation that manifested itself was that friendly societies should be given a legal status. Friendly societies rose into prominence at a time when all combinations of laboring men were looked upon with suspicion. In common with other labor organizations, they had no position before the law; they could hold no property as organizations; they had no rights against defaulting treasurers; no right to appeal to the courts to restrain abuses. The first special friendly society act was that known as the Rose Act, passed in 1793, by which a fixed legal status was granted to all societies which should become registered. The nature of this act is characteristic of all the legislation that followed. So abhorrent to the spirit of the English workingman was any suggestion of compulsion, that, neither in this nor in any subsequent laws, has the government made compliance with their provisions obligatory. The government has said in substance, if you will voluntarily come forward and consent to be registered, and thus undertake to comply with certain regulations, the chief of which is that of making reports, you can profit by the benefits offered by these acts. The result has been that throughout their subsequent history there have always remained the two classes of registered and unregistered societies.

It will result in needless detail to follow all of the twenty or more subsequent acts relating to friendly societies which were passed prior to the general act of 1875. The tendency of all was to make the provisions of the law somewhat more comprehensive, the benefits of registration greater, and the control stricter. But one or two provisions need to be specially mentioned. Registration, as at first required, was made before the justice of peace of the districts in which the societies were located. There was, therefore, no attempt to exercise a unifying influence on societies or to collect information concerning them.

It was not until 1846 that the service of registration was centralized in the general office of Registrar of Friendly Societies, and not until 1857 that the publication of the yearly reports was begun by the registrar. A second important provision was one first introduced by the act of 1819, by which permission was given to registered friendly societies to invest their funds with the National Debt Commission. They were thus placed on the same footing as savings banks, and enabled to get a higher rate of interest than was current in the market.

For twenty years prior to 1875 no legislation relating to friendly societies was enacted. In 1871 a royal commission was appointed to inquire into all questions relating to friendly societies. The report of this commission, consisting of four volumes, the last of which appeared in 1874, constitutes a mine of information concerning these societies, their origin and past history, their organization, methods, and results. The immediate effect of this investigation was the passage of the law of 1875, the purpose of which was to consolidate all previous legislation and introduce certain new conditions. As another consolidating act has recently been enacted, that of 1895, we will not enter into a consideration of the details of that of 1875, but pass directly to the latter act, which will enable us to study the law as it is in force at the present time.

The most concise and at the same time the clearest exposition of this law is found in the Guide issued by the Friendly Society Registry Office. The principal provisions of existing legislation can be summarized from it, it being understood, of course, that many of these provisions were in force prior to the enactment of the law of 1895.

Provision is made for a central registry office, at the head of which is the Chief Registrar, with assistants for England, Scotland, and Ireland. This office exercises functions in regard to a great variety of workingmen's organizations, of which the friendly societies constitute by far the most important group. Registration on the part of these societies is voluntary. The advantages of registration are that the society can legally hold land and other kinds of property in the name of trustees; that it has greater rights of action against defaulting officers; that it can compel its officers to render accounts, and one-fifth of the members, or a certain number according to the size of the society, can demand an investigation, and, if necessary, the winding up of the affairs of the society. In the way of direct benefits, it can invest money with the National Debt Commissioners; it is exempted from the payment of certain stamp duties; and it can avail itself of the public auditors for the auditing of its accounts, or the valuing of its assets and liabilities.

On the other hand, registered societies must assume certain obligations, many of which, however, may be considered as advantages. A large, and certainly the most important, part of these obligations relate to the securing of publicity of operations. In addition to filing copies of its constitution and rules, which must correspond to certain general requirements,[1] each

---

[1] The registry office issues model constitutions and rules, but their adoption is not obligatory.

registered society must make three kinds of reports; first, an annual report of its operations during the year; secondly, a quinquennial return of its sickness and mortality experiences during the preceding five years; and thirdly, a quinquennial valuation of its assets and liabilities. Among the restrictions placed upon the operations of the societies, the most important is that forbidding the granting of an annuity in excess of £50 ($243.32), or a gross sum, on death, of over £200 ($973.30).

The above are some of the principal positive requirements of friendly society legislation. It is of equal importance to notice some of the things that are not done. In the first place, registry, while it induces good management, by no means guarantees that such is the case. As the registrar says, "It cannot be too strongly insisted upon that the registrar cannot ensure the good management of societies, and that the mere fact of registry affords no guarantee that a society is solvent or even honest." In other words, the registrar is given no power similar to that of many of our bank examiners of declaring an institution insolvent, unless, as previously stated, an examination of its affairs has been demanded by a certain proportion of its members. It is about this consideration that the great debate has always taken place whenever the subject of friendly societies has been under discussion. The principle of non-intervention has thus far prevailed. Whether this has been wise or not remains an open question. That a great deal of mismanagement or bad practice could have been avoided had greater power been given to the registrar cannot be doubted. On the other hand, it is scarcely likely that there would have been developed under that system a similar degree of voluntarily undertaken reform with its consequent educational influence in the art of self-government. At the present time, however, the undoubted tendency is toward giving the registrar more power; first, to require new societies to be based upon sound financial principles; and secondly, to pass upon the solvency and general conditions of societies as revealed by their reports from year to year.

It is important to notice that practically no restriction is placed upon societies in regard to the investment of their funds. Though losses have resulted from bad investments, it cannot be said that this liberty has in general been abused.

Turning now to a consideration of the effects of these laws, the consequences of their permissive character are plainly seen. In spite of the advantages of registration, a considerable proportion of the societies have neglected in the past and still refuse to become registered. The number of registered societies is, however, steadily growing, and it is probable that this is a relative increase over the number of those unregistered. It should also be taken into account that those registered represent the strongest and best-managed organizations. The great workingmen's orders, representing as they do the highest type of voluntary insurance, have taken the lead in this matter, and are doing a great deal in the way of encouraging the registration of other societies. As regards compliance with the provisions of the acts on the part of the registered societies, only an indifferent success has been obtained. Even the annual reports have by no means been made in such a shape that they could always be utilized by the office. The quinquennial returns of sickness and the quinquennial valuations, by far the most important of the reports demanded, have not been made by all the societies.

The great benefits of the system of government registration have been indirect. It is impossible to calculate the good which has been done by the registry office in the way of encouraging societies to put their affairs upon a sound mathematical basis, and in providing model constitutions, tables of premiums and benefits, etc. The single fact that societies have been impressed with the necessity for periodical valuations has been extremely instrumental in furthering this reform. In all this work the office has been ably seconded by the large orders, and it is difficult to say to which is due the greater credit for the reforms of recent years.

Of the three branches of the history of friendly societies in England, that of their internal reform is the most important. The great interest in this subject attaches from the fact that in it is contained the entire history of the evolution of a scientific insurance institution from a relief society. From an organization differing at times little from a charitable society, and in no way based upon any attempt to make contributions of members proportionate to the probable charge that they might be expected to entail upon the society, there has been developed an organization, the operations of which are based upon the most approved principles of actuarial science, and in which there is no suggestion of charity. This, moreover, has been accomplished by the unaided efforts of the workingmen themselves. A study of this development, therefore, affords us an insight into all the difficulties encountered in the organization of voluntary insurance, and of the methods by which they can be overcome; while an examination of these societies, as organized at the present time, affords the best idea obtainable of the manner in which a voluntary insurance society should be organized, the tables of contribution and benefits that most nearly correspond to actual experience, the best methods of conducting the business, etc.

To understand the great improvement that has taken place, one must know the character of these societies in the early part of their history. In their origin, the friendly societies were little more than benevolent organizations in which the members united to assist each other in case of death or sickness. As long as these societies consisted of but a few members, who were for the most part well known to each other, they in the main served their purpose. As soon as they began to develop and to attempt to accomplish more ambitious purposes, difficulties of all kinds became manifest. The primitive financial system was that of payment by assessments. On the occurrence of illness or death, a collection was made among the members for the benefit of the sufferer or his family. The first step toward systematization was the fixing of the amount of relief that would be granted and the amount that could be assessed against each member. The next advance was the practice of doing away with assessments altogether and substituting in their place a regular periodical payment of dues, and the consequent maintenance of a greater or less sum of money on hand to meet obligations. This once done, the insurance principle, that of fixed payments for fixed benefits, may be said to have been fairly introduced.

Far from scientific methods, however, were followed in the application of this principle. The practice of making contributions uniform for all ages constituted the greatest violation. It is evident that liability to sickness increases with age. Under a system of uniform contributions the younger members take upon themselves the burden caused by the greater amount of sickness among the older members. Unless, therefore, a society of this character constantly receives new blood, it must sooner or later come to grief. Thus, as Mr. Baernreither says, it was a matter of accident, or exceptionally cautious management, when societies remained solvent for any length of time. Even as late as 1867, the registrar reckoned that from 1793 to 1867, out of the 38,315 friendly societies registered in England and Wales, no less than 13,935 had collapsed, this notwithstanding the fact that the registered societies represent the most solvent organizations. From the standpoint of the development of insurance, a great damage was caused by the direct discouragement of workingmen to join friendly societies until they were old and enfeebled. The correct system is that whereby contributions are graduated according to the ages of members upon admission to the society. It was, however, by no means an easy matter to establish such a system. The plan of uniform contributions had a strong hold upon the workingmen on account of its simplicity. A system of graduated contributions required the use of tables based upon statistics of morbidity and mortality. Such tables, to correspond to actual conditions, could only be compiled from data relating to a large number of persons, during a period of years. This information was absolutely wanting during the early history of friendly societies. With the organization of societies on this basis, came the demand for a better order of book-keeping, for the introduction of rational rules, the accumulation of reserve funds, and their investment. To recapitulate, then, in the words of Mr. Baernreither, the problems confronting the friendly societies were: "Firstly, to discover the proper transition from the system of levies or incomplete or insufficient contributions to a safe and well-calculated system of premiums; secondly, to improve their management by the introduction of rational rules, correct book-keeping, and a safe investment of capital; and, lastly, to perfect the system of workingmen's insurance by a separation and independent constitution of its different branches."

The great orders, and particularly the Manchester Unity and Foresters, were the first to recognize the importance of these reforms. For years they have striven to put their operations upon a scientific basis. In so doing they have not only indicated to other societies the path of reform, but have labored unceasingly to induce them to follow it. They have made extensive and costly statistical compilations in order to prepare tables of sickness and mortality. On this basis, they have compiled tables of premiums and benefits which they have encouraged other societies to adopt, and have likewise issued model rules and regulations. They have stood by the registrar in emphasizing the advantages of registration. The history of the reform of friendly societies is, therefore, largely that of the reform of these orders. It should be understood, however, that, in general, reform in the case of the other societies has not been so thorough, and that to-day there are many societies whose organization presents all of the defects of those of the earlier period.

As this reform has been largely the preparation and adoption by the orders of approved tables, its progress can best be traced in the rise of the literature of this subject. To Dr. Price belongs the credit of the first efforts to compile tables of mortality and sickness. In 1770 he published his famous Northampton Tables of Mortality, based upon the lists of births and deaths in the various parishes of that town. These tables, important as a beginning, were far from accurate. In 1824 a decided advance was made by the publication by the Highland Society of tables showing the average duration of sickness of persons according to ages, based on the experience of 73 friendly societies of Scotland, and representing 104,218 years of life. Ten years later Mr. Charles Ansell published tables of sickness relating to 5000 members of friendly societies for five years, 1823-1827, and embracing 24,323 years of life.[1] In 1845 appeared what Mr. Baernreither calls

[1] Charles Ansell, *A Treatise on Friendly Societies*, London, 1835.

an epoch-marking book, *Contribution to Vital Statistics,* by Mr. F. G. P. Neison. Mr. Neison in this work not only gives tables of sickness and duration of life based upon the quinquennial returns of the registrar from 1836 to 1840, but presents a scientific discussion of the principles that should govern societies which desire to put their operations upon a sound actuarial basis.[1]

To the Manchester Unity, however, belongs the credit of the most important work in this direction. This order, through its corresponding secretary Mr. Ratcliffe, made at its own expense three elaborate statistical investigations concerning its experience as regards sickness and death among its members. The first of these related to the period 1846–1848, and embraced 621,561 years of life and 609,112 weeks of sickness; the second to the period 1856–1860, embracing 1,006,272 years of life and 1,321,202 weeks of sickness; and the third to the period 1866–1870, embracing 1,321,006 years of life and 1,975,032 weeks of sickness; or a total for the three of 2,948,839 years of life and 3,905,346 weeks of sickness.[2] The cost of this work was in the neighborhood of $50,000. Its character is of the highest order. Based as these investigations were upon a broad basis of the best data, and compiled by an actuary of unusual attainments, it is difficult to

---

[1] See Baernreither, pp. 236–240, for a description of the contents and nature of this book. In a small pamphlet, *Observations on Odd Fellows and Friendly Societies,* Mr. Neison puts in a popular form the information contained in this work.

[2] Wilkinson, p. 88. The titles of Mr. Ratcliffe's works are: (1) *Observations on the Rate of Mortality and Sickness amongst Friendly Societies,* Manchester, 1850; (2) *Ditto,* Colchester, 1862; (3) *Supplementary Report,* 1872.

overestimate their value. For the first time, friendly societies were provided with adequate statistical tables from which to construct their schedules of contributions and benefits. Actuarially speaking, a revolution was worked in the organization of friendly societies. The era of scientific insurance by the friendly societies may be said to date from their compilation.

The Foresters, some years later, undertook a similar work. In 1878 it directed its secretary, Mr. Neison, the younger, to compile the experience of the order during the period 1871–1875. Mr. Neison published his work in 1882.[1] It is in every respect a valuable work and deserves to rank with the efforts of Mr. Ratcliffe. In some respects it is of even greater value, owing to the careful selection of the data considered. It contains thirty-one admirably constructed tables, from which branches of the order or other friendly societies can prepare tables of premiums applicable to their conditions.

The possession of these tables enabled the orders to put their operations upon an insurance basis where premiums were closely calculated according to risks, and, what is of equal importance, enabled them to make periodical valuations of assets and liabilities. The Manchester Unity and the Foresters about this time made the rendition of quinquennial valuations obligatory upon all their branches, thus voluntarily taking this important step fifteen years or more before it

---

[1] The title of this work is *The Rates of Mortality and Sickness according to the Experience for the five years 1871–1875 of the Ancient Order of Foresters Friendly Society*, by Francis G. P. Neison, London, 1882.

was rendered obligatory by law upon all registered societies.

Constituting, as they do, probably the best tables for voluntary sick and accident insurance in existence, it will be of value to reproduce at least one of them in order to show their character. In so doing, there is at the same time presented in the most concise way the expense which insurance entails upon the members, and the corresponding benefits which they receive in return. The table selected is one used by the Manchester Unity, as given in the book of rules of that order. This table constitutes one of a series, the adoption of which is obligatory upon all newly formed lodges, or for all new members of old lodges.

The tables of the order offer a choice of five classes of insurance, as far as the amount of the benefit is concerned, and in each of these classes a further choice of five classes as regards the length of time that the benefit will be paid. But one of the five tables will be given, that showing the amount of contribution required according to the age of the members on joining the order for each of the five classes of benefits; when these benefits are given in full for the first twelve months of sickness; and, in half, for the subsequent period of incapacity. The other tables are similar in every respect to the one given except that they show respectively the contribution demanded when: (1) the benefit is given in full for six months and in half thereafter; (2) in full for twelve months, one-half for twelve months, and one-fourth thereafter; (3) in full for six months, one-half for six months, and one-fourth thereafter, and (4) in full for six months, three-fourths for six months, and one-half thereafter.

Age.	Class I. Sick Benefit 7s. Burial Money £7 and £3 10s.		Class II. Sick Benefit 8s. Burial Money £8 and £4.		Class III. Sick Benefit 9s. Burial Money £9 and £4 10s.		Class IV. Sick Benefit 10s. Burial Money £10 and £5.		Class V. Sick Benefit 12s. Burial Money £12 and £6.	
	s.	d.	s.	d.	s.	d.	s.	d.	s.	d.
18	1	1	1	2	1	4	1	6	1	9
19	1	1	1	2	1	4	1	6	1	9
20	1	1	1	3	1	4	1	6	1	10
21	1	1	1	3	1	5	1	7	1	10
22	1	2	1	3	1	5	1	7	1	11
23	1	2	1	4	1	6	1	8	1	11
24	1	2	1	4	1	6	1	8	2	0
25	1	2	1	4	1	6	1	8	2	0
26	1	3	1	5	1	7	1	9	2	1
27	1	3	1	5	1	7	1	9	2	2
28	1	4	1	6	1	8	1	10	2	2
29	1	4	1	6	1	8	1	11	2	3
30	1	4	1	7	1	9	1	11	2	4
31	1	5	1	7	1	10	2	0	2	5
32	1	6	1	8	1	10	2	1	2	6
33	1	6	1	9	1	11	2	2	2	7
34	1	7	1	9	2	0	2	3	2	8
35	1	7	1	10	2	1	2	3	2	9
36	1	8	1	11	2	1	2	4	2	10
37	1	9	1	11	2	2	2	5	2	11
38	1	10	2	0	2	4	2	6	3	1
39	1	10	2	1	2	4	2	7	3	2
40	1	11	2	2	2	5	2	8	3	3
41	2	0	2	3	2	6	2	10	3	4
42	2	0	2	4	2	7	2	11	3	6
43	2	1	2	6	2	9	3	0	3	9
44	2	2	2	7	2	10	3	2	3	9

The first amount of burial money is paid upon the death of the member himself, and the second upon the death of his wife.

Government Insurance. — The subject of the direct efforts on the part of the government to provide for the insurance of workingmen can be dismissed in a few words. Experiments in the way of life and old-age insurance by the state were first made many years ago. In 1771 a scheme was brought forward for establishing life annuities, but a bill introduced for that purpose failed in 1773 and again in 1787. Somewhat similar schemes proposed in 1790 and in 1818 likewise failed of enactment. The foundation of the present system was laid by the act of 1833.[1] This act permitted the purchase of annuities, either deferred or immediate, through the medium of savings banks or other societies, the minimum amount of which should be £4, and the maximum £20. This system, under which practically nothing was done, was further elaborated by the acts of 1864[2] and 1882.[3] These acts as originally introduced provided for a much more comprehensive scheme than that finally erected. The determined opposition of the friendly societies and the private insurance companies was responsible for this result. The essential provisions of the system created in 1864 were: that annuities could be purchased through the post-office savings banks from the National Debt Commissioners; these annuities could not be greater than £50 or £100 of life insurance; the rate of premiums was calculated on a basis of an interest of three per cent on investments; applicants for insurance were required to be between the ages of 16 and 60 years; after paying premiums for five years

---

[1] 3-4 Will. IV. c. 14. [2] 27-28 Vict. c. 43. [3] 45-46 Vict. c. 51.

the policy holder could surrender his policy and receive in return either a cash sum, a paid-up life insurance policy, or an immediate or deferred annuity.

The operations of this system were insignificant. The act entered into force in 1865. During the 17 years ending with 1882 only 6524 contracts for life insurance and 11,646 annuities were taken out. In 1882 the attempt was made, through the act of that year, to modify the system so that it would appeal to a larger class. The minimum limit for life insurance, which had been £20, was removed, as well as the age limit of 16 years, the experience of the friendly societies having proven that the working classes in England largely desired to insure the lives of their children; a change was made so that policies could be surrendered after two instead of five years; the number of stations at which insurance could be contracted was increased; and other facilities provided.

The system as it exists to-day, therefore, provides that immediate or deferred annuities of not less than £1 and not more than £100 can be purchased through the postal savings bank, on the life of any person over five years of age. The lives of persons between 14 and 65 years of age may be insured for any amount not less than £5 and not more than £100. The lives of children between 8 and 14 years of age may be insured for £5. The cost of the insurance of course varies according to the age of persons applying for insurance. A male 24 years of age can purchase an annuity of £1 to commence running on his reaching the age of 54 years by the annual payment of 4s. 4d., or the immediate payment of £3, 19s. 10d. The life of a person between the age of 21 and 22 years may be insured for £10 by an annual payment through life of 4s. 4d., or an annual payment to the age of 60 years of 4s. 8d., or by a single payment of £4, 4s. All persons insuring their lives or purchasing annuities must become, if they are not so already, savings bank depositors, so that their premiums can be deducted from their deposits.

In spite of these changes, the system of government insurance in England has absolutely failed to accomplish results of importance. It is not an easy matter to give an explanation for this failure. The fundamental reason undoubtedly lies in the temper of the English people, which does not take kindly to a government institution of any kind, and in the fact that the government has not been able, or at least has never made any active effort, to encourage workingmen to take advantage of its institutions. The friendly societies, on the other hand, being institutions which the people can call their own, have succeeded in constantly increasing the number of their members. It seems to be the general opinion, however, that the establishment of the government system has exerted a beneficial effect upon the friendly societies in urging them, through the fear of its competition, to place their operations upon a sounder financial basis.

Employers' Liability. — In England and the United States the problem of accidents to labor is still in the stage when a solution is sought in the modification of the law in relation to the liability of employers for accidents to their employés. A study of the question in these countries, therefore, involves a consideration of these laws rather than that of insurance institutions actually in operation.

The law now in force is the outgrowth of the fundamental legal principle that makes every man liable for his own wrong-doing or breaches of contract whenever actual or legal damages result in consequence of them. From this was evolved the doctrine of *respondeat superior*, that a man is liable not only for his personal acts but for those of his agents as well. This extension of liability was inevitable. The operations of business are so complex and varied that in all large undertakings the director must act through other hands. There was no other consistent course for the law, than to declare these hands to be in effect the hands of the director as the responsible head of the enterprise. This became settled law as early as the reign of Charles II.

This would seem to establish the broadest possible principle of employers' liability for all accidents resulting either to outside parties or to employés from the negligence of either the employer himself or of any of his employés. So, in fact, it did. In 1837, however, an important innovation was made in this rule by the judicial decision rendered in the case of *Priestly* v. *Fowler*. There are few cases in English law of greater importance. It makes a new departure, and constitutes the fundamental precedent upon which rests all modern English and American law regarding the liability of employers for accidents to their employés. A butcher sent one of his men on a wagon which had been loaded by another employé, but loaded too heavily. The wagon broke down and the man's thigh was broken.

The court decided that the butcher was not liable for the injury. The reason for this decision, as stated by the court, was: "That if the master is liable, that liability will be found to carry us to an alarming extent. The master, for example, would be liable to the servant for the negligence of the chambermaid for putting him into a damp bed; for that of the upholsterer for sending in a crazy bedstead whereby he was made to fall down while asleep and injure himself; for the negligence of the cook in not properly cleaning the copper vessels used in the kitchen," etc.

The result of this decision has been the development of the modern doctrine of common employment. In the leading case of *Hutchinson* v. *The York, Newcastle and Berwick Railway Company*, decided in 1850, this doctrine is clearly defined. The court in its decision says: "The difficulty is as to the principle applicable to the case of several servants employed by the same master, and injury resulting to one from the negligence of another. In such a case, however, we are of the opinion that the master is not in general responsible where he has selected persons of competent care and skill." The reasons for this rule, it says, are: "They (the employés) have both engaged in a common service, the duties of which impose a certain risk on each of them; and in case of negligence on the part of the other, the party knows that the negligence is that of his fellow-servant and not of his master. He knew when he engaged in the service that he was exposed to the risk of injury, not only from his own want of skill and care, but also from the want of it on the part of his fellow-servant; and he must be supposed to have contracted on the terms that as between himself and his master he would run this risk."[1]

Like all legal doctrines, this rule involved principles of justice. The absolute liability of the employer did require restriction. In practice, however, the interpretation of the principle of common employment has gone to the other extreme, and has led to the gravest injustice. Under a régime where an employé worked in a small shop with but few fellow-workers, the reasoning upon which this principle is founded may be valid. With the development of the conduct of industry upon a large scale, the entire argument falls to the ground. As the law stood, the employé was in a less advantageous position than any outsider. If an accident caused injuries to both, the latter could recover damages while the former had absolutely no legal claim. The engineer or conductor of a train has as little opportunity to determine the capacity of the switchman to whose negligence an accident is due, as any of the passengers. If the company is liable for damages for one, there is no reason why it should not be equally so for the other. If an explosion of a steam boiler in a factory causes an injury to a visitor and an employé, there is no real reason in equity why the one should not be entitled to damages as much as the other. It cannot be too distinctly stated that the common-law doctrine of employers' liability is one that works a grave injustice to the workingmen.

[1] Quoted from Massachusetts Labor Report, 1883.

In the application of this principle, of course, the employer is not exempt from liability if it can be shown that the accident causing the injury was due to his or his direct representatives' fault or neglect. On the other hand, if it can be shown that the injured person was himself in any way at fault, he loses all rights to an indemnity. These and similar considerations, however, bring up such questions as contributory negligence, what constitutes common employment, what is reasonable care in the selection of agents and tools, etc.; questions into which it would manifestly be out of place for us to enter. The important point that it is desired to bring out is that, under the common law, employés are able to obtain indemnification for accidents received during their work, though they themselves may not be to blame, in but an insignificant number of cases. The hardships resulting from industrial accidents is thus made to fall upon the employé instead of the industry.

The injustice of this condition of affairs could not fail to lead to efforts to provide a remedy. One of the earliest employers' liability bills was introduced in 1872. Years of discussion and investigation by parliamentary committees followed before the passage of the Employers' Liability Act of September 7, 1880, was obtained. This act was originally passed for a provisional period of seven years, but has, since the expiration of that time, been periodically renewed. The object of this act was simply to lessen the rigor of the doctrine of common employment, by extending the liability of employers to the five special cases, where personal injury to a workingman was due to accidents caused: (1) By reason of any defect in the condition of the ways, works, machinery or plant connected with or used in the business of the employer; (2) By reason of the negligence of any person in the service of the employer who has any superintendence entrusted to him, whilst in the exercise of such superintendence; (3) By reason of the negligence of any person in the service of the employer to whose orders or directions the workman at the time of the injury was bound to conform, and did conform, where such injury resulted from his having so conformed; (4) By reason of the act or omission of any person in the service of the employer done or made in obedience to particular instructions given by any person delegated with the authority of the employer in that behalf; and (5) By reason of the negligence of any person in the service of the employer who has charge or control of any signal, points, locomotive engine, or train upon a railway.

This law, as will be seen, made but a slight advance. It merely made employers liable to their workmen for the negligence of persons in authority over them. Except in the case of railroad employers, their liability went no further. Moreover, the employé was not entitled to recover if he was aware of the defect or negligence which caused his injury and failed to report it to his superior, or where the defect was not connected with any negligence on the part of the employer or his foreman. Finally, the power was given to the employer to "contract out" their employés, that is, make the employés on entering his service renounce their claims to compensation under the act. The act provided for special procedure in the county courts, and limited the sum recoverable as compensation to the estimated earnings, during the three years preceding the injury, of a person in the same grade, employed during those years in the like employment.

As far as accomplishing any direct good is concerned, this act may be said to have been almost a failure. Mr. Geoffrey Drage, Secretary of the Royal Commission of Labor, in his report to the Milan Congress in Relation to Accidents to Labor, 1894, said: "Experience has shown that it has neither confirmed the hopes of the workman nor the fears of the employers. In the first place, only a comparatively small proportion of the total number of accidents which occur, estimated at about one in ten, were found to come under the act. In the second place, in only a small proportion of these did the workmen either attempt to enforce, or succeed in enforcing, their claims under the act."

In consequence of this failure, the agitation for the enactment of a law increasing the liability of employers became even more active after the act was passed than before. This agitation resulted in the introduction, in 1893, of a new employers' liability bill, which, after various legislative experiences and modifications, became a law, August 6, 1897, under the title of "Workmen's Compensation Act." Unlike its predecessor, this act is no halfway measure. It completely abolishes the doctrine of common employment in the industries to which it relates. The principle of the compulsory indemnification of injured workingmen by their employers is as unequivocally accepted as in Germany and Austria. Thus the position, so long striven for, that the burdens entailed by industrial accidents should be made to constitute a normal item in the cost of operation or production, and therefore to be borne by the employers, has triumphed in England as on the Continent. More than this, the necessity has been recognized that the amount of the indemnity should, as far as possible, be determined in advance according to a fixed scale, and not left to the slow, vexatious, and expensive judgment of a court of law. Thus far England has followed the German legislation. The first material difference arises in regard to the precaution taken in each case that the employers will be able in all cases to pay the indemnities. In Germany and Austria, the government has required employers to insure themselves against these risks in certain state-controlled institutions. In England, the employers have been left entirely free to protect themselves by insurance in private companies, or not, as they deem advisable. In case of insolvency, however, on the part of a concern, it is provided that the indemnities shall constitute the first charge against its assets.

The general importance and significance of this act have been shown. The details of its provisions are of not less interest. The indemnification of workingmen injured while in the performance of their work is made compulsory upon employers in the following industries: railways; factories, including under this head all establishments coming under the provisions of the factory acts; mines; quarries; engineering work; construction work in connection with the making or alteration of railways, harbors, canals, sewers, and the like, or in and about any building which exceeds thirty feet in height, and is either being built, repaired, or demolished by means of a scaffolding, or on which machinery driven by steam, water, or other mechanical power is being used. It is thus evident that, though the act is restricted to certain specified undertakings, it is by no means limited in its scope. A classification that includes all railway, mining, quarrying, factory, and important construction work embraces a large proportion of workingmen to whom the principle of the compulsory indemnification of accidents can well be applied.

The accidents for which indemnification must be made include all resulting in death or an incapacity on the part of the victims to earn full wages, at the work at which they were employed, during at least two weeks. The only exception made is that when the accident is proven to have been caused by the "serious and wilful misconduct" of the workingmen claiming damages. But even in this case, it will be noticed that the victim has a *prima facie* claim, and the burden of proving such misconduct as will defeat it, is placed upon the employer.

The schedule of indemnities is as follows:—

(1) In case of death, if the workingman leaves any dependants who were wholly dependent upon his earnings at the time of his death, there is paid to them a sum equal to his earnings in the employment of the same employer during the three years next preceding the injury, or the sum of £150 ($729.98), whichever of these sums is the larger, but not to ex-

ceed in any case £300 ($1459.96). If the workingman has been in the employment of his last employer less than three years, the amount of his earnings is deemed to be 156 times his average weekly earnings during the time he has been employed. If the workingman leaves persons only partly dependent upon his earnings for support, the amount paid is somewhat less, and, unless an agreement can be reached, is determined by arbitration as provided for in this act. If there are no dependants, the reasonable expenses of his medical attendance and burial, not exceeding £10 ($48.67), are paid.

(2) When total or partial incapacity for work results from the injury, there is paid during the incapacity, after the second week, a weekly benefit not exceeding 50 per cent of the average weekly earnings of the victim during the preceding year, if he has been employed so long, but, if not, then for any less period during which he has been in the employment of the same employer, but in no case can the benefit exceed £1 ($4.87). In fixing the amount of the weekly payment, regard must be had to the difference between the amount of the average weekly earnings of the workingman before the accident, and the average amount that he is able to earn afterwards.

The sum allotted in any case as compensation to a dependant may be invested, or otherwise applied, as agreed or ordered by the arbitrator. Thus provision is made whereby this sum may be deposited in the Post-office Savings Bank, or be used for the purchase of an annuity from the National Debt Commissioners. In order to provide against imposition, the injured workingman is required to submit to an examination by a duly qualified practitioner provided and paid by the employer, or, if he desires, by a practitioner the method of the selection of whom is provided by the act. If he is in receipt of a weekly benefit, he must submit to such examination from time to time, as deemed necessary.

Reference has been made to the settlement of the amount of the indemnities, and of certain other questions, by arbitration. It is unnecessary to enter into the details of the manner of proceeding or the appointment and powers of the arbitrators. It is sufficient to say that, in case an agreement between the employer and the injured person or his representatives cannot be reached, an arbitrator is appointed by the county court judge.

There are at least two collateral provisions incorporated in this act which are of special importance. The first is that this act shall in no way abridge the right of employés to sue their employers for damages in the common law courts. The employé, however, must make his option, and either claim compensation under the act, or take the same proceedings as were open to him before this law was enacted. If, however, he decides upon the latter course, and in that action it is determined that the injury is not one for which the employer is liable in such action, but that he would have been liable to pay compensation under the provisions of the act of 1897, the court shall, if the plaintiff so desires, proceed to assess such compensation, in doing which, however, the judge shall, in his discretion, deduct from the amount awarded all the costs resulting from the plaintiff having brought the action instead of proceeding under the compensation act. It would be difficult to conceive of any provision regarding this point that could be fairer to the workingmen than the one just described.

The second provision relates to the vexed question of "contracting out." This difficulty seems to have been solved in a skilful and equally just way. It was desired, if possible, to encourage the organization of accident insurance associations, rather than to displace them by the system provided in this act. Permission is therefore given to employers, either alone or in co-operation with their employés, to organize schemes of accident insurance which shall take the place of the provisions of this act. Before such schemes can enter into operation, they must be submitted to the Registrar of Friendly Societies, and be certified by him that they are on the whole not less favorable to the general body of workingmen and their dependants than the provisions of the compensation act. No scheme can be certified which contains an obligation upon the workingmen to join the scheme as a condition of their employment. Such schemes, moreover, are always subject to the examination of the Registrar upon the complaint of any person, and the certificate may be revoked at any time. The Registrar is also ordered to include in his annual report full particulars of his proceedings under this act.

It needs but a cursory examination to show that this law is in almost every respect an admirable measure. It definitely establishes the principle that employers must indemnify their employés for all serious accidents suffered by them during the time that they are at work, according to a predetermined scale, — a principle which it has been an effort throughout this work to establish as the only one doing full justice to the workingmen, and obviating the unbearable hardships consequent upon the effort to provide compensation through the law courts. The act is one for compulsory compensation, but not for compulsory insurance. That the employers, however, will in great part insure against this risk is certain, and in no country can the efforts of privately organized insurance institutions be more depended upon. The clause permitting employers to organize insurance institutions of their own is a particularly happy one, for under it the creation of such funds as that of the *Comité des Forges de France* is not only permitted but encouraged. That insurance against accidents will receive a great development as the result of this act is certain. The exact form that it will assume, however, only the future can reveal.

Proposed Schemes for Old-Age Insurance. — Until a comparatively recent date the problem of workingmen's insurance in England was concerned primarily with the development and reform of the friendly societies, and with the attempt to secure to workingmen injured by accidents while at work an adequate indemnification by increasing the liability of employers. To these two efforts must now be added a third. Within late years, the subject of state insurance of workingmen has entered upon a new phase. It was inevitable that the rapid development of compulsory insurance on the Continent, and the great attention everywhere paid to this question, should lead Englishmen to study anew the principles involved in state insurance.

The great development of the friendly societies, the operations of which are chiefly concerned with sick and accident insurance, has caused attention to be chiefly directed toward old-age and invalidity insurance, for which, as we have seen, these societies make almost no provision. Schemes providing for the creation of a national system of old-age insurance have been brought forward by various persons and have received a widespread discussion. Two royal commissions have investigated the subject of the condition of the aged poor, and all of the political parties have been forced to take notice of the question in their political programmes.

There is no doubt that the problem of the aged poor in England is one of tremendous importance. In 1892 Sir Hugh Owen found that there were 1,372,000 persons over 65 years of age in the country. Of these, 114,000 were indoor, and 287,000 outdoor, paupers. Deducting 25,000 who received medical relief only, there remained 376,000, or over one-fourth of the entire population of the country over 65 years of age, who were dependent upon the poor-law authorities for support. The calculations of Mr. Charles Booth have made him place these figures even higher. As the result of his inquiries, he estimates the ratio of paupers over 65 years of age to the total population of that age to be 25.9 per cent. Five-sixths of this pauperism, he says, must be accounted old-age pauperism. Canon Blackley found, by an independent inquiry in 26 parishes, that no less than 42 per cent of the old persons dying during a certain period had had relief during the closing years of their life. Regarding this inquiry Mr. Booth says, "I cannot think that the average all over the country would be so high, but 30 per cent would not be an impossible estimate." [1]

The question in England, therefore, is not whether the state should aid the aged poor, for that it already does through its poor-law service, but whether it could not better aid them by some systematic plan of insurance. It is important to note that in England the problem of old-age insurance is posed as a poor-law reform, and not, as on the Continent, as a pure workingman's question.

The father of the movement in favor of old-age pensions is Canon Blackley. Mr. Blackley's original idea, which dates from the year 1878, was for the state to establish a compulsory system by which the whole sum needed for the constitution of an old-age pension should be collected from each individual between the ages of 18 and 21 years. In the light of criticism, however, he has been forced to modify his propositions so that he is now willing to admit state aid, and even to abandon the general compulsory character of his scheme, and accept any system of voluntary state-aided insurance. He still maintains his opinion, however, that the desired results can only be obtained by a compulsory scheme.

In 1880 the National Provident League was organized to promote the discussion of this question. This

[1] *Pauperism and the Endowment of Old Age*, London, 1892, p. 165.

organization elaborated a proposition, the essential principle of which was that every one should be encouraged to provide for an old-age pension of £6, 10s. per annum, by a promise that an equal sum would be added by the state so as to secure, in all, £13, or 5s. a week to each old person. There are numerous objections that can be raised to both Mr. Blackley's and the Provident Association's schemes, chief among which is the one that results would not be apparent for a great many years, as no provision is made for the cases of the present generation of old and middle-aged persons.

A third proposal is that brought forward by Mr. Chamberlain. This scheme Mr. Chamberlain states had its origin in a voluntary committee composed of about 80 members of the House of Commons. As this scheme may be said to hold the field politically, its provisions should be at least briefly stated. The plan comprehends the establishment of a voluntary state old-age pension institution. Every man is encouraged to make deposits in this institution early in life by the promise on the part of the state to add £15 to the account of every one who shall have deposited the sum of £5 by the time he is 25 years of age. The account so started must then be kept alive by a payment of £1 each year for 40 years. If the person lives to be 65 years of age, he will then be entitled to a pension of 5s. a week for the remainder of his life. If he dies before that time, his widow will receive 5s. for 26 weeks, with an additional 2s. for each child until 12 years old. If neither widow or children are left, the original £5 will be returned to the deceased's representatives. Provision is also made for the state to assist persons now over the age of 25, but not more than 50 years of age. Slightly different provisions are made for women. Other alternative schemes have been proposed by Mr. Chamberlain, the most important of which is the one providing for co-operation with the friendly societies and trade unions. Thus it is proposed that any one who will provide for a pension through these organizations shall have his pension doubled by the state when he reaches the age of 65 years.

There are, of course, a great many other schemes which have been advocated by one or another person. Of these but one, that of Mr. Charles Booth, deserves particular attention. The essential feature of Mr. Booth's proposal is that the state should grant free and universal pensions for old age. This feature differentiates it radically from all the voluntary schemes which require the insured themselves to make substantial contributions. Mr. Booth's plan does not provide for any elaborate system of insurance; it simply says that any one on reaching the age of 65 years shall be entitled to a weekly pension of 5s. from the government, the cost of which shall be raised by taxation, each year being made to pay the expenses of that year. Mr. Booth's reasons for his proposal, as summarized by Mr. Geoffrey Drage, are: "A large proportion of the aged poor are suffering from destitution due to causes over which they had no control, and in such cases it is unjust that their necessary relief should be accompanied by any degradations such as now attends the reception of poor-law relief or even to a less extent of private charity. Since, however, the investigation of the causes which have led to each individual case of destitution would be a work of too great magnitude to be undertaken by the state, and since, moreover, the materials for such an investigation are often inaccessible, justice to all the deserving poor can only be ensured by a method of state relief, which does not take into account the question of desert. Again, it is argued, if such relief be given to the destitute because they are such, it will, on the one hand, be impossible to disassociate this relief from some stigma of social inferiority, whilst, on the other hand, it will come too late to save the recipient from the suffering involved in sinking into this condition. Therefore, the relief must be given to all persons alike irrespective of their necessity for it, and, further, it must be given if possible before this necessity becomes urgent."

It is not our intention to enter into a discussion of measures as long as they remain merely propositions. To do so would carry us far from our purpose. Mr. Booth's scheme, we can only remark, is not an insurance scheme, it is rather an alternative solution of the old-age problem. At best, it is a desperate remedy, and there is little likelihood of its adoption. The foregoing consideration of the various old-age pension schemes that have been proposed serves, however, to show us the general drift of opinion on this question, and the condition of the problem at the present day.

CHAPTER IX.

Workingmen's Insurance in the United States.

Introduction. — The problem of workingmen's insurance up to the present time has been essentially an Old World question. In America, whatever attention the subject may have received, it is certainly not presented as a separate problem. The reasons for this are easily found in the conditions surrounding American labor. The whole spirit pervading the life of the workingmen is unfavorable to the practice of economy, or especially that form in which present sacrifices are made for remote benefits. In general, the artisan has been able to make money more easily than in European countries. The American workingman rarely, if ever, looks to the poorhouse as his inevitable home in old age, as do many laborers in England. Sickness, while resulting in suffering, does not, even as a rule, necessitate outside assistance. In the field of accidents alone is the question of insurance one of as much interest in the United States as in European countries.

Though there exists no system of workingmen's insurance, either state or private, more or less has, of course, been done in the line of workingmen's insurance in one way or another. Chief among these efforts are those of the relief departments of a number of the most important railway companies, and the insurance work of some of the stronger labor organizations. The fraternal orders of course insure a great many persons. Their work, however, though important, will not be considered, since it is not primarily workingmen's insurance, and because few points of interest would be presented that have not been considered in connection with the friendly societies of Great Britain. Our study, therefore, will relate chiefly to the insurance work of railway companies and labor organizations, and the subject of accidents to labor and employers' liability.

As regards the first of these, the courtesy of the railway officials having charge of the relief departments enables us to make an exceptionally complete study of the insurance work done under their auspices.[1] In regard to the second, that of insurance by labor organizations, it has been impossible to make anything like an accurate statement of the extent of their work. In general, it may be said that most of the stronger organizations make some, and many considerable, provision for sick, accident, and disability benefits. Desirable as a complete statement of the insurance work of labor organizations in this country would be, the account here given of that done by a number of the more important organizations will serve to describe practically every point of importance so far as a study of insurance methods is concerned. It will give the data necessary to enable us to make a comparison of the methods here followed with those of other countries,

---

[1] On this subject, see articles by Dr. E. W. Bemis in Conrad's *Handwörterbuch der Staatswissenschaften*, and by Mr. Emory R.* Johnson in the *Bulletin of the Department of Labor*, No. 7.

and to determine the chief lines along which this question is moving. The third branch, that of accidents to labor and employers' liability, may be said to be the most important feature of the whole question at the present time. As a legal study its consideration is, however, quite outside the plan of this work. Here we are interested only in determining its present basis, its economic effects, and whether it corresponds to our idea of equity and justice.

Railroad Employés' Relief Departments. — The demand for the insurance of railroad employés rests upon exceptionally strong grounds. Railroad employés, not only pursue a calling which is particularly hazardous in its nature, but their connection with large undertakings and the general permanency of their occupation make the introduction of insurance institutions a comparatively simple matter. The managers of American railways have to a certain extent recognized their responsibility in this matter, and a considerable number of roads make provision in one way or another for the relief of employés who are injured in the performance of their duties. Certain it is that no other industry has given an equal attention to this matter. Of the railroads which have done something in this direction, but six have created regular insurance institutions: the Pennsylvania Railroad Company; the Pennsylvania Company, lines west of Pittsburgh; the Chicago, Burlington, and Quincy; the Philadelphia and Reading, and the Plant System. In each case these companies include a number of affiliated lines which it is unnecessary to enumerate. The similarity of the organization of the name of the Relief Department of the Baltimore and Ohio Railroad, was created March 15, 1889. By an agreement with the members of the defunct association, it came into possession of the latter's assets and in return assumed all the obligations that it had incurred. As practically no change was made in the organization of the system of contributions and benefits, the relief department may be deemed to have had a continuous existence since 1880.

Membership still remained obligatory upon all employés joining the service after March 15, 1889, or all old employés as a condition of their promotion. Employés over 45 years of age, or who do not pass satisfactory medical examinations, cannot, however, be enrolled as members. That the employés had by this time come fully to realize the advantage of the department is shown by the fact that 19,467 out of the 20,626 members of the old association voluntarily joined the new department.

The constitution of the Baltimore and Ohio relief department differs materially from those of the other departments that will be described, in that it is made to subserve other purposes than that of insurance proper. It is, in fact, organized into three sections, consisting of a relief department proper, the object of which is the relief of members when incapacitated for work as the result of accidents or sickness; a pension department, to make provision for employés who by reason of age or infirmity are compelled to retire from the service of the company; and a savings and loan department, to enable members to make small savings and to borrow money at moderate rates of interest for the purpose of acquiring a home. We are here interested only in the first two sections. Fortunately the accounts of each section are kept rigorously distinct, and the different sections are for all practical purposes separate societies.

The resources of the relief and pension funds are derived from contributions required from the members, from interest on investments and current balances, and from contributions by the railroad company. These latter consist of the annual payment by the company of $6000 to the relief fund, $25,000 to the pension fund, $2500 for the physical examination of employés, and the assumption of the whole burden of administration. In case all of the $6000 is not needed by the relief fund, the balance is paid over to the pension fund.

For the purpose of determining the amount of contributions required of members, and the value of the benefits to which they are entitled, all members are first divided into the two classes of those operating trains and those not so engaged; and, secondly, into five classes according to the amount of the wages received by them. The first division is made on account of the greater risk of accidents run by the first class, it being considered but just that their contributions should be correspondingly greater. The accompanying table shows, in a condensed form, this division into classes, the amount of the contributions required, and the character and value of the benefits offered.

The death benefit shown in the table represents only the benefit the member is entitled to as the result of his membership in the department. Provision is made in the constitution whereby members may, if they choose, provide by additional payments for higher death benefits. The extra dues required is 25 cents a month for each additional $250 of insurance. To be entitled to take out this extra insurance, however, members must be under 50 years of age and pass a new physical examination. The maximum additional death benefit that can be contracted for is $1250.

Classes.	I.	II.	III.	IV.	V.
Highest monthly pay of members	$35.00	$50.00	$75.00	$100.00	over $100.00
Contributions per month, class *a*	1.00	2.00	3.00	4.00	5.00
Contributions per month, class *b*	.75	1.50	2.25	3.00	3.75
Benefits.					
Accident, first 26 weeks, per day [1]	0.50	1.00	1.50	2.00	2.50
Accident, after first 26 weeks, per day	.25	.50	.75	1.00	1.25
Sickness, for 52 weeks [1]	.50	1.00	1.50	2.00	2.50
Death, accident	500.00	1000.00	1500.00	2000.00	2500.00
Death, natural causes	250.00	500.00	750.00	1000.00	1250.00

The superannuation service forms a most interesting part of the department's relief work. This service is maintained entirely at the expense of the company. The appropriations made by it for this purpose are declared to have for their object; first, the support of members of the old relief association after they have been in the employ of the company 10 consecutive years, have reached the age of 65 years, and have been honorably relieved from duty;

[1] Sundays and legal holidays not included.

secondly, the pensioning of the members filling the same conditions when voluntarily retiring from the service; and, thirdly, if the conditions of the fund permit, the provision of pensions for other employés according to their merit as determined by the governing committee. The following summary shows the value of the daily benefit that is granted to employés transferred to the pension list. The amount of the pension varies according to the length of time the recipients have been members of the department and the wage class to which they belonged. It is expressly provided, however, that all of the pensions may be subjected to a percentage reduction, or the class of persons to whom pensions may be given may be restricted if the conditions of the fund demand it.

10 years' membership	$0.25	$0.50	$0.75	$1.00	$1.25
15 years' membership	.26¼	.52½	.78¾	1.05	1.31¼
20 years' membership	.27½	.55	.82½	1.10	1.37½

The membership has remained fairly constant. In 1889, the end of the first fiscal year after the department supplanted the old association, there were 22,930 members. The membership for succeeding years was 22,313 in 1890; 21,920 in 1891; 19,894 in 1892; 22,637 in 1893; 20,479 in 1894; and 20,710 in 1895.

The workings of the department have varied but little from year to year. A showing of the results of the last fiscal year for which information could be obtained is, therefore, sufficient for all practical purposes.

Receipts.	1894-1895.
Balance on hand	$ 301,063.18
Contributions	365,993.47
Interest	13,117.03
Other	4,187.79
Total	$ 684,361.47
Expenditures.	
Benefits, including surgical expenses	$ 307,454.28
Medicine furnished members	702.60
General expenses	49,326.56
Contributions refunded members leaving service	2,654.75
Advances to members for artificial limbs, etc.	1,052.98
Other	9.14
Total	$ 361,200.31
Assets after deducting liabilities	$ 334,410.59

It is interesting to make a further analysis of the purposes for which benefits were paid. To do this there is given on the opposite page a statement of the amounts paid for each kind of benefit for the year 1894-1895, and for the whole period since the organization of relief work in 1880.

The Pennsylvania Railroad Company was first to follow the example of the Baltimore and Ohio, and create a relief service. In 1886 it organized a Voluntary Relief Department with purposes similar to those of the Baltimore and Ohio department. In organization, however, it presents several important points of difference. The relief department constitutes a distinct service of the company, with its own account of receipts and expenditures. Membership in it is entirely voluntary on the part of the employés, thus differing essentially from that of the

	May 1, 1880–June 30, 1895.			July 1, 1894–June 30, 1895.		
	Number.	Amount.	Average.	Number.	Amount.	Average.
Death, accident	1,014	$1,073,044.22	$1,058.22	55	$61,812.00	$1,123.85
Death, natural causes	1,996	912,690.50	457.25	155	91,400.00	589.67
Disablement, accident	56,168	720,384.55	12.82	4,738	58,299.74	12.30
Disablement, sickness	80,026	1,179,252.55	14.73	5,720	87,913.98	15.36
Surgical expenses	32,678	157,963.26	4.83	3,087	8,028.56	2.60
Total	171,882	$4,043,335.08	$23.52	13,755	$307,454.28	$22.35
Other expenses	....	574,210.70	....	....	53,746.03	....
Total expenditure of department	....	$4,617,545.78	....	....	$361,200.31	...

Baltimore and Ohio system. The management, however, frankly states that it was its desire to introduce the compulsory feature, and only refrained in deference to the wishes of its employés. Only employés not over 45 years of age, and having passed a satisfactory medical examination, are eligible to membership.

The relief operations consist in the granting of benefits for sickness and accidents, and the gradual accumulation of a fund for the ultimate granting of old-age and invalidity pensions.

Receipts are derived from the contributions of members, interest on investments, and the contributions of the company. The latter consist in the payment of all operating expenses and the covering of any deficits that may arise.

A division of members into classes, in order to determine the amount of their contributions and benefits, similar to that found in the Baltimore and Ohio, is made, except that no distinction is made between employés operating trains and other workingmen. This division is shown in the following statement:—

Classes.	I.	II.	III.	IV.	V.
Highest monthly pay of members	$40.00	$60.00	$80.00	$100.00	over $100.00
Contributions per month	0.75	1.50	2.25	3.00	3.75
Benefits.					
Accident on duty, first 52 weeks, per day	0.50	1.00	1.50	2.00	2.50
Accident on duty, after first 52 weeks, per day	.25	.50	.75	1.00	1.25
Accident off duty, first 52 weeks, per day	.40	.80	1.20	1.60	2.00
Accident off duty, after first 52 weeks, per day	.20	.40	.60	.80	1.00
Sickness, first 52 weeks, per day	.40	.80	1.20	1.60	2.00
Sickness, after first 52 weeks, per day	.20	.40	.60	.80	1.00
Death	250.00	500.00	750.00	1000.00	1250.00

Members also have the opportunity of securing additional death benefits. The extra payment required is 30 cents for each $250 of insurance for members not over 45 years of age, 45 cents for those over 45 but not more than 60 years of age, and 60 cents for those over that age. The maximum benefit that can be taken out for each class is twice the amount of the ordinary death benefit.

The scheme, as has been said, also comprehends the creation of a fund for the ultimate payment of old-age and invalidity pensions. At the end of each three-year period, the accounts for the three years are balanced. If any deficit has resulted during that time, the company makes it good. If, on the other hand, there is shown a surplus, this surplus is carried to a special fund for the ultimate establishment of a superannuation service. The relief fund thus starts with a clear balance-sheet every three years. The actual workings of this scheme have been such that on the 1st of January, 1895, there had been accumulated in this fund, through successive surpluses and interest, the important sum of $273,750.95. All of this had thus really been created through the contributions of the members. The company, however, has also made important sacrifices for the same purpose. It has assumed the entire burden of providing for superannuated members during the time this fund was and is being accumulated, but no pensions are being paid. This the company has done quite outside of any obligations imposed upon it by the constitution of the relief department. The amount expended by the company in this way since the inauguration of the relief department to January 1, 1895, is $136,644.60. In other words, these departments, representing as they do but two types, that of the Baltimore and Ohio Relief Department and the Voluntary Relief Department of the Pennsylvania Railroad Company, would seem to indicate the possibility of a general treatment. Such a method, however, though it would make possible a considerable economy of space, must inevitably make it more difficult to understand each system as a whole. As we are here chiefly concerned with the study and comparison of systems, the separate consideration of each fund has been deemed the preferable method.

The Baltimore and Ohio Railroad was the first railway company in the United States to organize a relief or insurance department for the benefit of its employés. Its relief work originally took the form of an independent association, organized May 1, 1880, and subsequently, May 3, 1882, incorporated under the title of " Baltimore and Ohio Employés' Relief Association." The provision in the constitution of this association, whereby membership was rendered obligatory upon all employés of the company, immediately subjected it to adverse criticism. In spite of the undoubted advantage which it offered to the workingmen, the latter saw in it an insidious attack against their own organizations. It is now generally believed that the motive of the management was the honest desire to improve the condition of its employés. The opposition, however, was sufficiently strong to cause the state of Maryland, in 1888, to revoke the charter which it had granted. The company, however, immediately organized a practically identical institution as an independent branch of its service. This department, under the company has in substance said to the men, you provide for the future granting of old-age and invalidity pensions and we will look after present deserving cases.

In a pamphlet recently issued, the company has summed up the operations of the department from its organization in 1886 to December 31, 1894. To this statement we can add the accounts of the last year, 1895, and thus show in a single table the operations for the last year, and for the whole existence of the department.

Receipts.	1895.	1886–1895.
Contributions of members	$641,849.12	$4,599,091.90
Contributions of company, operating expenses and deficiencies	98,658.53	869,039.13
Contributions of company, extra relief	40,834.83	168,497.17
Interest	8,832.14	102,557.44
Total	$790,174.62	$5,739,185.64
Expenditures.		
Disability benefits, accident	$112,125.00	$834,690.15
Disability benefits, sickness	225,072.33	1,512,292.81
Death benefits, accident	63,000.00	483,944.45
Death benefits, natural causes	191,298.64	1,470,513.09
Operating expenses	98,658.53	869,039.13
Total	$690,154.50	$5,170,479.63

These figures show the great importance of the insurance work that has been done by this department during the brief period of 10 years. The actual receipts of the whole period have been over five millions of dollars, and those for the last year were considerably over three-quarters of a million. It will be seen that the employés receive back, practically the entire amount of their contributions in death and disability benefits, the amount of their benefits for the period being $4,301,440.50 as against $4,599,091.90 contributed by them; while the contributions of the company and interest have served to defray all operating expenses and build up a strong reserve fund for the future· payment of old-age and invalidity pensions. This fund was materially increased during the last year. On January 1, 1895, it amounted to $238,085.56. During the year there was added to it $11,086.54 interest earned, and $35,665.39 transferred to it from the surplus of the relief fund. The amount of the fund at the end of the year was, therefore, $284,837.49. The directors in their report state that plans are now under consideration for the utilization of this fund, and that it may be confidently expected that before long the superannuation feature will be in full operation.

The growth in membership of the department since its organization has been fairly constant, as is shown in the following statement: —

1886,	members	19,952	1891,	members	27,200
1887,	"	18,744	1892,	"	31,640
1888,	"	19,322	1893,	"	32,827
1889,	"	21,457	1894,	"	33,405
1890,	"	24,984	1895,	"	36,432

The data is not at hand to determine accurately the number of cases in which each kind of benefit was granted for the whole period. The statement prepared by the company, to which reference has been made, states that during the nine years 1886–1894, payments were made for nearly 140,000 cases of disablement by sickness and accidents, and in the case of 2948 deaths. We are able, however, to give this information in detail for the last year, 1895, and thus show the average value of the relief given in each case.

Benefits.	Number aided.	Amount of Benefits.	Average.
Disability, accident	8,765	$112,125.00	$12.79
Disability, sickness	23,112	225,072.33	9.74
Death, accident	99	63,000.00	636.36
Death, natural causes	343	191,298.64	557.72
Total	32,319	$591,495.97	...

The relief department of the Pennsylvania Company, which has just been described, relates only to employés on lines of the company east of Pittsburgh. Satisfied with its experiment here, the Pennsylvania Company, July 1, 1889, created a similar department for its western lines. This department is identical in all practical features with that of the older system, the division of employés into classes, their contributions, and the schedules of benefits being precisely the same. Any further description of the system is, therefore, unnecessary.

This latter fund has now been in operation seven years. Its growth in membership from year to year is shown below.

1889–1890	. .	12,168	1893–1894 . .	11,463
1890–1891	. .	11,606	1894–1895 . .	13,619
1891–1892	. .	11,391	1895–1896 . .	15,884
1892–1893	. .	12,462		

The financial operations are shown in the table below in a similar way to that followed in the case of the other departments.

Receipts.	1895–1896.	1889–1896.
Contributions of members . .	$295,962.20	$1,650,007.79
Contributions of company, operating expenses	48,999.86	315,982.13
Contributions of company, extra relief	10,156.75	31,180.15
Contributions of company, deficiencies	. . . .	21,269.35
Interest	4,248.07	16,227.90
Total	$359,366.88	$2,034,667.32
Expenditures.		
Disability benefits, accidents . .	$80,802.90	$434,545.80
Disability benefits, sickness . .	91,596.80	541,778.40
Death benefits, accident . . .	18,500.00	152,716.69
Death benefits, sickness . . .	66,310.00	456,757.78
Company relief	10,156.55	30,155.75
Operating expenses	48,999.86	315,982.13
Total	$316,366.11	$1,932,936.55

In making up this statement, the operations of the relief fund and the so-called surplus fund have been combined. This has been done for the reason that, though the same provision exists, as in the case of the other relief department, that all surpluses found at the end of each three years must be carried to a special fund, this surplus fund is not set aside for a superannuation fund, but is used for the granting of additional relief.

After allowing for existing liabilities, the report for the last year showed a balance on June 30, 1896, of $35,331.72 in the relief, and $37,216.40 in the surplus fund, or total assets for the department of $72,548.12. The report for 1895 states that during the six years that the department had been in operation, payments of benefits had been made on account of 14,359 cases of disability resulting from accidents, 22,129 cases of sickness, and 857 cases of death, of which 224 were due to accidents and 633 to natural causes, to the total amount of $1,315,212.82. The company during this period also granted relief in 235 other cases, to the amount of $20,999.20. The grand total of death and disability cases was, therefore, 37,580, and the amount of the benefits $1,336,212.02.

An analysis of the number aided and the average amount of relief granted is given on the opposite page in greater detail for the last year, 1895–1896.

March 15, 1889, the Chicago, Burlington, and Quincy Company associated itself with four other roads with which its relations were very close, and organized a common employés' relief department. In general, it adopted the Pennsylvania system. Membership is

UNITED STATES.

Benefits.	Number aided.	Amount of Benefits.	Average.
Disability, accident . .	5350	$ 80,802.90	$ 15.10
Disability, sickness . .	7113	91,596.80	12.88
Death, accident	31	18,500.00	596.77
Death, natural causes. .	105	66,310.00	631.52
Total	12,599	$ 257,209.70	. . .

entirely voluntary, and is open to all employés not more than 45 years of age who can pass a satisfactory physical examination.

As in the case of the other relief departments, the funds of the department are derived from the contributions of members, interest on investments and balances, and the contributions of the company. The latter consist of the payment of all operating expenses, and the covering of any deficit that may occur.

The division of members into classes, their contributions and benefits, are shown in the following table: —

Classes.	I.	II.	III.	IV.	V.
Highest monthly pay of members, less than	$ 35.00	$ 55.00	$ 75.00	$ 95.00	$ 95.00 or over
Contributions per month	0.75	1.50	2.25	3.00	3.75
Benefits.					
Accident, first 52 weeks, per day . .	0.50	1.00	1.50	2.00	2.50
Accident, after first 52 weeks, per day	.25	.50	.75	1.00	1.25
Sickness, first 52 weeks, per day . .	.50	1.00	1.50	2.00	2.50
Death	250.00	500.00	750.00	1000.00	1250.00

The Burlington system has likewise incorporated in its scheme provisions whereby members may secure additional death benefits. The maximum death benefit that can be acquired is fixed at the very liberal sum of one, two, three, four, and five thousand dollars for the five classes respectively. The additional contribution required is 30 cents a month for each additional $250 of insurance for members not more than 45 years of age, 45 cents for those over 45 and not more than 60, and 60 cents for those over that age. It will be seen that this is the identical scheme of charges used by the Pennsylvania department. Applicants for additional insurance must pass a satisfactory medical examination.

The Pennsylvania system, whereby accounts are balanced every three years and the deficit is met by the company, has likewise been adopted. If there is a surplus, however, it is not set aside as a superannuation fund, but is carried to the new account. There is thus no provision looking toward the ultimate granting of old-age pensions.

The membership of this department shows the following increase: —

1889 5,027	1893 11,476
1890 9,407	1894 11,768
1891 10,336	1895 13,463
1892 12,283	

The receipts and expenditures of the department during the fiscal year ending December 31, 1895, are shown in the statement immediately following.

Receipts.

Balance on hand	$48,285.00
Contributions of members	267,161.45
Contributions of company, deficiencies	. . . .
Contributions of company, operating expenses	50,699.29
Interest	2,698.07
Total	$368,843.81

Expenditures.

Disability benefits, accident	$68,640.75
Disability benefits, sickness	67,658.63
Death benefits, accident	24,250.00
Death benefits, natural causes	46,814.85
Surgical attendance	9,458.35
Operating expenses	50,699.29
Total	$267,521.87
Surplus	$101,321.94

Since the organization of the department in 1889, the total receipts of the department have amounted to $1,759,582.08, of which $1,475,985.71 was derived from the contributions of members, $5725.89 from interest, and $379,192.42 from the company. Of this latter sum $236,659.48 was contributed to defray operating expenses, and $42,532.94 to meet deficiencies. The total amount paid out was $1,422,922.60 for benefits, and $336,659.48 for operating expenses, thus leaving a balance on hand, as shown in the table of receipts and expenditures, of $101,321.94.

The following statement shows the number of cases

of sickness and accident, and deaths reported during the year, and the average payment on each case.

Disability, accident	3019	$24.91
Disability, sickness	5295	28.65
Death, accident	35	808.33
Death, natural causes . . .	66	668.78

The Philadelphia and Reading Railroad organized a relief service October 30, 1888. Though called an association, it in reality differs little from a department of the company's service. Here again the Pennsylvania system has been followed. Membership is voluntary and is limited to employés not more than 45 years of age who pass the required medical examination. The exception however was made, that all employés then in the service of the company, and joining within the first six months, might become members without regard to their age, if they were physically able to perform the duties of their positions.

The relief afforded by this department consists only in the granting of benefits in case of sickness or accident and death, no provision being made for old-age or invalidity pensions.

The receipts of the association are derived from the contributions of the members, from interest on investments, and from contributions by the company, consisting of an annual payment equal to 10 per cent of that contributed by the members, until the total of these contributions amounts to $1,000,000, after which its contribution will be reduced to 5 per cent of that paid by the employés. The company also pays all operating expenses. Further than this there seems to be no guarantee by the company of the engagements of the association.

The division of members into five classes for the purpose of determining the amount of their contributions and benefits is shown in the following table: —

Classes.	I.	II.	III.	IV.	V. over
Highest monthly pay of members	$40.00	$60.00	$80.00	$100.00	$100.00
Contributions per month	0.75	1.50	2.25	3.00	3.75
Benefits.					
Accident, for 52 weeks, per day	0.50	1.00	1.50	2.00	2.50
Sickness, for 52 weeks, per day [1]	0.40	0.80	1.20	1.60	2.00
Death	250.00	500.00	750.00	1000.00	1250.00
Death, additional payment	100.00	100.00	100.00	100.00	100.00

The additional payment of $100 in case of death is made in accordance with a provision of the constitution, that if during any period of three successive years a surplus should be accumulated, it could be used for the establishment of a superannuation fund or in any other way for the benefit of the members. This case having arisen, it was decided to apply the surplus to increasing death benefits. No provision is therefore made for old-age and invalidity insurance. It will be noticed, also, that provisions allowing the contracting of additional death benefits are also lacking.

[1] Not including first seven days.

The following statements giving the number of members each year, receipts and expenditures for 1895, the last year for which information could be obtained, and the number and average value of benefits granted during the year, will serve to show the operations of this fund, and render any extended comment unnecessary.

1889,	members	13,030		1893,	members	14,748
1890,	"	14,596		1894,	"	15,160
1891,	"	15,035		1895,	"	15,781
1892,	"	15,216				

Receipts.

Surplus on hand	$314,704.89
Contributions of members	222,170.66
Contribution of company, cash	11,087.24
Contribution of company, operating expenses	15,020.81
Interest	14,158.98
Total	$577,142.58

Expenditures.

Disability benefits, accident	$66,480.00
Disability benefits, sickness	53,015.90
Death benefits, accident	31,501.53
Death benefits, natural causes	50,027.42
Expenses, medical examination	8,716.26
Operating expenses	15,020.81
Total	$224,761.92
Surplus on hand	$352,380.66

Benefits.	Number.	Average Value.
Disability, accident	3085	$17.13
Disability, sickness	5602	15.75
Death, accident	59	462.50
Death, natural causes . . .	118	427.35

The important Plant system of railway and steamship lines is the latest company to inaugurate a system of workingmen's insurance. Its department was only created in 1896, and did not go into operation until July 1 of that year. As yet, therefore, it is only possible to describe the system, without giving any information concerning the extent of its operations.

The Baltimore and Ohio system has been more closely patterned after than that of the Pennsylvania Company. Membership is limited to employés not more than 45 years of age who can pass a satisfactory medical examination, but for such it is obligatory. As in the case of the Philadelphia and Reading department exception is made of those employés already in the service of the company, to whom membership is voluntary. Persons can also become members without regard to their ages or physical condition. To such as do not join, however, membership is made obligatory as a condition precedent to promotion.

The work of this department is limited to the provision of free hospital treatment when required, and the granting of benefits in cases of accidents, sickness, and death. The resources of the fund are derived from the contributions of members, interest, and the contribution of the company, consisting of the payment of all operating expenses, a cash contribution of $12,000 per annum, and the meeting of all deficits that may occur.

The division of members into classes made use of by the Baltimore and Ohio has been adopted. Though the scale of benefits is precisely the same, the contributions required, it will be seen, are somewhat higher.

Classes.	I.	II.	III.	IV.	V. over
Highest monthly pay of members	$35.00	$50.00	$75.00	$100.00	$100.00
Contribution per month, class a	1.25	2.50	3.50	4.50	5.50
Contribution per month, class b	1.00	2.00	2.75	3.50	4.25
Benefits.					
Accident, first 26 weeks, per day [1]	.50	1.00	1.50	2.00	2.50
Accident, after first 26 weeks, per day	.25	.50	.75	1.00	1.25
Sickness, first 52 weeks, per day [2]	.50	1.00	1.50	2.00	2.50
Death, accident	500.00	1000.00	1500.00	2000.00	2500.00
Death, natural causes	250.00	500.00	750.00	1000.00	1250.00

In addition to these benefits, the employés enjoy free hospital treatment in the hospitals maintained at different points by the company. Any member under 50 years of age who can pass a satisfactory medical examination can take out additional death benefit insurance to a total maximum amount of regular and additional benefit of 12 times the death benefit

[1] Not including Sundays.
[2] Not including first six working days and Sundays.

granted for death due to natural causes to members of the lowest class, or $3000. The cost of this additional insurance is 25 cents per month for each $250 of insurance.

The employés' relief system established by the Lehigh Valley Railroad, though it is of such a nature as not to merit the designation of an insurance institution, is yet deserving of short mention. The system is briefly this: A fund is accumulated by the voluntary contributions on the part of employés to the amount of one day's wages or less, but in no case to exceed three dollars, as called for by the administration of the fund, to meet demands for the payment of benefits. The company on its part makes a contribution equal in amount to the total contributions of the employés. Benefits are only paid in the case of accidents, and to employés who responded to the last call for contributions. The value of the daily benefit is equal to three-fourths of the amount contributed by the injured member on the last call, during a period not exceeding nine months. In case of death, $50 is immediately paid for funeral expenses, and subsequently to the family of the deceased, during two years, the accident benefit to which the deceased would have been entitled.

This system was created in 1878. Its operations down to 1895 can be seen from the statement on the following page.

The study of the organization and operations of the insurance departments created by railroads that has just been made, shows that a very considerable prog-

Operations of Lehigh Valley Railroad Relief Fund.

Year.	Contributions by Employés.	Contributions by Company.	Total.	Payments to Beneficiaries.	Average Number of Contributors.
1878	$3,953.00	$3,953.00	$7,906.00	$4,857.00	1269
1879	5,234.00	5,234.00	10,468.00	9,875.25	1609
1880	6,586.00	6,586.00	13,172.00	13,836.75	1978
1881	13,786.63	13,786.63	27,573.26	22,502.95	2143
1882	7,539.91	7,539.91	15,079.82	15,972.71	2305
1883	9,298.64	9,298.64	18,597.28	19,965.86	2867
1884	10,112.31	10,112.31	20,224.62	19,489.67	3104
1885	8,360.89	8,360.89	16,721.78	16,334.86	2524
1886	4,248.55	4,248.55	8,497.10	10,618.83	2664
1887	5,335.25	5,335.25	10,670.50	13,706.23	3071
1888	12,235.02	12,235.02	24,470.04	18,592.65	3619
1889	13,915.09	13,915.09	27,830.18	21,036.29	4007
1890	16,611.20	16,611.20	33,222.40	32,391.85	4661
1891	18,568.11	18,568.11	37,136.22	40,903.85	5243
1892	26,266.70	26,266.70	52,533.40	42,678.93	4805
1893	17,873.05	17,873.05	35,746.10	46,358.13	4813
1894	16,890.28	16,890.28	33,780.56	37,082.02	4497
1895	19,607.89	19,607.89	39,215.78	41,053.05	5332
	$216,422.52	$216,422.52	$432,845.04	$426,755.88	
Total payments			426,755.88		
Balance on hand Dec. 31, 1895, . .			$6,089.16		

ress has been accomplished within the past decade. Prior to 1886 there was existent but one relief department, that of the Baltimore and Ohio Company, with about 20,000 members. In the ten years that have succeeded, five other important railway systems have followed suit. The increase in the total number of employés embraced in insurance departments, that has in consequence resulted, is shown in the following statement: —

1886	19,952	1891	86,157
1887	18,744	1892	90,424
1888	19,332	1893	94,252
1889	62,444	1894	92,275
1890	83,468	1895	102,270

On June 30, 1895, there were, according to the report of the Interstate Commerce Commission, 785,034 men in the employ of railways in the United States, and of these it is shown by the table that 102,270 were members of regularly constituted insurance departments. These figures do not include the membership of the Lehigh Valley system, nor of the department of the Plant system of railways, which, if added, would materially increase the total. Though but a fraction of all the employés, about one-seventh, are as yet embraced in insurance departments, the important fact is that so great a progress has been made in one decade. There is, moreover, every reason to believe that the existence of these departments will exert an increasing influence upon other roads, and that the latter will be compelled to establish similar services in order to escape the stigma of indifference to the welfare of their employés.

In a way it may be said that the future of workingmen's insurance in this country is largely involved in these institutions; since, should they be generally adopted by railroads, they could not but exercise a great influence in bringing about the inauguration of similar efforts in other industries. This being so, it is of great moment to determine if the systems that have been adopted are such as can be commended. As would be expected, such an inquiry cannot be answered categorically. The points to be considered relate to: first, the technical excellence of the scheme of organization, and, secondly, the equity with which the relations between the employés and the companies have been adjusted.

Fortunately, as regards the first, we find that the financial requirements of a well-organized scheme of workingmen's insurance have in most respects been met. The financial basis of the departments are perfectly sound, and experience has demonstrated that a very accurate adjustment of contributions to expenditures has been made. In all cases the departments have been fully able to meet their statutory obligations without any modification of the original contract.

The fivefold division of members into classes according to the amount of their wages, perfectly serves the purpose of making the expenses and benefits of insurance proportionate to the abilities and needs of the different classes of employés. Further elasticity has been secured by the provision in the constitutions of practically all of the departments, that members may, if physically sound, be assigned to a higher class than that to which the amount of their wages would entitle them, and by the opportunity offered them to take out additional death-benefit insurance.

The scheme of benefits has been organized on a very liberal scale. The substantial character of the benefits is shown by the following table, which gives the average value of the benefits granted by each department during the year 1895:—

Departments.	Disablement from		Death from	
	Accident.	Sickness.	Accident.	Sickness.
Baltimore and Ohio ...	$ 12.30	$ 15.36	$ 1123.85	$ 589.67
Pennsylvania.......	12.79	9.74	636.36	557.72
Pennsylvania lines, West	15.10	12.88	596.77	631.52
Philadelphia and Reading	17.13	15.75	462.50	427.35
Burlington	24.91	28.65	808.33	668.78

These funds, therefore, make quite adequate provisions against accidents and sickness. As regards old-age and invalidity insurance, but little has as yet been accomplished. Considering the newness of workingmen's insurance in this country, it has probably been a fortunate thing that attempts to provide for this kind of insurance, with the infinitely greater difficulties that they involve, have been postponed until the other kinds of insurance are firmly established. Old-age and invalidity insurance is, however, an important branch of workingmen's insurance, and it is much to be desired that an advance be made in this direction.

In several important respects, however, the technical organization of the scheme is open to criticism. In the adjustment of contributions, the element of ages of members has been largely disregarded. Were the benefits entirely paid by the companies, or were there no life-insurance feature, there would be but little ground for complaint upon this score. But inasmuch as benefits are largely provided for by the contributions of the members themselves, equity demands that the payments of the latter should be graduated according to their ages when joining the department. Under the system adopted, the contributions of all members are uniform. This is a great hardship upon the younger members. This is particularly true in regard to that portion of their contributions which is applied to the death-benefit service, though it is also true to a less degree as regards disability and sickness.

Secondly, in at least three of the departments, a far from adequate protection is accorded to the rights of members leaving the employ of the companies maintaining the funds. The contributions of members are for two distinct purposes: for assistance in case of temporary disability resulting from accident and sickness, and, secondly, for life insurance. Enough has been said in preceding chapters to show that these two kinds of insurance are essentially different in their nature. In regard to the first, the contributions of members only pay for the immediate benefit of assurance of relief in case of disability, and all claim upon the funds of the department ceases with the discontinuance of contribution payments. In the second case, however, contributions are made during a series of years with the object that the contributors' families may ultimately profit from the sacrifices which they have made. Each such payment, therefore, gives rise to a claim against the fund by the payer, that should not be subject to forfeit.

The Baltimore and Ohio and the Plant systems have recognized this obligation, and permit members to continue their natural death-benefit payments after severing their connection with the departments. The Burlington system does the same, with the exception that it limits this right to those who have been in the employ of the company three years and have been members of the relief fund during the year immediately preceding the termination of employment. The two Pennsylvania systems, however, absolutely fail to provide for such continuance of death-benefit payments, and members on leaving the employ of the companies forfeit all right to death benefits. In this respect they violate a fundamental insurance principle, that under no circumstance should acquired rights be forfeited. The existence of these inequitable principles is to be regretted, not only on account of the positive injustice done, but because it cannot but exercise a deterrent effect upon employés becoming members of the funds.

This condition shows the importance of keeping separate insurance operations which are different in their nature. In all of the departments it would be a distinct advance if the two services could be separated, and each member thus be in a position to know exactly how much he pays for disability and how much for death benefits.

As regards the great advantages that the employés enjoy through membership in these funds, over and above those which any private insurance company could offer them, there cannot be two opinions. These advantages have been so clearly set forth in the sixth annual report of the Burlington Relief Department that the paragraphs relating to this subject are here introduced *in extenso*. The facts there shown are equally true of the other departments.

"The best accident insurance companies," the report reads, "report that from 40 to 50 per cent of their premiums is consumed in operating expenses. The operating expenses of our relief department, as previously given, are less than 24 per cent of the contributions of members. It cannot be assumed that the relief department could be operated independently of the railroad companies more cheaply than the best accident insurance companies, so that the operating expenses represent but about one-half the normal cost of operating. Leaving out of consideration that part of the cost of operating which has been given by the railroad companies without charge, and leaving out of consideration also the liability existing December 31, 1894, let us see what the result would have been if the operating expenses had been paid from the contributions of members. The contributions from members, with interest, amounted to $1,211,852.08; if we deduct the operating expenses, $285,960.19, there is left available for the payment of benefits $925,891.89. If we further assume that the benefits paid on account of sickness and death from sickness, $552,842.02, were paid entirely from the contributions of members, there would be left available for the payment of accident benefits $373,049.87, whereas the actual payments on account of disability and death from accident were $653,258.00 ; so that there would have been a deficiency of $280,208.13. This deficiency, plus the balance on hand in all relief funds having a balance December 31, 1894, $48,285.00, represents the amount paid by the railroad companies from their own funds, namely, $328,493.13. It makes no essential difference as to what the railroad companies have done for the maintenance of the relief department, whether we say that they have contributed the operating expenses, $285,960.19, and have made up deficiencies of $42,532.94, amounting together to $328,493.13, or whether we say that they have made up a deficiency of $280,208.13 in accident benefits and have contributed in addition $48,285.00, which remains on hand as an unexpended balance, amounting together to $328,493.13, which is more than one-half the total amount paid for accident benefits.

"The most valuable part of the contribution of the railroad companies to the relief department is their guarantee of the payment of benefits as they become due. It furnishes to the association the essential elements of security, stability, and prompt payment, and obviates the necessity of a provision for assessments on the members in addition to fixed rates on the establishment of much higher fixed rates."

But it is not sufficient to show that the railroad employés find membership in these departments of greater advantage than that in an ordinary accident insurance company. That part of the work of the departments that relates to insurance against accidents should be almost, if not wholly, at the expense of the employers. This is an opinion which to-day finds scarcely an opposing voice in Europe. As we have pointed out elsewhere in our work, the remuneration of victims of accidents should be considered a normal item in the cost of operation of any industry.

Accidents are inevitable, and their burden should be borne by the employers, who determine the working conditions, rather than by the men. In failing to do this, the roads are distinctly behind public opinion upon the question. An analysis of the receipts and expenditures of the different departments shows that, apart from operating expenses and those surpluses carried to a superannuation fund, the departments are largely supported by the men themselves.

Moreover, the charge that these departments are but inadequately supported by the roads is not the only criticism that can be directed against them in this respect. Even the little contribution that they do make is more than offset by the fact that the companies have used these departments to protect themselves against suits for damages on the part of their employés. The regulations of all of the departments stipulate that members, or their beneficiaries, must elect, whether they will sue the companies for damages on account of the injuries they have received, or accept the benefits of the relief fund. If they choose the former, they thereby forfeit all claim to the latter, and the acceptance of the latter acts as a renunciation of all legal claims they may have against the companies. Mr. Johnson, in his paper, states that he believes this to be only just. From this position we must absolutely dissent. The departments are largely supported by the members themselves, and the receipt of benefits in return should in no way abridge their legal rights. The provision that the benefits, as far as they are paid from contributions made by the roads, should be considered as a part payment of any damages that might be recovered against the company might possibly be defended, but that the act of bringing suit should work a forfeiture of acquired rights is thoroughly unmoral and contrary to public policy. The men have made payments for a particular purpose. That to cancel their rights is an injustice, it would seem must be beyond question.

Finally, the objection has been raised against these departments that they have been organized by the roads in order better to control their employés, to prevent their striking, and to undermine the influence of their organizations. This is a question the discussion of which does not fall within the scope of our work. It is one, moreover, upon which it would be quite impossible for us to pass judgment. There is no doubt that this consideration, as well as that of protecting the roads against damage suits, did enter to some extent in the motives of those organizing the departments. It would be more than unfair, however, to maintain that the roads are not also actuated by the honest desire to better the conditions of their employés.

In thus subjecting these departments to a more severe criticism than they have in general received, we do not want to be understood as condemning them. They have led the way in inaugurating workingmen's insurance in this country, and they are proving an undoubted benefit to the workingmen. It is only regretted that the companies, while doing so much for the cause of workingmen's insurance, should have thus thrown themselves open to the accusation of having sought their own selfish interests, and it is hoped that, as the true nature and objects of workingmen's insurance become better known, the system of these departments will be improved along the lines that have been suggested.

Insurance Work of Labor Organizations. — No comprehensive investigation has yet been made of the relief work performed by labor organizations in the United States. Such an inquiry could be undertaken only by an official bureau or by an individual possessing exceptional advantages. The character of their work, however, can be shown by describing the insurance features of a number of typical organizations. A selection has therefore been made of the three orders, the "United Brotherhood of Carpenters and Joiners of America," the "Cigarmakers' International Union of America," and the "Brotherhood of Locomotive Firemen."

The Cigarmakers' International Union is one of the strongest and best-organized labor organizations in the United States. It was created in 1864. In 1896 it had 28,700 members. Its constitution provides for five classes of insurance benefits; viz. strike, sick or disability, death, out-of-work, and travelling benefits. Of these, those of strike, travelling, and out-of-work do not enter strictly within the scope of workingmen's insurance as treated in this work. The death benefits are determined according to the length of time that the deceased had been members of the union. Upon the death of a member, there is paid to his widow or heirs the sum of either $50, $200, $350, or $550, according to whether he had been a member 1, 5, 10, or 15 years. In addition there is paid to the member of two years' standing the sum of $40 upon the death of his wife or widowed mother dependent upon him for support.

The sick or disability benefit consists of the payment to members of at least one year's standing of $5 per week in case of sickness lasting over a week, for a period not exceeding 13 weeks in any one year. In all cases no benefit is paid where the death or sickness was the result of intemperance, debauchery, or other immoral conduct.

BENEFITS GRANTED BY THE CIGARMAKERS' INTERNATIONAL UNION OF AMERICA, 1879–1895.

Year.	Strike Benefit.	Sick Benefit.	Death Benefit.	Travelling Benefit.	Out-of-Work Benefit.
1879 ..	$ 3,668.23	....	....	....	....
1880 ..	4,950.86	....	....	$ 2,808.15	....
1881 ..	21,797.68	$ 3,987.73	$ 75.00	12,747.09	....
1882 ..	44,850.41	17,145.29	1,674.25	20,886.64	....
1883 ..	27,812.13	22,250.56	2,690.00	37,135.20	....
1884 ..	143,547.86	31,551.50	3,920.00	39,632.08	....
1885 ..	61,087.28	29,379.89	4,214.00	26,683.54	....
1886 ..	54,402.61	42,225.59	4,820.00	31,835.71	....
1887 ..	13,871.62	63,900.88	8,850.00	49,281.04	....
1888 ..	45,303.62	58,324.19	21,319.75	42,894.75	....
1889 ..	5,202.52	59,519.94	19,175.50	43,540.44	....
1890 ..	18,414.27	64,660.74	26,043.00	37,914.72	$ 22,760.50
1891 ..	83,531.78	87,472.97	38,068.85	53,535.78	21,223.50
1892 ..	37,477.60	89,906.30	44,701.97	47,732.47	17,460.75
1893 ..	18,228.15	104,391.83	49,458.33	60,475.11	39,402.75
1894 ..	44,966.76	106,758.87	62,159.77	42,154.17	174,517.25
1895 ..	44,039.06	112,567.06	66,725.98	41,657.16	166,377.25
Total .	$ 623,151.44	$ 894,542.84	$ 353,894.90	$ 590,414.00	$ 491,742.00

The character and importance of the relief afforded to members is shown in the preceding table, which gives the expenditures for benefits of all kinds during the years 1879 to 1895.

As the various benefits are all paid from the same general fund, it is impossible to make any accurate analysis of the cost of insurance. The secretary of the order, however, in his annual report for the year 1895, states that the cost per member for benefits during the year was $14.04; of which $4.05½ was for sick benefits, $1.58½ for strike, $5.99½ for out-of-work, and $2.40½ for death benefits. The year 1895 was a panic year. The same benefits for 1892, which was a normal year, were $3.37 for sick, $1.40½ for strike, $0.65 for out-of-work, and $1.67½ for death, or a total of $7.11. It is interesting to contrast the value of the benefits granted with the dues paid by members. During the five years 1891 to 1895, the average dues paid by members, not including special assessments, was $12.15. The total average cost of benefits per member for the same period was $10.57. This shows to how large an extent the Cigarmakers' Union is a beneficial or insurance organization.

The United Brotherhood of Carpenters and Joiners of America also ranks as one of the strong labor unions of America. It was established in 1881, and in 1894 had 33,917 members in good standing, that is, members whose dues were not three months in arrears. The United Brotherhood provides for death and invalidity benefits, and leaves to the individual lodges the privilege of creating sick insurance funds if they desire to do so. The death benefit consists of the payment of $100 on the death of members of six months' standing, and of $200 if the deceased has been a member one year or more. In case of total disability the members of one year's standing receive $100; those of two years', $200; those of three years', $300, and those of five years' standing, $400. There is also paid a benefit of $25 to defray burial expenses on the death of the wife of a member of six months' membership, and $50 of one of one year's standing. Persons desiring to become benefit members must be not more than 50 years old and pass a satisfactory medical examination. No specific contribution is required for the maintenance of the benefit department. All contributions go into a general fund which is devoted to all the purposes of the order. The table on the following page shows the membership of the union, and the number and amount of benefits paid since the organization of the union in 1881 to 1894.

In 13 years, therefore, the order has paid 2888 claims for benefits, amounting to $353,520.60. During that period the secretary reports that $685,434.00 was expended by the local branches for sick benefits to their members. The general secretary, in his biennial report for 1891–1892, makes an analysis of the figures for those two years that shows in greater detail the character of the relief granted. During the two years, 994 claims, amounting to $117,346, were paid. Of these 484 were for death benefits, 487 for benefits paid on the death of members' wives, and 23 for disability. Estimating on the average member-

MEMBERSHIP, AND BENEFITS GRANTED BY THE UNITED BROTHERHOOD OF CARPENTERS AND JOINERS OF AMERICA, 1881 TO 1894.

	Members.	Number of Benefits.	Amount of Benefits.
1881	2,042	...	...
1882	3,780	...	...
1883	3,293	6	$ 1,500.00
1884	4,364	9	2,250.00
1885	5,789	36	5,700.00
1886	21,423	54	9,200.00
1887	25,466	139	16,275.16
1888	28,416	172	18,750.00
1889	31,494	224	25,575.00
1890	53,769	254	32,267.49
1891	56,937	374	44,732.65
1892	51,313	620	72,613.35
1893	54,121	538	64,684.45
1894	33,917	462	59,972.50
Total	...	2888	$ 353,520.60

ship for the years 1889 and 1890, the cost of the benefit system was 80 cents per member per year, or 6¾ cents per month. For the year closing June 30, 1891, the cost was 8¼ cents per month, and for 1892, 11½ cents or $1.37 per year.

The Brotherhood of Locomotive Firemen was organized in 1873. With the exception of the year 1893, when the number of railroad employés fell off in consequence of the industrial depression, it has increased steadily in membership. In 1881 it numbered 2998 members; in 1885, 14,694; in 1890, 18,637, and in 1896, 22,461. The present constitution of the order, as amended in 1894, makes provision for three grades of life insurance, $500, $1000, and $1500, from which each member can make a choice. It is obligatory upon all members upon joining the union, if they pass a satisfactory physical examination, to contract for one of these grades of insurance. These sums are paid to the heirs of deceased members no matter what the cause of the death, or to the members themselves in case of total disability to follow their profession. By total disability is meant total blindness, loss of hand or foot, or disability caused by consumption, Bright's disease, or paralysis.

To provide for this insurance, each member belonging to the beneficial department is assessed $0.75, $1.50, or $2.00, according to the grade of insurance assumed, as often as it is necessary to meet the obligations of the fund. The table (p. 324) shows the number and amount of benefits paid each year since 1880.

This single order has, therefore, paid out during a period of 16 years a total of $3,836,621.20 in death and invalidity benefits. The Brotherhood of Locomotive Engineers has paid in similar benefits the sum of $5,771,214.61. The local lodges are permitted to organize systems of sick insurance if they desire to do so.

An examination of the benefit features of these three orders affords sufficient information to enable us to study the main feature of workingmen's insurance as practised by labor organizations in the

BENEFITS GRANTED BY THE BROTHERHOOD OF LOCOMOTIVE FIREMEN, 1880–1881 TO 1895–1896.

Year.	Number of Benefits.	Amount.
1880–1881	25	$12,104.00
1881–1882	30	23,937.00
1882–1883	61	55,000.00
1883–1884	86	77,035.00
1884–1885	122	149,960.00
1885–1886	146	227,900.00
1886–1887	163	225,166.50
1887–1888	145	217,500.00
1888–1889	186	280,150.00
1889–1890	165	247,500.00
1890–1891	209	359,000.00
1891–1892	270	399,250.00
1892–1893	...	476,750.00
1893–1894	...	435,467.90
1894–1895	...	333,816.50
1895–1896	...	316,084.30

United States. The first point that is evident from this account is that labor unions, while making substantial provision for the relief of members, have by no means provided industrial insurance of the most desirable order. They have not as yet progressed beyond the "benefit-giving" stage. Little attempt is made to establish a scientific relationship between the contributions demanded and the probability of charges resulting from sickness or death. The amount of benefits is determined solely according to the general resources of the union. As regards that important branch of workingmen's insurance that relates to old age, the labor unions do practically nothing, and but few make any adequate provision against disability. The best-organized branch of insurance is probably that of insurance against sickness. In the majority of cases sick relief has been left to the local unions. This is strictly in line with the best ideas of insurance, which call for the centralization of old-age and invalidity insurance, and the localization, as far as possible, of insurance against sickness.

It is in those branches of insurance where definite engagements are made to pay certain benefits or pensions in the future, that defects in the financial basis of systems become apparent. It is extremely fortunate that the unions have made no attempt to provide for old-age pensions; for, with the existing knowledge on the subject, nothing but disaster could have resulted. An inspection of the operations of the unions that have been considered will show that even in the much simpler operations of giving death benefits, the unions have seen their expenses for this purpose increase more rapidly than receipts; and, unless checked, it would seem that disaster or partial failure to meet obligations is inevitable. In the case of the Cigarmakers' Union, for example, expenditures for death benefits have advanced in the 15 years, 1881 to 1895, from \$75.00 to \$66,725.98, an increase altogether out of proportion to the increase in membership. This result is inevitable as a union grows older, unless contributions are rigidly fixed according to the ages at which members join the order. The period has now been reached when the new and younger members must pay for the insurance of their older companions. Even should the accession of new members be sufficient to accomplish this, it is nevertheless an injustice to make present members defray expenses incurred in the past. From the standpoint of the union itself, the greatest damage results from the fact that the increased contributions demanded, if they do not cause local unions to drop out, at least deter new members from joining. The experience of the carpenters and joiners is an actual demonstration of this result. It has been seen that the cost of the benefit system, which in 1889 and 1890 was but 80 cents per member, rose in 1891 to 99 cents and in 1892 to $1.37. As the result of this increase, regular dues have been altogether insufficient, and it has been necessary to resort to special assessments. Concerning the result of one of these assessments, the secretary wrote in his report: "The levying of that assessment of 25 cents, imperatively necessary and small as it was, caused considerable dissatisfaction. Many of the locals were suffering at the time from impoverished finances, owing to heavy drains on them for payment of local sick benefits. Hence the general executive board refrained from levying this assessment until no other course was left them. And when it was levied, it caused quite a number of unions to break up and lapse. Until we have a system of higher dues, this condition of affairs is apt to occur."

Generally, then, the result of our investigation of the insurance work of labor organizations is that, though the efforts on the part of the orders in the past to assist their members, through the payment of death benefits and relief in the case of sickness, cannot be too highly commended, the time has come when these operations should be placed upon a securer footing.

The first and most imperative reform called for is that the contributions for insurance should be kept rigorously distinct from those for the general purposes of the order. Especially should they be kept separate from those for the strike fund. It is always of the greatest importance that members of an insurance institution should know exactly the amount of the benefits to which they are entitled, and how much they are paying for them. Secondly, the different kinds of insurance should be kept separate. The practice of leaving sick insurance to the local branches should become universal. Thirdly, the granting of death and invalidity benefits should be put upon a better mathematical basis. To do this, contributions should be made to vary according to the ages of the members on joining the order, and, finally, it should be provided that acquired rights can never be forfeited; that, if at any time the payment of dues is arrested, the payments that have been made shall be converted into a paid-up policy, or some other equitable adjustment arranged.

Employers' Liability. — In regard to the question of the provision of old-age pensions, or a national system of sick insurance for the benefit of the laboring classes, it can possibly be alleged, with considerable show of reason, that conditions in the United States are so different from what they are in Europe, that the action of the latter furnishes but an indifferent guide as to what should be done here. The same, however, cannot be claimed in the case of accidents to labor. Here, on the contrary, the necessities for measures of reform are even more pressing than in Europe. Accidents are, if anything, more frequent, and the demand that the workingmen who are injured should be indemnified by their employers is equally imperative.

Step by step we have seen almost all of the European nations abandon the position that employés have no claim for damages except when they can prove negligence on the part of their employers, in favor of the one where their compensation by the employers should be compulsory in all cases except where they are wilfully and seriously at fault. The indemnification of injured workingmen has thus been made one of the normal items in the cost of operation, to be taken account of as any other charge. At the same time, the effort to enforce this system through the law courts has been abandoned, and the position taken that adequate and prompt compensation can only be secured where the amount of the compensation is determined in advance by a fixed scale of indemnities. It is only as thus organized, moreover, that employers are able to take account of the risks that they run, and provide against them by means of insurance.

While this movement has been going on in Europe, the United States has stood practically still. Scarcely a beginning has been made towards modifying the unjust provisions of the old common law. It is quite beyond our field to attempt any description of the state of the law regarding employers' liability in the United States at the present time. The subject is one of great complexity, and here we are concerned with the principle rather than the details of legislation. It is sufficient to say that the United States are in the position where the injustice of the common law in respect to this question is more or less recognized, and attempts are being made to bring about a reform through legislation and judicial decisions. The states are thus still in that primitive stage where a solution is sought in the timid modification of the doctrine of common employment, of what constitutes negligence, and other subtilities of the law. They are thus attempting a method of reform long since abandoned by European nations as one which not only does not do justice to the workingman, but is thoroughly inadequate to solve the difficulties of the question. It would be difficult to think of another field of social or legal reform in which the United States is so far behind other nations.

The most depressing feature of the situation lies in the fact, that the very principles involved in this gradual evolution from the limited liability of employers to that of the compulsory indemnification by them of practically all injured employés, are as yet not even comprehended in the United States. Evidently it is useless to expect any decided legislation until the people generally are made to see the justness and correctness of the position for which we are contending, and which has so recently been assumed by Great Britain. The first step, therefore, consists in the education of public opinion. This once accomplished, legislation will inevitably follow.

CONCLUSION.

We have now, in a measure, covered the field marked out in undertaking this study. After a preliminary examination of the various kinds of workingmen's insurance, and the chief methods by which its provision can be accomplished, we have considered the history and present condition of the problem in each of the great countries of Europe and in the United States. In so doing we have studied in detail both the organization and practical operations of the leading examples of every important type of institution that has been created in any country for the insurance of workingmen. It now remains to pass in review the whole field, to contrast, in a measure, the various policies that have been pursued, and to indicate some of the ways in which this rich experience can be of assistance in any attempts that may be made in this country to further similar movements.

The history of workingmen's insurance, we have seen, presents three great movements, which, though for the most part operating independently, yet are all directed toward the same end.

First and foremost, there is that general movement which is taking place in practically every country, the object of which is the transformation of the old mutual-aid and charitable relief societies into scientific insurance organizations. Mutual-aid societies are ancient institutions. True insurance, as applied to the contingencies we are considering, is of recent development. The progress of this evolution from one form to the other constitutes the real history of the question. Workingmen's insurance thus, as almost all measures of social reform, is one which has had to pass through long periods of change, during which its features have been gradually perfected. To neglect this movement, and consider only the modern proposals for state insurance, would be to omit the most significant feature that our subject has to present. The benefits of organized charity have been much and justly vaunted. The powerful co-operation that improved methods of workingmen's insurance lends to this effort to put relief upon a proper basis, is not likely to be overestimated.

The second movement is the direct consequence of the evolution of industrial methods, by which large numbers of workingmen are grouped under the same roof, or employed in the same undertaking, and consists in the profound change that has taken place in public sentiment regarding the obligation of employers to indemnify their employés for accidents received by them while in their service. We have seen that this position has only been reached after a hard struggle. Efforts at first assumed the form of increasing the liability of employers, by restricting the doctrine of common employment, and of bettering the position of employés as litigants in various ways. It was only after experience had demonstrated that this gave rise to intolerable litigation, and that practically the employés were but slightly benefited, that the system of compulsory compensation was accepted, with the equally important corollary, that the value of the indemnities should be fixed in advance. Whether the employers should be compelled to insure themselves against this risk in certain institutions, or be left a free choice as to the manner in which they would provide for this extra charge, is a matter of less importance. This movement, as far as Europe is concerned, may almost be said to be completed. That it will sooner or later triumph in America is one of the certainties of the future.

Thirdly, there is the recent rapid development of the idea of compulsory insurance. Undoubtedly, the most important question to be answered at the present time in regard to the general problem of workingmen's insurance, relates to this last movement. Whatever our attitude on this question may be, we must recognize that the policy of compulsory insurance has rapidly gained ground in recent years. Germany enacted her first compulsory insurance law in 1883. Not only has she persistently continued the elaboration of her system, but other nations have followed suit. Austria and Norway have no less unreservedly accepted the policy of compulsion. In France, where the principle of obligatory insurance has been fought with the greatest determination, a law has been passed providing for the compulsory insurance of miners, and measures have been repeatedly accepted by one or the other legislative branch for the compulsory insurance of workingmen generally against accidents. The legislative history of these proposals shows how steadily the people have been converted to this principle. In Italy, when the first proposal for a general system of workingmen's insurance was introduced in 1880, the idea of compulsion was summarily and almost unanimously rejected. Step by step, however, this position had been abandoned, until the more recent propositions embody this principle. In Switzerland, the people, through the referendum, pronounced overwhelmingly in favor of compulsion in some form or other. In England itself, that stronghold of individualism, the compensation of injured workingmen by their employers is now obligatory, and measures looking toward compulsory, or at least liberally state-aided, insurance have received serious consideration and the endorsement of at least one of the great political parties. State-encouraged, state-aided, or state-compelled insurance must therefore be accepted as the definitely adopted policy of European nations.

Turning now to the actual problems involved in the organization of systems of workingmen's insurance, we have seen that its different branches are essentially different in character, and consequently require quite different measures to meet the special difficulties of each. The consequence of this dissimilarity is that an independent organization should be provided for each one. This does not mean that all cannot be under the administration of one department; but that, if a scientific organization is to be obtained and justice done as between the different industries and individuals, the accounts, that is, contributions and expenditures, of each, must be kept rigidly distinct. It is hardly necessary to repeat in detail the reasons for this policy. They have been constantly adverted to throughout this work. Of these points, the chief, however, is the different policy that should be followed regarding the extent to which insurance should be centralized in general institutions or decentralized in more or less independent local societies. This point must be determined for each branch of insurance separately. In general, it may be said that the provision of old-age insurance requires the greatest centralization, that of accidents the next, while insurance against sickness should be accomplished, as far as possible, through small independent societies. This is due because, in the first two, provision is made for the payment of pensions, and risks consequently have to be calculated for a great many years in advance. Stability, therefore, can only be obtained when large numbers are insured in organizations, the permanency of which is beyond question. In the third case there is no such necessity: on the other hand, it is only by having very small and local societies that the evils of simulation and malingering can be kept in check.

These elementary principles have been recognized wherever a system of compulsory insurance has been either adopted or proposed. In Germany, for example, old-age insurance is provided for through central insurance institutions created in each of the 31 great divisions of the country; accident insurance through 64 institutions, each representing a group of industries; while sick insurance is accomplished through over 22,000 financially independent societies. In Austria an almost exactly similar system has been created for sick insurance. For insurance against accidents, however, the radically different policy has been pursued of providing for insurance through seven central institutions organized according to territorial divisions, instead of according to industries. Account is then taken of the different risk of accidents in different industries by the construction of a table of trade risks, which determines the contributions of employers in different industries. This feature constitutes one of the essential differences between the German and Austrian systems, and the relative merits of each kind of organization have been subjected to a great deal of discussion.

A second important point, as regards organization, is that of the financial system employed in making provision for the payment of pensions. In Germany, each year is charged with the payments made during its course, while in Austria each year is charged with the liabilities incurred. The differences in these two systems have already been fully described. There can be no doubt that the system of making each year responsible for all charges resulting from accidents occurring during it is theoretically the more scientific method. It not only corresponds to the idea of justice, but makes it possible to organize the system upon a more accurate mathematical basis. Under the German system, new employers have to contribute for the payment of indemnities on account of accidents incurred before they had even begun business. Again, should the membership of an institution decrease, the remaining members would have to bear the burden of charges created by a larger number of persons. It should be stated, however, that Germany has, in great measure, prevented any grave injustice by the creation during the early years of substantial reserve funds, the purpose of which is to make face against increasing charges. Advocates of the latter system, moreover, claim that it has substantial advantages through the fact that the employers of labor were not suddenly subjected to a new and heavy expense, and that time was thus given to them to accustom themselves to the new charges; and, secondly, that the necessity of withdrawing from industry large sums of money for investment in the special pension funds was obviated. After all is said, however, the Austrian system cannot but be considered as the preferable practice.

The grouping of the different kinds of insurance institutions which have been organized in the various countries into certain general classes has been one of our efforts. Diverse as they are, our study has shown us that they can be referred to a few types, the essential differences between which lie in the extent to which the state exercises a control or supervision over their operations. We will devote a few words to the summing up of the peculiarities of each.

First in this scheme of classification, we have the system of compulsory state insurance. In its introduction the two policies have been pursued of, either creating a general system, as has been done by Germany and Austria, or of providing for the insurance of a particular class of workingmen, as has been done by Belgium, France, and Roumania. If the desirability of compulsory insurance is once accepted, the first method is, of course, the more thoroughgoing and courageous. The difficulties of creating such a system, however, are enormous. To a country making the first step in the execution of this policy, the method of treating each industry separately simplifies matters greatly. In the case of insurance against accidents, but one trade risk has to be calculated; the persons insured receive about the same scale of wages, thus permitting a simple scheme of premiums and benefits; and in general the difficulties of administration are reduced to a minimum. With the best of preparation it is impossible accurately to predict future charges. The first few years of any system must be experimental in character. The policy of providing for a single homogeneous class of workingmen thus permits this experiment to be made upon a small scale, and under the most advantageous conditions. With the experience thus gained, the work of gradually extending the system to other classes can be pursued with far greater certainty and ease. Thus, if we should suppose that the United States became convinced of the desirability of compulsory insurance, the preferable line of action would be, first, to provide for the insurance of railway employés, then of miners, and only gradually to extend the system to other classes of the working population.

Finally, it is important to notice the manner in which the principle of compulsion is applied. We speak of the compulsory insurance of workingmen, as if the workingmen were compelled to insure themselves. In point of fact this is not the case at all. The obligation has in all cases been put upon the employer and not the employé. The more correct way to speak of the system is, therefore, the compulsory insurance of workingmen by their employers. The insurance is in all cases done by the latter, though they are permitted, in certain cases, partially to recoup themselves by retaining a portion of the wages of their employés. It is upon them that falls all the burden of keeping records of the amount paid out in wages, of notifying the insurance institutions of cases of accidents, invalidity, etc. The workingmen in reality do scarcely anything, except submit to the deduction that is made from their wages. It is difficult to see how the law could be enforced in any other way; how the members could, otherwise, either be compelled to affiliate with the insurance institutions, or their contributions afterwards collected. The system of deducting contributions from wages, moreover, possesses the great advantage of presenting this obligation so that its burden is met in the easiest way, and in making the determination of the relative contributions of the employers and employés a simple matter.

We have, it is hoped, gained a general idea of the mechanism of compulsory insurance. Let us now attempt to contrast the advantages and disadvantages that are claimed for and alleged against it. The great argument for compulsory insurance is, not that it is the best form of insurance, but that it is the only method by which all workingmen can be reached. Voluntary insurance, it is said, may be the desirable form, but it cannot reach more than a small proportion of the working classes. No one has put this argument more forcibly than Professor Schaeffle. "Experience," he says, "has everywhere demonstrated that the great mass of those workingmen who are poorly off will not voluntarily insure themselves. Furthermore, the great majority of those who would like to do so cannot on account of the smallness of their earnings. In other words, it is exactly that class which is most in need of insurance that either will not, or cannot, avail themselves of this device. This is the fundamental weakness of voluntary insurance. It fails to reach the class most in need of it. Obligatory insurance, and obligatory insurance alone, by making the support of insurance an indispensable item of the family budget, will act upon wages in such a way as to raise its standard, which increased expenditure will be shifted upon the cost of production and prices, and thus made a general industrial condition to be borne without any appreciable extra hardship."

Though we cannot but admit the force of this argument, a partial reply to it can be made. No one can follow the history of the movement for workingmen's insurance in each country, as traced in the preceding chapters, without being struck with the fact that really desirable forms of workingmen's insurance institutions are of comparatively recent creation. Voluntary insurance in the past has been hopelessly hampered by defective forms of organization. We are but entering upon the period of scientific insurance against sickness, accidents, and old age. It is thus too early to say that voluntary efforts cannot possibly solve the problem. In the short period that has elapsed, really remarkable results have been accomplished, and there is every reason to believe that the movement will continue to advance with increasing strength. A most momentous change has also taken place in regard to the conception of the obligation of employers for accidents to their employés; and we see such organizations as the national associations of iron and steel manufacturers and textile-mill owners of France voluntarily organizing at their own expense institutions for the insurance of their workingmen against accidents, and initiating and contributing liberally toward similar institutions for their insurance against old age and invalidity. Other forces are also working toward this end. The concentration of industries into large establishments will facilitate this greatly. The growth in importance and strength of labor organizations is practically certain, and, with this growth, will be developed organizations admirably adapted to certain classes of insurance.

It is not on this ground, however, that the introduction of compulsory insurance is chiefly resisted. It is generally admitted that voluntary efforts cannot hope to provide as complete a system as legal compulsion. The criticism that is made, is that the increased efficiency of compulsory insurance is gained at too great a cost. The arguments against it can briefly be summed up as follows: —

Compulsory insurance is class legislation, in that it places the laboring or wage-receiving classes under a special régime, and in a way makes them the wards of the nation; it is socialistic; it lessens the quality of self-help and reliance in the individual, by substituting state aid for personal economy; it necessitates the creation of a vast bureaucratic system; it is inelastic, and cannot adjust itself to the varying needs of particular industries and localities; it is conducive to fraud upon an enormous scale, as it is impossible to guard against imposition, feigned illness, etc.; the expense of administration is disproportionate to the benefits conferred; it leads to carelessness, and has caused the number of accidents rapidly to increase; and, finally, it imposes upon industry a burden that places it at a disadvantage in foreign competition.

Certain of these objections, it will be seen, are fundamental. They are not directed against any particular disadvantage of the system, but assert that the policy itself is based upon a destructive theory of the powers of the state. Such are the objections that compulsory insurance is socialistic, class legislation, and relates to duties which should be left to private efforts. The others relate to the practical difficulties with which the organization and administration of such a system has to contend.

The first of these involves a consideration of the problem of the proper sphere of the state, the determination of which constitutes the great political question of the present time. Compulsory insurance is but one of the ways in which this question has arisen as a practical problem. It is manifestly impracticable for us to attempt any general consideration of this question. That compulsory insurance does mean an enormous extension of the power of the state, there can be no doubt. Whether this is theoretically desirable or not, must be determined by each one according to his position in regard to the general principles of state action. Personally, we do not believe that this is a question that can be settled *a priori*, as is done by Mr. Spencer or the socialists. We believe that there are many things that the state can do better than the individual, and others that the individual can do better. Each question, therefore, should be decided upon its own peculiar merits.

The second class of objections relate directly to the disadvantages of compulsory insurance. They are ones upon which it is by no means an easy matter to pass judgment. Both the German and Austrian insurance officials are forced to acknowledge that the administration of their systems has developed a number of undesirable features. Litigation over the adjustment of benefits and contributions has far exceeded expectations. The burden of administrative detail is enormous. The problem of keeping in check fraud and simulation of illness has not as yet received a solution. Finally, the workingmen themselves are not wholly satisfied with the system that has been created for their benefit. Mr. Brooks' report to the Department of Labor on Compulsory Insurance in Germany contains a chapter on public opinion and state insurance, that presents in the most judicial way the objections that the Germans themselves find against their system. The perusal of this chapter, as well as the current criticism contained in the periodical press, exhibits one important fact. Numerous and, in general, as well founded as are these criticisms, the principle itself of compulsory insurance is generally accepted. Important modifications in the system are urged, but there is no real effort looking toward its abandonment. The complaints that are made are almost wholly directed to the trouble of complying with the provisions of the law. Red tape, vexatious requirements, the arbitrary action of officials, unjust discrimination, the inconvenience of being transferred from one class to another, the trouble of "sticking in" stamps, of keeping accounts, of making reports, etc., are samples of the objections that are urged. The reply that is made to these criticisms is that it is impossible to construct in advance a complicated system of insurance. The first organization must necessarily be in some degree experimental; and it is unfair to judge a system until time has been given to perfect it as defects are shown by practical experience. To the writer it would seem that these difficulties have largely been due to the fact that too much has been attempted at once. The general insurance of miners in Belgium has given rise to no such objections. Insurance has there worked with almost no friction, and the expenses of administration have been reduced to a minimum. Had the policy been pursued of providing for the insurance of workingmen in each industry in turn, time would have been given to the working classes and employers gradually to accustom themselves to the system; and difficulties as they arose could have been more easily met.

Finally, in attempting to reach a conclusion upon this matter, it should be remembered that each kind of insurance should be considered separately. Arguments and criticisms that can justly be made in reference to one kind have no application as regards the others. Thus, of the three, the arguments in favor of compulsion are much stronger in the case of insurance against accidents. The necessity for a state institution, however, is much greater in the case of old-age insurance. As regards insurance against sickness, nothing short of absolute necessity would seem to warrant the intervention of the state. The report addressed by the federal council of Switzerland to the federal assembly in 1889, to which reference has been made, lays down this distinction with exceptional clearness and accuracy. Though arguing for state insurance against accidents, it says:—

"It should be noted, however, that the organization of insurance against sickness should have quite a different character from that of insurance against accidents. As far as possible, insurance against sickness should not be provided by the state, but should continue to repose on private associations now in existence, the numerous sick funds, etc. The great and disastrous abuses that insurance against sickness by the state gives rise to, demands a decentralization as complete as possible, because it is only through a control exercised directly, and within a limited circle, that simulation can be guarded against. Insurance against sickness ought to preserve its private character, because it will be less bureaucratic, possesses a less complicated legislative machinery, and is less costly to the country. It goes without saying, however, that the state should make general regulations concerning the operation of the societies. It should determine to what point slight accidents should be assimilated with cases of sickness, and be provided for by these funds; in other words, to make the system of insurance against sickness supplement that of insurance against accidents, so that the two will together cover the whole field."

Turning now to the consideration of state but voluntary insurance institutions, we are confronted with quite a different problem. The arguments which can be made against compulsory insurance are here totally inapplicable. The theory of the intervention of the state in this way is exactly analogous to that of its action in creating a postal savings bank. In creating an insurance bank of its own, the state in no way contravenes the principles of self-help and self-reliance. On the other hand, it can serve as a useful agent in stimulating these qualities, in the same way that postal savings banks stimulate saving among the poorer classes. The organization of a state insurance department, moreover, is a comparatively simple matter. There is no necessity for the creation of a new and elaborate service. Use can be made of the post-offices in the same way as is done by the postal savings banks.

A state institution, as long as its use is voluntary, has manifest advantages over those privately organized and managed. In the first place, it can offer a security impossible to be obtained by a private corporation. It is able to gain the attention of workingmen without the great expenses of agents' commissions, advertising, fees, large salaries, etc. How important this is can be seen from the fact that the acknowledged cost of operation of our strongest life insurance companies frequently exceeds one-fourth of the amount paid in benefits. Finally, the government institution does not have to make profits.

These, however, are but the smallest part of the advantages of government insurance. The great services of a government institution are, first, that it appeals to a class, and furnishes a kind of insurance that is offered, to but a limited extent, by private companies; and, secondly, it offers facilities for the collective insurance of workingmen by their employers. Private companies do not attempt to reach the laboring classes, on account of the disproportionate expense of collecting premiums. They also do not provide the most valuable of all kinds of workingmen's insurance,— invalidity pensions. Finally, their method of requiring a fixed contract, necessitating the payment of fixed dues at certain periods, does not adapt itself to the conditions of the workingmen. Workingmen are unwilling to assume obligations that they have to meet for a long time. Under the system of government insurance, as practised in Europe, each workingman can make use of the insurance institution exactly as he would a savings bank. He has an account book, makes deposits when he is able to do so, and can see by reference to a simple table exactly the effect of each payment upon his prospective pension.

We have left to the last the consideration of the greatest service performed by these institutions: that of their provision of collective insurance. We have seen that it is hopeless to expect all, or even an important portion, of the working classes voluntarily as individuals to insure themselves against such contingencies as accident and invalidity. If insurance is to become general, it must come through the employers. The experience of the French, Belgian, and Italian banks is conclusive on this point. The great advantage of state institutions is that they adapt themselves to this kind of insurance. They offer facilities by which employers so inclined can insure their employés. The establishment of an insurance system on a correct actuarial basis is a complicated matter. It is difficult for any but the large employers of labor to attempt the creation of such a system. The state thus offers to small employers an institution in which all these calculations have been made for them; and assumes for them all the expenses and inconveniences of management, the investment of funds, the subsequent payment of pensions, no matter where the recipient may be located, etc. At the same time, it leaves the employers and employés absolute freedom to make what arrangement between themselves they deem fit. The employer can elect to pay all the premiums, or merely encourage and assist the employés to insure themselves, by agreeing to contribute a certain amount if the latter will agree that a portion of their wages shall be retained and devoted to insurance payments. To the employé the great advantage of the system lies in the fact that his right to a pension is not conditional upon his remaining in the service of a particular employer, or dependent upon the latter's financial stability. A payment once made is carried to his individual account, which he retains wherever he goes.

If properly organized, there would seem to be no reason why such a state institution might not accomplish a great good. Indeed, under a policy of voluntary insurance, it may almost be said to constitute an essential part of any system. It in no way interferes with individual efforts. On the other hand, it provides for that branch of insurance which it is almost impossible for mutual-aid societies to offer. It encourages, by offering suitable facilities, employers to insure their employés against accidents and invalidity. Finally, it sets a standard, provides tables of risks and premiums, and in other ways assists the cause of voluntary insurance.

In the practical constitution of such an institution, the most important consideration to be observed, is that it should be made self-supporting. The pensions offered should be calculated in strict accordance with the risks run and the rate of interest that can be earned upon investments. To secure this, an absolutely independent institution should be created. The histories of the French banks are of especial interest from this point of view, showing, as they do, the various dangers that must be guarded against, and the means that can be devised for best accomplishing the ends in view.

Our third group of institutions, in the classification that we have adopted, includes all efforts made by the workingmen themselves for their insurance through association in mutual-aid societies. In many respects this form represents the ideal type of workingmen's insurance.

The great superiority of these societies over other forms of organization lies in the fact, that the expenses of administration are reduced to a minimum, since for the most part officials are not paid a salary, and expensive headquarters do not have to be provided, and, because in no other way can imposition be so effectively guarded against. In addition to these financial considerations, it should be remembered that these societies are often real fraternities. When a member is sick, he is not simply paid certain benefits. Friends visit him and assist him in every way. This feature alone would make this form of organization the one to be preferred over all others. Unfortunately, it is adapted to but one form of insurance, — that against sickness. It is possible, however, through the association of societies, as in the case of the strong orders of Great Britain, for other kinds of insurance to be attempted as well.

The two important types of these institutions are the friendly societies of Great Britain, to which are assimilated the insurance work of labor organizations, and the mutual-aid societies of the Continent of Europe. These two classes, though belonging to the same group of insurance institutions, yet present fundamental differences. The friendly societies represent, to a much greater degree, the result of individual efforts. Not only has the government assisted them to but a slight extent, but it does not even interfere in their management sufficiently to ensure that they are conducted upon an honest or safe basis. The mutual-aid societies of the Continent, on the other hand, were early taken under the fostering care of the government, and regulated and aided in various ways. They have also received assistance through the adhesion of honorary members.

A second important difference between the two consists in the fact, that in England there has taken place a process of consolidation, that has resulted in the building up of great central orders comprising, some of them, over a half a million members each, with branches all over the country. This phenomena of consolidation is one of the most interesting phases of the evolution of insurance methods.

The important problem in connection with these societies is the extent to which the state should interfere in their management. In England the effort has been made to do with as little legislation as possible. One cannot but admire this independence; but, at the same time, one cannot but recognize that great abuses and hardships might have been averted by timely legislation. The state undoubtedly has a rôle to play in this movement. It can do a great deal without interfering with free action to a detrimental degree. If it can, in any way, ensure that these are organized upon a suitable basis, and that they are honestly administered, the result would be, not to stifle private efforts, but to encourage them, by removing the feeling of insecurity that is the chief obstacle to their development. Publicity of accounts, through the requirement of annual reports, is the first requisite. Following this should come the power of the state to make regular examinations of the financial conditions of all societies of a certain importance, in the same way that the accounts of savings and other banks are now examined by state and federal bank examiners. The extent to which this power of regulation should be carried must be determined by each country according to the extent to which its societies have voluntarily put their operations upon a proper foundation, and the extent of the evils that it is desired to remedy.

As regards the technical organization of mutual-aid societies, the important considerations to be regarded are; first, the elimination of charity, or at least its rigid separation from the insurance work proper; secondly, the separation of the various kinds of insurance, so that separate contribution will be required for each kind; and, thirdly, the preparation of premium tables, in order that justice may be done between old and new members, and members of different ages. The English societies have reached the point where these principles are being observed. Much still remains to be done, however, by kindred organizations in this country, as evidenced by the benefit work of our labor organizations.

The variously organized funds created by employers for the insurance of their employés constitute the fourth class into which we have divided workingmen's insurance institutions. Diverse as these are, we have found it necessary to make but one important classification of them: independent funds organized by large employers of labor, as best seen in the case of the funds organized by the railway and mining companies, and, those where smaller and less permanent establishments have joined forces and created central funds for the common insurance of their employés. Funds of the first class have had a long existence. Until very recently, however, it had seemed impracticable to attempt the organization of such funds for small establishments. The creation, however, within the last few years, of the really admirable insurance institutions by the general associations of iron and steel and textile manufacturers of France has pointed out the way by which practically all manufacturers can insure their employés if they desire to do so.

These funds should not be looked upon as charitable institutions maintained by employers for the benefit of their employés. This, to be sure, has frequently been their character in the past. At the present time, however, the charitable feature has been entirely eliminated in the better funds, and they represent merely special institutions for each establishment or group of kindred establishments. As far as insurance against accidents is concerned, the relief afforded by them is relief to which employés are justly entitled. In regard to insurance against invalidity and old age, it is usual for the employés to contribute largely to the support of the fund. Just as mutual-aid societies represent the best type of institution for insurance against sickness, so these employers' funds represent the simplest and most direct way of providing for insurance against accidents and old age.

The organization by an employer of a fund for the insurance of his workingmen against accidents is a simple matter. The furnishing of insurance against old age and invalidity, however, presents a number of special considerations. Here provision must be made for the cases where members sever their connection with the insurance institution, or cease making payments in any way. It is imperative that no system of forfeiture of rights should be tolerated. Neither should the enjoyment of the pension be in any way dependent upon the workingmen remaining in the employ of the particular firm which may be maintaining, in whole or in part, the insurance fund. It has been this feature that has made the attempt to found purely private old-age insurance institutions so difficult and unsatisfactory. The continuance in the employ of the firm as a condition to the right to a pension, has been a provision in a great many privately organized company funds, and, more than any other feature, has given ground for the accusation that such funds are but the means to bind the employé to the interests of his employer. This accusation is a perfectly just one. Whether supported by the employer alone, or in co-operation with his employés, the interest of the workingman in the fund should always be in the nature of a right, from which he cannot be divested. Justice and public policy alike demand it. The most successful method of meeting these requirements that has yet been tried is for employers to avail themselves of the state institutions, where such are in existence, or to combine forces and form general funds.

The organization of general insurance funds by a

number of employers presents difficulties which do not exist in the case of funds relating to a single establishment. The chief of these is the determination of the basis according to which each establishment shall contribute to the support of the fund. As the risk in one establishment varies greatly from that in another, an equitable system demands that the contribution of each should be in proportion to the charges it entails upon the fund. By so doing, also, account is taken of the important consideration that each manufacturer should have an immediate interest to take every possible precaution against accidents. These various considerations have been solved in the most satisfactory way by the French institutions, through their system of granting rebates.

We have attempted in the foregoing paragraphs to indicate the chief advantages and disadvantages of each system of insurance, and the particular consideration that should be observed in the organization of each kind. There remains, however, a number of other points more or less common to them all, which, though they have frequently been alluded to in describing particular institutions, should be included in any attempt to recapitulate the ground covered.

The determination of upon whom shall fall the burden of maintaining the insurance funds is, of course, a vital feature of any system, and has been one of the chief points of controversy in all modern discussion. It would seem that, in the case of accidents at least, this burden should be chiefly, if not wholly, borne by the employers of labor. In the case of sickness, the workingmen themselves should be depended upon. The same is theoretically true for old-age insurance, though here practical experience would seem to indicate that workingmen unaided are unable to make the necessary payments, and that employers, or the state, must assist in some way, if anything like a general system is to be established.

The fixing of the amount of dues, and the determination of the manner in which they shall be collected, while matters of detail, are yet of importance. In Europe, the almost universal method is to fix the dues of members at a certain percentage of their wages, which amount is retained from wages by the employers and paid into the fund. It is evident that under this system the amounts of the payments of members differ widely from each other. This is compensated for by the provision that indemnities are likewise proportional to the wages of the recipient. This method has the great advantage that, not only are dues proportionate to the paying abilities of the members, but benefits in like manner correspond to the income that each has been accustomed to receive. One of the difficulties in carrying on insurance under a system of fixed premiums is the necessity that these payments should be made under all circumstances. When premiums are determined according to wages, however, members, if out of employment, have no payments to make, though, of course, the amount of the benefits to which they will be entitled is proportionately diminished. In the case of the working classes, therefore, where instability of employment is always a more or less important feature of their life, this elasticity is of almost imperative importance. At the same time it is essential that this elasticity should not extend to the extent of allowing to each member the determination of the amount he must contribute, for in many cases they would make no savings at all, and it is just this class that insurance is intended to aid. The feature of having contributions deducted from wages may seem a trivial point, but, as a matter of fact, it is of vital importance. Owing to the fact that the member never receives this money, he becomes accustomed to its non-receipt, and in the end scarcely misses the deduction from his wages. Saving is thus presented to him in the easiest way.

The determination of the cases in which relief shall be given is a special problem for each kind of insurance. In the case of accidents, there is offered the choice of the two systems: where indemnities are classified according to the nature of the injury received, and where they are apportioned according to the length of time the person is incapacitated for work. The latter is not only the simpler, but much the more effective system, and has, therefore, been generally adopted in European countries. In its application, accidents are usually divided into the five classes of those causing (1) death; (2) total permanent disability; (3) partial permanent disability; (4) total temporary disability; and (5) partial temporary disability, or those causing inability to labor for a minimum number of days.

In the case of sickness the problem is a very simple

one. The only questions are, how serious must be the sickness in order to entitle members to relief, and for what length of time this relief shall be granted. The usual method is to provide that any sickness resulting in incapacity for work lasting more than a certain number of days will give rise to a claim upon the funds, and that relief will be granted a maximum number of weeks or months.

The determination of the scope of insurance against old age involves the single element of fixing upon the age at which the right to a pension shall accrue. In European systems the various age limits of 55, 60, 65, or even 70 years have been fixed. Whatever the age fixed, it is desirable in all cases to provide that it shall be optional for the workingmen to continue to work after reaching this age, and thereby secure a pension proportionately greater, in accordance with the length of time that he postpones its enjoyment. In case of invalidity before reaching the minimum age, the pension should begin to run immediately.

It is impossible to lay down any rules generally applicable in regard to the amount or character of the benefits to be granted. A pure insurance system comprehends only the payment of cash indemnities in the case of certain contingencies. In many cases, however, especially where these funds are maintained by the employers, it has been found desirable to join with the granting of these indemnities a medical or hospital service. This is especially the case with coal-mining companies, and other industries necessitating the creation of special industrial communities. In such cases it is usual to provide for the free care of workingmen while incapacitated for labor through injuries, and the payment of a small cash indemnity. This is a consideration that must be decided according to the conditions of each case. In America, the general feeling would undoubtedly be for the granting of maximum cash payments, leaving to the men themselves the expense of medical attendance.

In terminating this chapter, though it is contrary to the purpose of our work to pass a final judgment as regards the superiority of any particular system, we cannot refrain from indicating, in a general way, the policy that it is believed should be followed in this country for the development of workingmen's insurance.

The first step should be that of the general education of the people concerning the real nature and benefits of workingmen's insurance. Employers and employés alike should be made to see the importance of separating insurance from general assistance or charitable aid of any kind; of providing for each of the three kinds of insurance by independent organizations, or at least through independent contributions; of constructing tables of contributions and benefits according to actuarial calculations based on risks incurred; and generally of putting insurance operations upon a business basis. As regards sick insurance, it would seem that immediate efforts should be directed toward the development and betterment of the work now done by labor organizations. The latter should be especially cautioned against the attempt to provide invalidity or old-age insurance except in accordance with the most carefully constructed tables of mortality and probable invalidity. There is also, of course, great room for the development of the great orders of friendly societies, such as the Manchester Unity and the Foresters.

As regards insurance against accidents, progress should be made along two lines: the reform of our employers' liability laws, and the development and improvement of relief departments similar to those already inaugurated by a number of the important railway corporations. Should resort ever be had to the principle of compulsion, it should first take the form of compelling railways to maintain insurance funds of a certain character. This is one of the few cases in which the federal government could act. As the provision of relief or insurance departments by railways becomes more general, it is inevitable that similar efforts will be made in other industries requiring the aggregation of large numbers of men under the same management, such as the iron and steel industries, coal mining, etc. Finally, if the manufacturers themselves could be made to see the advantages of insurance, and our great industrial organizations, such as the American Iron and Steel Association, be induced to create funds on the pattern of that of the *Comité des Forges* of France, the greatest advance would be made both in educating the people up to the advantage of insurance and in providing means for its accomplishment.

The provision of insurance against old age and invalidity is at once a work of very great difficulty and one concerning which the future does not hold out much hope of immediate progress. With employers' funds for the insurance of workingmen against accidents once in general operation, the creation of similar funds for old-age and invalidity insurance might possibly be anticipated. Until then, however, the emphasis should be placed upon the development of sick and accident insurance. It is possible, however, that the government might accomplish something by creating a national old-age insurance bank similar to the Belgian and French institutions. Such an institution, being voluntary in operation, could do no harm. On the other hand, it would enable small employers to insure their employés; it would provide an institution through which individual workingmen could provide for their old age; and could not fail to exercise an important influence upon the development of correct ideas concerning insurance principles.

APPENDIX I.

INSURANCE AGAINST UNEMPLOYMENT.

The purpose of workingmen's insurance is to make provision for the assistance of workingmen when, through any incapacity, they are unable to earn their usual wages. A workingman may be unable to work as the result of any of four contingencies: accident, sickness, old age or invalidity, and the inability to obtain employment. A complete system of provision of assistance must necessarily embrace all four of these cases. It is now very generally accepted that insurance of some kind, either mutual or state-aided, voluntary or compulsory, offers the best device for providing for the first three contingencies, or those relating to physical disability. It remains for us to determine to what extent the same device can be used in making provision for the fourth, or inability to earn wages as the result of involuntary idleness.

It has been deemed desirable to consider insurance against unemployment in a special chapter for various reasons. In the first place, it is by no means certain that it is practicable to apply insurance principles to the solution of this problem. Secondly, it will be seen that, even if such insurance is possible, the conditions involved in its organization are so different that its application must be studied as a distinct problem. Insurance against the various forms of physical disability are so intimately related to each other, that together they form one general system. Lack of employment is a problem that stands by itself; and provision against it is in no way connected with any other kind of insurance. Finally, the cases in which attempts have been made to provide for such insurance are so few that they can better be studied in one place than noticed under the institutions of the particular countries in which they have been made.

Fortunately, we are not under the necessity of studying this problem from the purely theoretical standpoint. The widespread industrial depression of recent years, and the consequent extent to which workingmen have been forced to remain in involuntary idleness, has caused attempts to be made in various countries to make provision against unemployment through some system of insurance. Such are the out-of-work insurance institutions created in several of the cantons of Switzerland, at Cologne, and at Bologna. Of these, those established in Switzerland are of much the greatest importance. Our account will, therefore, be chiefly devoted to their operations. A consideration of the efforts there made will not only serve to illustrate by a practical example the principles involved in the organization of this kind of insurance, but to show the practical difficulties with which its administration is attended.

The experiments inaugurated in Switzerland relate to ; first, the voluntary insurance institution against lack of employment, organized as a municipal institution by the town of Berne; second, the obligatory insurance institution against lack of employment created by the town of Saint Gall; and, third, the various propositions to introduce similar institutions in Basel, Zurich, and Lausanne.

The first attempt to provide for insurance against unemployment under government auspices was made by the town of Berne. January 13, 1893, the town council provided for the creation of a municipal institution for the insurance of workingmen against unemployment. Though a municipal institution, membership was left entirely voluntary. Practically, the only condition of membership was the payment of monthly dues of 40 centimes ($0.077). To the fund thus accumulated, the town agreed to add a subsidy, the maximum amount of which was limited to 5000 francs ($965) a year. The constitution also provided for the receipt of gifts from employers and other individuals.

The value of the out-of-work benefits was fixed at 1 franc ($0.19) for unmarried, and 1½ francs ($0.29) for married men, per day. This relief is granted only during the three months of December, January, and February. To be entitled to receive it, members must have paid their dues regularly during the six preceding months, and have been unable to obtain work during at least fifteen days. If relief was granted, however, it began to run after the first week of unemployment. Various conditions are placed upon those receiving benefits, in order to protect the institution against imposition. Members out of work must present themselves twice a day in a room set aside for that purpose, where they can spend the day if they desire. A workingman who refuses work of any kind loses all right to aid. Members thus do not have the right to refuse work because it is not in their trade. There are various other cases in which the workingman loses his right to a benefit, as, for instance, when he is unemployed as the result of his own fault, and especially when he engages in a strike. The administration of the fund is entrusted to a commission of seven members, three of whom are named by the municipal authorities, two by the employers contributing to the fund, and two by the workingmen.

This institution has now been in existence a sufficient length of time to furnish some indication of the character of its results. The number of members during the first year, 1893–1894, was 404. Of these 166 were aided during the year. There was paid to them $1319.16, or an average of $7.95 each. The highest sum paid to any one person was $20.27. The total expenditure of the year was $1508.30. Receipts for the year consisted of $212.30, dues of members; $382.14, gifts from employers and others; and $913.86 municipal subsidy.

It will be seen that the members contributed but 14 per cent of the total receipts, and that they received, in actual benefits, six times the amount paid by them as dues. One would think that under such favorable circumstances membership would increase rapidly. Such, however, has not been the case. During the second year, 1894–1895, there were but 390 members, or 14 less than the preceding year. Two hundred and nineteen persons, or more than half the members, were aided. They received $1869.06, or an average of $8.53 each. But $263.79 out of a total receipt of $2249.86 was from members' dues. The ratio of this sum to the amount paid out in benefits is 14 per cent, the members thus receiving on an average seven times the amount contributed by them.

The institution had been founded for but two years as an experiment. In 1895, the two years having elapsed, the town council determined by an almost unanimous vote to continue it in operation. Some modifications, however, were introduced in its organization. Dues were raised from 40 to 50 centimes ($0.077 to $0.096) per month, and the maximum amount of the municipal subsidy was raised from $965 to $1351. Daily benefits were also increased from 1 to 1.50 francs ($0.193 to $0.29) for single, and from 1.50 to 2 francs ($0.29 to $0.386) for married members. In addition, the municipal employment bureau, which until then had been an independent service, was attached to the insurance fund.

The result of these changes was to increase the operations of the system. On December 31, 1895, there were 605 members enrolled, of whom 169, or 49 more than during the preceding year at the same date, had been aided. The total receipts during the year 1895–1896 were $2213.99, of which $312.70 was derived from dues. Total expenditures were $2121.30, of which $1932.22 was for benefits. In this third year, therefore, slightly over six times the amount received as dues from the members was paid in benefits.

Saint Gall, a town of about 30,000 inhabitants, was the first to follow the example of Berne, and provide for the insurance of workingmen against unemployment. Its policy, however, differs radically from that of Berne, in that it adopted the policy of compulsory insurance. By the law of May 14, 1894, the Canton of Saint Gall authorized any of its communes that desired to do so to create a compulsory unemployment insurance institution, and provided further that several communes might combine and organize a general insurance fund. On the basis of this law the town of Saint Gall, after an abortive attempt to unite with the neighboring communes of Tablatt and Straubenzell, founded, by act of June 23, 1895, its unemployment insurance fund.

The principal features of this institution can be summarized as follows: Membership was made obligatory upon all workingmen whose daily wages did not exceed 5 francs ($0.97), excluding youths and apprentices earning less than 2 francs ($0.86) a day. Weekly dues were fixed at 15 centimes ($0.03) for members earning 3 francs ($0.58) or under, 20 centimes ($0.04) for those earning not more than 4 francs ($0.77), and 30 centimes ($0.06) for those earning more than that sum. The amount of the benefit was determined according to which of these three classes the recipient belonged, being 1.80, 2.10, and 2.40 francs ($0.35, $0.41, and $0.46) respectively per day. Benefits could not be paid to any person for more than 60 days in any one year.

In order to be entitled to a benefit, members must have paid dues uninterruptedly for at least six months, and show that for at least five days they had not been able to secure work suitable to their occupations at the usual wages of the season. All those who were without work as the result of their own fault, who had participated in a strike, or who refused, without a good reason, work assigned to them by the employment bureau, which was operated in connection with the insurance fund, were debarred from any right to a benefit. Workingmen incapacitated for labor through sickness or accident were not entitled to a benefit, when otherwise insured against these two contingencies.

In addition to dues, the fund had as receipts a subsidy of the town which, according to the law, could not exceed a maximum of 2 francs ($0.86) for each person insured, and a subsidy from the canton. No account, apparently, was taken of gifts and donations from employers or other persons. The fund was administered by a commission of nine members, two of whom were appointed by the municipal authorities, and seven by the workingmen belonging to the fund.

This institution commenced operations July 1, 1895. The law being obligatory, the first duty of the commissioners was to see that all persons to whom the law applied became members. As the result of the first publicity, 1535 persons became members; a new call, a month later, added 579 names; and, as the result of further efforts, the total number of persons inscribed during the first year was increased to 4220. This was only secured after over 150 convictions had been had of persons neglecting to answer the summons to affiliate with the fund. Of the total number secured, 2895 were members of the first class, or those earning not more than 3 francs; 179 belonged to the second class, and but 146 to the third, or those earning over 4 francs a day.

During the year, 430, or about 10 per cent of the members, registered themselves as without work. Of these but 363 were granted benefits, since a number of them had not made the required six months' contributions. To these there was paid a total of 23,504 francs ($4536.27), or an average of 54.66 francs ($10.55) each. The highest amount received by one person was $24.32, and the lowest $1.74. Receipts and expenditures during the year were as follows:—

Receipts.	
Contributions of members	$4183.14
Municipal subsidy, cash	772.00
Municipal subsidy, payment of operating expenses	1084.44
Interest	21.81
Total	$6061.39

Expenditures.	
Benefits	$4536.30
Operating expenses	1084.44
Total	$5620.74
Balance on hand	440.65

It will thus be seen that the year closed with a surplus in the bank, in spite of the fact that the city only paid a portion of the sum that could be required of it. It should be remembered, however, that as this was the first year that the fund had been in operation, no benefits were paid during the first six months, as no member could before that have made the required number of payments. The officials thus estimated that future charges would be much heavier, and that it would be necessary, either to increase contributions or reduce benefits.

This institution, like that at Berne, had been created for a provisional period of two years. Before the end of the second year, however, the council, on November 8, 1896, by a decisive vote ordered its suspension after June 30, 1897. The first experiment in compulsory insurance against unemployment was thus declared a failure. It is worthy of note, also, that this suppression was accomplished on the motion and through the votes of representatives of the working classes in the council.

A detailed account of the organization and operations of the Saint Gall institution has been given, even though its suppression has been definitely decided upon, since in matters such as this information can be gained from failures as well as successes. It is worth our while, therefore, to examine some of the objections that were raised against this scheme. The first was that which inevitably arose from the members who were forced to make contributions without receiving any benefits in return. This is a fundamental objection. The liability to lack of employment varies greatly in the different trades. To require all workingmen earning less than a certain sum to become members of an insurance fund, as was done at Saint Gall, results in positive injustice. Employés in trades having steady employment, such as factory operatives, are made to contribute to the insurance of workingmen, such as those in the building trades, who are certain to be unemployed more or less during the year.

The experience of the funds both at Berne and Saint Gall has shown that it is the workingmen in the building trades who suffer the most from lack of employment. Thus, in the former city, though membership is open to all occupations, and benefits are six or seven times the amount of dues, only day laborers, for the most part in the building trades, and other employés in the same trades, have availed themselves of the fund. Out of the 226 persons registered the second year as out of work, 163 were day laborers, 18 plasterers or painters, 13 roofers, 10 masons, 9 carpenters, 4 stone-cutters, 3 cabinet-makers, 2 locksmiths, and 1 each, wood-sawyer, cement worker, and fireman. It will be observed that factory employés proper were absolutely unrepresented. Turning now to the experience of Saint Gall under compulsory insurance, it is found that though both factory and building-trades employés were required to be insured, practically all the persons aided belonged to the latter class. Of the 430 persons registered as out of work during the first year, 205 were day laborers, excavators, etc., 47 masons, 18 porters, 17 house painters, 14 public messengers, 13 dressmakers, 12 plasterers, 11 carpenters, 10 roofers, while no other occupation was represented by as many as 10 persons.

A second objection was the great difficulty experienced in enforcing the compulsory feature. The administrators of the fund found it almost impossible to compel persons to become members, or afterwards to collect their dues, even though they resorted to prosecution in a great many cases. In the December following the commencement of operations, they found it necessary to send notices to 1110 persons who were behind in the payment of their dues. On April 1 over 4000 francs were owing by about 1300 persons.

Finally, it was complained that the indemnities were much too high. It was found that the efforts of those without work to gain employment were sensibly relaxed. Many seemed to use every effort to obtain as much relief as possible, only earnestly seeking work after they had been aided the maximum number of 60 days. In a word, the principle of self-help seemed to have been weakened in just the proportion that assistance was granted.

In spite of the check that the movement for the insurance of workingmen has received in Switzerland, through the suppression of the Saint Gall fund, efforts in this direction have not been abandoned. Though it is generally admitted that this and the Berne system had defects, it is claimed that they were such as lack of experience rendered inevitable, and that they can be eliminated by a more scientific organization. At Basel a plan is now under consideration that is of especial interest, since it involves an attempt to meet the objections that have been urged against the two older schemes.

In 1894 the council of state of Basel submitted

to the general council a proposition for the municipal insurance of workingmen against unemployment. This measure, after discussion, was first referred to a committee of experts, the leading spirit of which was M. Adler, professor of political economy at the University of Basel. This commission reported in April, 1896, a modified plan. After a full discussion this report was referred to a committee of the general council, which, after a further consideration, reported a specific bill differing in but slight details from the proposition of the committee of experts.

In its final form, the plan provides for the compulsory insurance in a municipal fund of all masons and excavators and all workingmen subject to the federal factory law who do not earn more than 2000 francs a year, excluding, however, young people and apprentices earning less than 300 francs a year. In adopting the principle of compulsion, however, an important option is given to the workingmen to insure themselves through self-organized institutions instead of through the municipal fund. This permission was granted in order to meet the objection that was urged against the bill as first framed by the committee of experts, that certain classes of workingmen had already voluntarily insured themselves through their labor organizations, and that it would be unjust to compel them to become members of the city fund. This was notably true of the members of the "Typographia," an organization of the printers of the city.

The receipts of the fund are made to consist of dues from members, contributions from employers, a subsidy from the city, and gifts and legacies. For the payment of dues and the determination of the amount of benefits to be given, members are first divided into the three categories of: factory employés, workingmen in the building trades the least subject to unemployment, and other workingmen in the building trades. The object of this division is to take account of the difference in the degree of probability that the members of the three classes will suffer from lack of employment. Within each of these categories there is a further division of members into three classes according to the amount of their weekly earnings. The dues of members of each of these classes are fixed at 10, 15, and 20 centimes a week respectively. The contribution of employers is fixed at 10 centimes per week per workingman insured in the first category, and 20 centimes for workingmen of the second and third categories. The city assumes all the expenses of management, and agrees to grant an annual subsidy of 25,000 francs.

The benefit granted to members out of work varies from 80 centimes to 2 francs a day. They are graduated in an ingenious manner according to the class to which the recipients belong, and according to their needs. The maximum length of time during which benefits can be paid is limited to 90 days. An important provision is that whereby there is paid, in place of the above indemnities, travelling expenses for as great a distance as 200 kilometres, and an indemnity of 1 franc to single and 2 francs to married men who desire to leave the city to obtain work elsewhere. This is to prevent workingmen who have an opportunity of finding work elsewhere from remaining a charge upon the fund.

No benefits are paid when the lack of employment is the result of a dispute of employés with their employer concerning the amount of their wages; when the member voluntarily quits his employment; when he has been dismissed for breaking the factory or other regulations; when the lack of employment is the result of sickness or accident against which the workingman is elsewhere insured; and when the person insured without a valid excuse refuses work offered to him.

The question of insurance against unemployment has also received attention in other Swiss cities, notably Zurich and Lausanne. As these efforts have not as yet resulted in any distinct propositions, it will be unnecessary to consider them. The institutions created at Cologne and Bologna offer few points of interest. That of Cologne was created in 1896, and is under municipal management. Insurance under it is purely voluntary. Any workingman over 18 years of age, and having resided in the city during two years, can become a member by paying a weekly contribution of 25 pfennigs. He thus acquires a "right to work" in case he is unemployed during the period from December 15 to March 15. If work cannot be found for him, he is entitled during the first 20 days of unemployment to a benefit of 2 marks, if he is married, and $1\frac{1}{2}$ marks, if single. A large guarantee fund has been created through gifts and the contributions of honorary members. In addition, the city itself has granted a subsidy of several thousand dollars as an encouragement to workingmen to become members.

At Bologna, a voluntary unemployment insurance

institution has been created which relates only to building-trades employés. Members must pay an annual contribution of 3.30 francs if they are under 20 years of age, and 5 francs if over that age. The out-of-work benefits consist of 60 centimes a day for members of the first, and 1 franc for members of the second class, during a maximum of 40 days, commencing with the sixth day of unemployment.

These experiments that have been made in Switzerland and elsewhere, while they are not sufficiently extensive to furnish conclusive evidence regarding the practicability of unemployment insurance, are fully adequate, to bring out the chief considerations that must be taken into account in any attempt to organize such a system.

An examination of the nature of the problem of unemployment shows that insurance principles are ill-suited for its solution. Insurance presupposes that the risk insured against shall possess two characteristics: it must be well defined, and be the consequence of a chance that can be estimated with some degree of certainty. The risk of unemployment fills neither of these conditions. It is not well defined, since it is difficult to say what work the unemployed should be required to accept. It does not depend upon chance, because the personal element involved in seeking and retaining work, to say nothing of the uncertainty of the employer's action, enters so largely. Though lack of employment is often unavoidable on the part of the workingman, the latter's will and energy play such an important part that any attempt to distinguish voluntary from unavoidable idleness is futile. Insurance concerns itself with a risk that can be calculated and provided for in advance. This cannot be done in regard to lack of employment. The study of the various systems that has just been made shows that, in spite of the fact that the term "insurance" has been employed, the effort has not really been made to create insurance systems. In no case has it been attempted to calculate risks and to adjust contributions accordingly, or indeed to make the system self-supporting. Nominal contributions only have been required from members, while the great burden of expense has been borne by the government and voluntary contributors. It is, therefore, scarcely proper to speak of these institutions as insurance organizations. What has been created is really a more systematized plan of granting relief to the unemployed.

Turning now to the actual organization of the Swiss systems, it will be seen that the radical mistake made was the failure to recognize the essentially different conditions obtaining in different industries. The problem of lack of employment in the factory trades, for example, is quite a different one from that in the building trades or among ordinary day laborers. It may be confidently stated that any attempt to introduce even a modified form of insurance against unemployment should follow strictly trade lines. In this respect the Basel proposition shows a marked advance over that of the other systems.

This, however, brings us to the consideration of the out-of-work benefit features of labor organizations. If unemployment insurance should follow trade lines, every argument would seem to indicate that such efforts should be made through existing organizations of workingmen. The great work done by these organizations in the way of aiding their members is well known. Thus, for example, the Chief Labor Correspondent of the British Board of Trade in his report on Trade Unions for 1895 reported that 100 of the principal unions expended during the year $2,121,775 in relief to the unemployed. In this country, a large part of the expenditures of the trade unions likewise go for this purpose, though it is not possible to make any exact statement of the amount. This mode of granting relief possesses manifest advantages over the granting of assistance through a municipal organization. The work of labor unions is not charity, but the highest order of mutual aid. These orders, moreover, are in a peculiarly favorable position to assist their members in obtaining work, and are able to guard against imposition. Finally, as we have seen, unemployment is not a condition beyond the control of individuals, and does not happen with a regularity that can be anticipated. Insurance proper affords little room for discretion in granting relief. Each case of unemployment should be considered upon its particular merits. Labor organizations can exercise this discretion in a way that is utterly beyond the power of a municipal institution.

The logical conclusion is that, in America at least, provision against lack of employment can best be made for the established trades by the men themselves through their organizations; and that this provision cannot be made according to hard and fast insurance principles, but must allow for a certain elasticity or discretion in the granting of relief according to the needs of the case and the amount of funds available for this purpose.

Though the Swiss efforts must be regarded as faulty, and as lacking the character of true insurance, it is not desired to give the impression that such municipal institutions cannot be made to serve a useful purpose. On the contrary, there are involved in their organization principles, which, when properly applied, can be of great assistance in solving the problem of unemployment. They may not provide insurance, but they constitute a vast improvement over the old methods of indiscriminate and uncertain relief. They require employés to register and to make some personal sacrifice in order to be entitled to relief; they ensure that relief will be granted only to *bona fide* residents of the city; and the unemployed are brought under the supervision of the public authorities. Workingmen can thus be more easily assisted in finding work, either through public employment bureaus, or can be directly employed by the government. To accomplish this work in the best way, however, the emphasis should not be placed upon the idea of insurance. The principle of registration, accompanied by the requirement of small monthly contributions, is the really valuable feature of their work. They should seek chiefly to reach those classes not possessing labor organizations. Finally, they should make assistance to the unemployed in finding work the most important part of their duties. Only after they have failed in this effort, should pecuniary relief be granted.

APPENDIX II.

BIBLIOGRAPHICAL NOTE.

In the account that has been given of workingmen's insurance in the preceding pages but few references have been made to authorities, since in practically every instance use has been made only of the official reports and other publications of the institutions that have been described. The attempt to give anything like a complete bibliography of all that has been written upon workingmen's insurance, even if only that of real value were included, would require the enumeration of thousands of titles. There is certainly no concrete labor question concerning which more has been written in Europe during the last ten or twenty years. No such effort of complete enumeration will therefore be made. It is intended in the present note but to indicate the official publications that have been used. These constitute the original sources of information to which recourse must be had in case a more detailed consideration of any institution is undertaken.

Germany. — The official reports of the state insurance institutions furnish the most detailed information concerning their operations. The information concerning accident and old-age and invalidity insurance is contained in the series of annual reports entitled *Amtliche Nachrichten des Reichs-Versicherungs-*

amts and *Geschäftsbericht des Reichs-Versicherungsamts.*
The reports of the operations of the institutions for
insurance against sickness are published by the Imperial Statistical Bureau in its regular series of publications, under the title of *Statistik der Krankenversicherung der Arbeiter.* The laws relating to these
institutions are contained in the *Reichs-Gesetzblatt,* the
official publication of laws of the empire. They can,
however, be best consulted in the Fourth Special Report of the United States Department of Labor, *Compulsory Insurance in Germany,* prepared by Mr. John
Graham Brooks, Washington, 1893, where the laws
then in force are not only translated, but their essential provisions brought out in brief analyses.

These laws and their operations have also been
made the subject of official investigations by various
other nations. The reports of these inquiries are of
great value in assisting in the analysis of the material
contained in the German reports. The French *Office
du Travail* has in particular followed the course of
German and Austrian insurance with great care. Its
publications on this subject now embrace six volumes,
entitled, respectively, (1) *Statistique des Accidents du
Travail, d'après les rapports officiels sur l'assurance
obligatoire en Allemagne et en Autriche,* 1892; (2) *Résultats Financiers de l'Assurance Obligatoire contre les
Accidents du Travail en Allemagne et en Autriche,* 1892;
(3) *Résultats Statistiques de l'Assurance Obligatoire
contre la Maladie en Allemagne,* 1893; (4) *Résultats
Statistiques de l'Assurance Obligatoire contre la Maladie
en Autriche,* 1893; (5) *Étude sur les Derniers Résultats
des Assurances Sociales en Allemagne et en Autriche,*

1e *Partie, Accidents*, 1894; (6) *Étude sur les Derniers Résultats des Assurances Sociales en Allemagne et en Autriche*, 2e *Partie, Maladie, Invalidité, et Vieillesse*, 1895. These reports make a very detailed study of the whole question. The Belgian *Office du Travail* has also made a very comprehensive study of the German system of old-age and invalidity insurance, which it has published under the title of *L'Assurance contre l'Invalidité et la Vieillesse en Allemagne*, 1895. The Swiss and English governments have issued reports on this question, which, however, are of less importance. For the more general statistics see the annual *Statistisches Jahrbuch für das Deutsche Reich*.

Austria. — Information concerning the operations of Austrian insurance institutions are given in the official reports entitled *Amtliche Nachrichten des K. K. Ministeriums des Innern betreffend die Unfall und Krankenversicherung der Arbeiter*. See also the two annual publications, *Die Gebarung und die Ergebnisse der Unfallstatistik der Arbeiter Unfall-Versicherungsanstalten* and *Die Gebarung und die Ergebnisse der Krankheitsstatistik*. The laws are contained in the *Reichs-Gesetzblatt*. They can also be easily consulted as translated into French in the publications of the *Office du Travail*. These reports, which have been mentioned under German authorities, are equally valuable for the study of Austrian as of German insurance. For general statistics see *Oesterreichisches Statistisches Handbuch*, published annually.

France. — In France the variety of institutions requires the consultation of a considerable number of different official publications. The operations of the national insurance institutions are published in the *Rapports Annuels de la Commission Supérieure de la Caisse Nationale des Retraites pour la Vieillesse* and the *Rapports Annuels de la Commission Supérieure des Caisses d'Assurances en Cas de Décès et en Cas d'Accidents*. The government also issued a very useful compilation on the occasion of the Paris Exposition of 1889, entitled *Caisse Nationale des Retraites pour la Vieillesse: Album de Statistique Graphique, Exposition Universelle de* 1889. These institutions also issue circulars and instructions giving the conditions of membership, the tables in use, etc., which can be had upon application. Finally, reference should be made to the report of M. Louis Fontaine, entitled *Rapports sur les Caisses de Retraites et de Rentes Viagères*, published in the report of the Section of Social Economy of the Paris Exposition, 1889.

The operations of the mutual-aid societies are very fully set forth in the *Rapports Annuels sur l'Opération des Sociétés de Secours Mutuels, Ministère de l'Intérieur*, a series of reports running back to the year 1852. A pamphlet published by the same department and entitled *Sociétés de Secours Mutuels: Statuts-Models, Lois et Décrets*, 1893, gives copies of all the laws and official regulations relating to these societies. The most important single document, however, is the special report entitled *Rapport Spécial sur les Sociétés de Secours Mutuels*, made in 1893 by the eminent actuary, M. Léon Marie. This report is the result of a specially authorized investigation of the whole question of the reform of mutual-aid societies, and sets forth with the greatest thoroughness all of the elements involved, and the lines along which such reforms should be conducted. Mention should also be made of the report of M. Louis Fontaine on *Sociétés de Secours Mutuels* contained in the report of the Section of Social Economy, Paris Exposition of 1889.

There is also a very extensive current literature relating wholly or chiefly to these societies. Such, for instance, are the *Bulletin Officiel des Sociétés de Secours Mutuels* and the excellent periodical *Revue des Institutions de Prévoyance* founded in 1887. Annual congresses of those interested in these societies have also been held since 1891, under the title of *Congrès National de la Mutualité Française*.

As regards information concerning the insurance funds organized by employers of labor, the author has depended almost entirely upon his personal investigations and the annual reports and other documents kindly furnished by the railway companies, the great mining corporations, the *Comité des Forges*, and other organizations. The report of M. Cheysson, entitled *Institutions Patronales*, contained in the report of the Section of Social Economy, Paris Exposition, 1889, as well as occasional articles in French economic reviews were, however, of some assistance.

All the laws relating to insurance matters and institutions can best be consulted in the admirable compilation *Lois Sociales: Recueil des Texts de la Législation Sociale de la France*, by Joseph Chailley-Bert and Arthur Fontaine, Paris, 1895. See the *Annuaire Statistique de la France*, for general statistics of the national insurance institutions and the mutual-aid societies. The monthly *Bulletin de l'Office du Travail* gives monthly reports of the operations of these institutions.

Belgium. — In Belgium the operations of the National Savings and Old-age Insurance Bank are published annually under the title, *Compte-Rendu Annuel des Opérations et de la Situation de la Caisse Générale d'Epargne et de Retraite*. The operations of the mutual-aid societies are published in the volumes, *Rapports de la Commission Permanente des Sociétés de Secours Mutuels*. Official documents concerning the miners' funds are the annual reports entitled *Caisses de Prévoyance en Faveur des Ouvriers Mineurs: Examen des Comptes de l'Année par la Commission Permanente, Ministère de l'Industrie et du Travail;* and the compilation of laws and decrees relating to them, *Caisses de Prévoyance en Faveur des Ouvriers Mineurs: Loi, Arrêtés Organiques et Statuts*.

The attempt will not be made to indicate, with the same particularity, the official authorities relating to insurance institutions in other European countries, because no such thorough study was made of their institutions. As regards England and the United States, such publications as there are have been indicated in foot-notes or in the text of the chapters devoted to those countries. Those desiring to know what are the most important privately published works relating to workingmen's insurance can avail themselves of the following sources. Undoubtedly the best bibliography relating to the insurance of workingmen against accidents is that contained in Circulaire No. 1, Series B, of the *Musée Social*, Paris, 1896. The first volume of the Bulletin issued by the *Congrès International des Accidents du Travail et des Assurances Sociales*, 1890, contains a brief bibliography of works relating to workingmen's insurance. Mr. Brooks' report for the United States Department of Labor on Workingmen's Insurance contains a list of works relating to workingmen's insurance in Germany. Finally, a consultation of the files of the bulletin of the congress in relation to accidents to labor, above referred to, will furnish the best idea of the general literature of the whole subject. The best consideration in a brief space of the subject can be found in the various articles of Conrad's *Handwörterbuch der Staatswissenschaften.*

Before terminating this note, however, an account should be given of a series of publications which, though not strictly official, are yet no less important and authoritative in their character. Reference is made to the publications of the *Congrès International des Accidents du Travail et des Assurances Sociales.* This congress was organized at Paris in 1889, and has since then held three other congresses, one at Berne in 1891, the second at Milan in 1894, and the third at Brussels in 1897. In addition to publishing the report of these meetings, the congress, in 1890, commenced the publication of a quarterly bulletin under the title of *Bulletin du Comité Permanent.* These publications now constitute a library of thirteen large octavo volumes and present the most valuable body of literature relating to the question of workingmen's insurance that exists in any language. The congresses have uniformly been attended by the chief officials of all of the state insurance institutions in Europe, and by those most prominent in insurance matters. In the Bulletins are not only given studies of particular insurance questions, but all important legislation or official reports are noticed, or even textually reproduced. While the official reports, therefore, constitute the records from which the facts relating to insurance must be obtained, the expert criticism, and analysis and comparison of institution with institution must be sought for in these reports. Finally, it is possible through the reports of these congresses, and especially through the *Bulletin*, to keep fully informed concerning what is being done in each country regarding this question.

www.ingramcontent.com/pod-product-compliance
Lightning Source LLC
Chambersburg PA
CBHW030430300426
44112CB00009B/929